Chelsea School Research Centre Edition
Volume 4

Sport in Divided Societies

D1342941

Chelsea School Research Centre Edition
Volume 4

John Sugden/Alan Bairner (eds.)

Sport in Divided Societies

Meyer & Meyer Sport

Die Deutsche Bibliothek – CIP-Einheitsaufnahme

Sport in divided societies /
John Sugden / Alan Bairner (eds.).
– Aachen : Meyer und Meyer, 1999
(Chelsea School Research Centre Edition ; Vol. 4)
ISBN 3-89124-445-2

© 1999 by Meyer & Meyer Sport, Aachen,
Olten (CH), Vienna, Oxford, Québec,
Lansing/ Michigan, Adelaide, Auckland, Johannesburg
Cover design: Walter J. Neumann, N&N Design-Studio, Aachen
Cover exposure: frw, Reiner Wahlen, Aachen
Typesetting: Myrene L. McFee
Printed and bound in Germany by
Firma Mennicken, Aachen
e-mail: verlag@meyer-meyer-sports.com • http://www.meyer-meyer-sports.com
ISBN 3-89124-445-2

Contents

ABOUT THE AUTHORS

Abdul-Karim Alaug has an MA in anthropology from Brown University (USA). His thesis focused on the acculturation of Yemeni immigrants in Detroit, Michigan. He is currently completing a doctoral degree in Women in Development at Tilburg University (Netherlands) and works for the Empirical Research and Women's Studies Centre in Sana'a.

Lincoln Allison is Director at the Warwick Centre for the Study of Sport and Reader in politics and international studies at the University of Warwick (UK). He is author of ten books and more than five hundred articles, mostly on political theory, environmental planning, sport and travel.

Alan Bairner is Lecturer in politics at the University of Ulster at Jordanstown (UK). He studied at the universities of Exeter and Hull and has written extensively on the politics and sociology of sport in Ireland, Scotland and Sweden. He is co-author with John Sugden of *Sport, Sectarianism and Society in a Divided Ireland* and is currently preparing a book on the relationship between sport and national identity.

Paul Darby is Lecturer in the sociology of sport at Liverpool Hope University College (UK). His research interests are in the political sociology of global sports.

Adrian Guelke was raised in South Africa. Currently he is Professor of Comparative Politics and Director of the Centre for the Study of Ethnic Conflict, at Queens University Belfast (UK). His main research interests are in the area of political cultures and political analysis, particularly in the context of South Africa. He has written and published widely on this subject.

John Hargreaves is Emeritus Reader in Sociology, University of London, Goldsmith's College (UK). He is a specialist on nationalism, and author of *Sport, Power and Culture*, and *Olympism and Nationalism: A Study of Catalan Nationalism, Spanish Identity and the Barcelona Olympic Games* (forthcoming).

Jean Harvey is Professor at the School of Human Kinetics, University of Ottawa (Canada). His research interests include sport and globalisation; sport and national identity; and sport and social class.

Ian McDonald is co-director of the Centre for Sport Development Research at Roehampton Institute London. His research interests are in sport, racism and national identity and the politics of sports policy. He is currently editing a book on racism in British sport and co-authoring a volume on sport and the making of modern India.

Udo Merkel is Senior Lecturer in sport and leisure cultures at the University of Brighton (UK). His research interests are in the sociology of sport and leisure and comparative studies of European sport. He is editor of *Racism and Xenophobia in European Football* (1996).

Thomas B. Stevenson holds a Ph.D. in anthropology from Wayne State University (USA). He has conducted research in Yemen since 1978. Dr. Stevenson is author of *Social Change in a Yemeni Highlands Town*, compiler of *Studies on Yemen: 1975–1990*, and author of articles on sport, migration and family. He teaches on Ohio University's regional campuses.

John Sugden is Reader in the sociology of sport at the University of Brighton (UK). His main research interests are in the political sociology of global sports and investigative and interpretive research methods. He is author of *Boxing and society: An International Analysis* (1996); and co-author with Alan Tomlinson of *FIFA and the Contest for World Football* (1998).

Alan Tomlinson is Professor and Reader in sport and leisure cultures at the University of Brighton (UK). His research interests centre on the application of critical sociology and social history in the study of sport and leisure cultures. He is co-author with John Sugden of *FIFA and the Contest for World Football* (1998).

Bart van Reusel is Professor in the Department of Physical Education and Sports Science at the Katholic University of Leuven (Belgium). His research interests are in the sociology of human movement and sport. He is the editor of *Sport and Contested Boundaries* (1994).

SPORT IN DIVIDED SOCIETIES

Alan Bairner
University of Ulster at Jordanstown

John Sugden
University of Brighton

This book resulted from a two-day symposium held at the Sussex Arts Club in May, 1997. Participation in the event was restricted to an invited group of scholars, each of whom was asked to present a paper which could then be discussed at length and in some depth by the other participants. Thus, with the exception of one of the articles in the book, all of the contributions first saw the light of day as conference papers. Needless to say, the contents of the book as well as its significant omissions reflect the interests of those who attended the symposium. Whilst this may be regarded as having had the effect of unnecessarily limiting the range of case studies included in the collection, the formula adopted had the obvious advantage of ensuring that each contribution was subjected to close scrutiny and each contributor, when rewriting for the purposes of this volume, was able to draw upon the critical observations of fellow contributors as well as the various different perspectives offered in Brighton. Opportunities for such exchanges of ideas between a relatively restricted group of people are few and far between. We are in no doubt that each contributor learned from the experience and that we left Brighton with a far greater appreciation of the place of sport in divided societies than had we continued to work alone or, alternatively, had we just left one of the larger academic conferences at which wood and trees become so easily confused.

The relationship between sport and identity politics has been increasingly well documented from a variety of theoretical perspectives covering gender, race, sexuality and so on. One area of growing concern has been that of sport's involvement in the construction and reproduction of national identities (Bairner, 1996; Blain *et al.*, 1993; Mangan, 1996; MacClancy, 1996). Some studies have

1

concentrated on particular sports, for example soccer (Sugden and Tomlinson, 1994; Wagg, 1995; Duke and Crolley, 1996). Other work has dealt with specific countries such as Scotland (Jarvie and Walker, 1994) and Ireland (Sugden and Bairner, 1993; Holmes, 1994; Cronin, 1994; Cronin, 1996). In general, sport has been recognised as having a role to play in the consolidation of certain nationalisms or the promotion of the interests of particular nation-states (Hill, 1992; Houlihan, 1994). In addition, considerable attention has been paid to the question of whether sport is able to play a role in resisting globalisation rather than simply becoming an aid to its growth by way of cultural imperialism and other related processes (Guttmann, 1994; Maguire, 1994; Donnelly, 1996; Harvey *et al.*, 1996). Only indirectly does this debate touch on the main concerns of the essays in this collection. Without wishing to exaggerate the extent to which societies are able to resist global forces (Donnelly, 1996: p. 251), it is clear that they remain distinctive in a variety of ways. What this book seeks to explore are the ways in which this distinctiveness is frequently characterised by political division and the degree to which sport has been implicated in the politics of divided societies.

It is a truism that all societies are divided. There are divisions between racial and ethnic groupings, between the rich and the poor, the young and the old, between men and women, adults and children, the healthy and the sick and so on. All of these, and numerous other divisions besides, impact upon the world of sport. They are reflected in the ways in which sports are played, watched and organised. Sport may also reinforce and, in some instances, exacerbate the divisions. In some instances, sport has also been used in attempts to defuse tension and bring rival communities together. Thus, the interplay between sport and a variety of forms of division is a matter of major concern for sports sociology. The United States of America, for instance, is remarkable divided along a variety of fault lines. This book is concerned, however, with a specific type of division, although this is not to suggest that the other ways in which societies are divided are of less importance.

The essays which follow examine a selection of societies which are deeply *politically divided* or which have found mechanisms whereby political differences are managed in such a way as to prevent or suppress deeper division. Naturally, some of these political divisions involve other forms of social division, most notably ethnicity. But we are not concerned with multicultural societies, like the United States, in which the legitimacy of the state goes largely uncontested and difficulties emerge, for the most part, only in relation to the manner in which life is organised within widely accepted constitutional boundaries. All of the societies discussed in these essays are, in varying degrees, multicultural. In every case, however, the divisions which exist have resulted in political or constitutional difficulties as opposed to purely internal social problems. This does not mean that the legitimacy of every society discussed in this book is currently being questioned by certain sections of the population, although this is certainly the case in both Northern Ireland and Quebec. In other countries, ethnic, linguistic and religious divisions have threatened the integrity of the nation state but, in general, they are managed by specific constitutional arrangements which render secessionist movements relatively powerless. Of the case studies which feature in this book, Belgium, India, Spain and Switzerland, albeit for different reasons, can all be placed in this category. The collection also includes two examples of the unification of previously separate political entities. Germany and Yemen, although distinct in many other ways, provide insights into the problems posed when societies with very different pasts are politically unified on the basis of national identity. India, itself the product of political partition, is commonly defined as the world's largest democracy. This does not mean, however, that it is free from internal divisions which could yet result in fundamental change. The particular source of division examined in this volume concerns the aspirations of those who would support the transformation of the country from a pluralist, secular society into a Hindu state. The remaining case study countries, Georgia and South Africa, would appear on the face of it to have little or nothing in common. What links them is the fact that both are in the throes of massive political change. In the case of Georgia, this involves working out a new set of relationships with Russia, of whose empire it was formerly a constituent element, as well as dealing with internal problems posed by ethnic diversity. As for South Africa, with its multiplicity of divisions, the task is to create a pluralist society, the legitimacy of which is unchallenged by the overwhelming majority of South African people.

Numerous 'divided societies' are absent from this book. At the start of the conference during which most of the chapters which appear in this book were originally presented as papers, there was a heated debate between European and British contributors concerning the United Kingdom's right to have four separate teams for the purposes of international football competition. Somewhat to the dismay of our overseas visitors, this general discussion soon led to an even more heated debate between the English and Scots over sport, political domination and cultural representation. It was a salutary reminder, if any were needed, that Britain is itself a divided society — a fact which is manifested in the world of sport as much as in any other area of human activity. Yet, the conference organisers (and editors of this book) had included a British dimension only to the extent that Northern Ireland is a constituent, albeit contested, element of the United Kingdom. The reason for the apparent omission is obvious. We had been thinking in terms of more visibly divided societies, ones in which there is a history of political violence stemming from division or in which there has been real constitutional division or where that might yet occur. Despite the proposals for devolved government to Scotland and Wales and the continuing threat to one part of the union posed by Irish nationalism, Britain is seldom regarded as a deeply divided society. Yet examples drawn from the world of sport illustrate all too clearly the multiple identities which flourish within this traditionally most centralised of states. As Moorhouse observes, "within Britain sport has been one of the main strands to which the submerged nations have clung in order to assert their distinctiveness" (1996: p. 71). As a result, this opening exchange of views concentrated the minds of the participants on the kind of issues which were to be discussed. We were meeting in a divided society in which sport is bound up with identity politics and, even if the UK was not to provide much of the material for our subsequent discussions, it offered an appropriate setting for the debate which was to follow.

Far more glaring omissions from the collection of essays than the United Kingdom are Cyprus, Israel, Sri Lanka and the states formed out of the ruins of the former Yugoslavia. The reasons for their omission and for the selection of case studies which do appear are twofold. First, there were pragmatic considerations concerning the number of essays which a collection of this type should contain and also the expertise which the editors could readily call upon. The second factor relates to the desire on the editors' part to offer examples of the involvement of sport in a range of politically divided contexts. To have concentrated solely on the best known examples of deeply divided societies would have failed to do justice to the varied ways in which political division manifests itself and becomes implicated in the sports process. We might also add that allowing such omissions leaves us plenty of scope for another book!

Authors have approached their subject matter in their own ways. Some have felt it necessary to devote more attention than others to explaining the political context of their particular case studies. Others have assumed more background knowledge on the part of our readers. In the case of Northern Ireland and South Africa, for example, it was felt that enough has already been written about the nature of the political problems involved and that it was possible to move with greater haste to a discussion of the current state of affairs as they affect sport. All of the contributors, however, regardless of their specific treatment of the material, have endeavoured to keep in mind the themes of sport, political division and the relationship between the two. In particular, they have sought to shed light on the extent to which sport contributes to division and the degree to which it can play a positive role in bringing that division to an end or, more realistically, assist in the process through which the more serious manifestations of division are eradicated.

The book cannot claim to compare the role of sport in identical or even essentially similar types of divided societies. Despite the manifest differences between the chosen case studies, however, comparable problems do emerge. It is undeniable that the problems of each society are unique and demand *ad hoc* responses. Indeed, what these essays reveal above all is the capacity of sport to embed itself in all kinds of social formations and to play an important role in their subsequent development. As Lincoln Allison suggests, in his study of sport in Georgia, there are settings in which the importance of sport is diminished in the face of the more serious considerations affecting human existence. In general, however, all of the essays presented here show sport's ability to thrive even in the most hostile of political environments. That it does so, however, is not a matter for unequivocal joy —particularly when, as the essays also reveal, sport may actually add to the feelings of mutual hostility and animosity which characterise most, if not all, divided societies.

Three main questions must be asked about the role of sport in divided societies. First, to what extent does the social organisation of sport reflect divisions in a given society? The answer to this question will clearly differ from one place to another. In some divided societies, the same sports are played and watched by everyone and the divisions which exist in those societies are manifested in the world of sport not in terms of the existence of rival sporting cultures but rather in the ways in which particular teams, clubs and individuals tend to become identified with particular identity groups. In other societies, different communities have created their own sports cultures in such a way as to consolidate separate identities whilst minimising the opportunities for direct rivalry on the field of play. In both cases, sport helps to emphasise division. To assess the different ways in which sport reflects divisions, it is important to understand the context in which it is obliged to operate. Here we can identify some broad themes, although each case study manifests its own peculiarities. In certain countries, the dominant problem is created by the existence of secessionist nationalism. Of the case studies examined in this book, this is particularly true of Canada, although it applies also to Spain. In each instance, nationalists (Québécoises in Canada, Catalans and others in Spain) seek varying degrees of autonomy from an existing nation state and sport has become one of the main vehicles through which a sense of national identity has been maintained despite centralising political tendencies. The situation in Ireland is rather different, although Irish nationalists on occasion liken their struggle to those of the Basques and Catalans in Spain. Whilst it is undeniable that the Irish nationalist movement demands political change, this aspiration is not couched in secessionist terms but rather in terms of the unification of what is regarded as the Irish nation. This demand is made with a degree of support from the government of the Irish Republic and despite the fact that a million Ulster Protestants do not wish this unification to take place and persist in defending their right to remain citizens of the United Kingdom. In this situation, many nationalists use sport to highlight their Irishness and to endorse their claim for a constitutional settlement which is consistent with their national identity. For many Protestants, on the other hand, sport is a means whereby their British identity can be expressed and reproduced. In Germany and Yemen, the problem has been to forge political unity between people who share cultural, ethnic and linguistic characteristics but who have been separated for strategic and ideological reasons in the recent past. It is important to understand, in each case, the ways in which sport reflects the old divisions and may yet prove resistant to aspirations towards unification. In both Belgium and Switzerland the divisions possess an essentially linguistic character, although this is clearly linked to the process whereby modern nation states have frequently brought together people with very different 'nationalist' pasts. Thus, language remains a potential focus for broader political and territorial division. Both democracies have sought to overcome the political difficulties which can result from such divisions although it is apparent, particularly in the case of Belgium, that the divisions are deep and continue to manifest themselves and thereby become reproduced through the agency of sport. In South Africa the divisions which the new regime is trying to heal have long been associated with sport, and sport in that country will continue not only to reflect racial, ethnic and cultural divisions but will also have an important influence on whether there can be a lasting resolution to the political problems which those divisions have engendered. In each of these cases, as well as in other divided societies which are not given separate treatment in this collection of essays, the world of sport provides a window through which we can view and understand political division.

As MacClancy suggests, "sports and sporting events cannot be comprehended without reference to relations of power" (1996: p. 5). Thus, dominant groups in society use sport to consolidate their control over particular societies by imposing a specific value system on the entire population. Those who do not internalise the dominant values — or, more aptly, 'play the game' — are marginalised as social outsiders, 'the other'. On the other hand, subordinate groups can also use sport to bring together oppositional forces and articulate challenges to the prevailing value system and the power relations which are dependent on it. Thus, sport is more than a mere barometer which gauges the levels of political division. It is also an integral element in the actual politics of division.

Thus, a second question follows hard on the heels of the first. How far does sport actually contribute to the divisions in society? Even to ask this question is to fly in the face of much conventional wisdom, particularly in sporting organisations themselves, concerning the 'healing power' of sport. Certainly it is always difficult to know whether sport acts as a safety valve which allows people to affirm their differences without actually entering into inter-community conflict or whether alternatively, given its immense popularity, it becomes such a significant vehicle for consolidating difference that ways in which divisions can be healed or rendered less important become increasingly difficult to find. In all the societies discussed in the book, and indeed in all modern societies, regardless of their political character, sport offers a venue for the expression of moderately excited behaviour which is largely kept under control courtesy of the rules of play and of civilised society (Elias and Dunning, 1986). Expressing one's identity by way of the sport which one plays or the team one supports may well represent a useful substitute for more aggressive tendencies. When Celtic and Rangers fans exchange insults during games, one can only imagine what would happen in the wider society if they had no such sporting channel for the expression of inter-community hostility. At the same time, lest one become too sanguine about the problem, one should bear in mind the significance of the fact that the two best supported football clubs in Scotland have traditionally owed their popularity in no small measure to the fact that their very existence is bound up with and serves to maintain the presence of rival and antithetical cultural and quasi-political identities. Similarly, although it may be of some value to the peace process in the Middle East that both Israelis and Palestinians play football, the fact that certain teams are clearly identified with one group rather than the other and are supported with considerable passion for that very reason suggests that clutching at straws could easily become an Olympic sport if it was left up to international mediators to decide such matters. When Croatia Zagreb played Red Star Belgrade in the preliminary round of the European Champions' Cup in 1997-8, it was a measure of the political progress that has been made in the former Yugoslavia that such a match could even be played. That the atmosphere in the stadia for each leg of the tie was so hate-filled, however, not only reminded us of the hostility that had gone before but also alerted us to the fact that the reasons for that hostility persist. This was war minus the shooting — but only just. Given that two countries, Honduras and El Salvador, once went to war with a football game being the immediate catalyst for the outbreak of conflict, the fact that a sports contest can be arranged between traditional enemies is not a sign that the causes of the original enmity have been eradicated. Indeed, the game between the representatives of Serbia and Croatia did more to rekindle the embers of war than to help to extinguish them. This is not to suggest, however, that sport can never play a part in bringing otherwise divided peoples together.

Thus, in each of the chapters there is a third consideration. In the light of sport's appeal, is it possible that it can also play a role in transcending division? This is, of course difficult to assess when, as in the case of Northern Ireland, there are distinctive sporting cultures. However, where everyone is attracted to the same games (and even in Northern Ireland, association football possesses a transcendent popularity), it is possible to imagine situations in which those who are otherwise resolutely at odds with one another might find in sport the temporary sanctuary of a 'no man's land' or even, perhaps, a single brick to add to the foundations of a lasting resolution to conflict. It was reported that the fighting in Sri Lanka between government forces and Tamil Tiger militia was temporarily suspended during 1997 whilst the country's cricketers scored the highest number of runs ever made in a single test match innings. In the same year, it was possible to organise a football game between Greek and Turkish Cypriot teams. It is much too early to suggest that such an event might pave the way for more harmonious relations on the island. But it represents an improvement in a situation in which there has been little or no contact between the two peoples.

Certainly, global governing bodies of sport have an extremely benign view of the role which sport can play in healing political division. One of the authors was present at the opening ceremony of the 1995 World Student Games in Fukuoka, Japan. Speaking 50 years after the dropping the atomic bombs on Hiroshima and Nagasaki, the President of FISU, the governing body for international student sport, Primo Nebiolo, stressed the unrivalled capacity of sport to heal old wounds and bring nations together. Such rhetoric is standard for the international Olympic movement whose representatives are forever extolling the cultural and political fraternity promoted by the Olympic Games. One of the International Olympic Committee's justifications for granting Seoul the right to host the 1988 Olympics was that it would help to bring North and South Korea closer to reunification. Likewise FIFA, world football's governing body, in deciding that Japan and south Korea should co-host the 2002 World Cup Finals, justified its decision on peace-making grounds. According to FIFA, this event will help to overcome 500 years of enmity between Japan and Korea. Also, FIFA have recommended that some of the venues for matches should be in North Korea, in the hope that this will improve relations between the South Koreans and their northern neighbours. In a similar vein, in 1997 FIFA announced that it was endeavouring to organise a 'friendly' football match between Israel and Palestine in New York, the home of the United Nations. In an interview with one of the authors, the President of FIFA, João Havelange, explained this as an initiative which would show that football could succeed where politicians have consistently failed (Sugden and Tomlinson, 1998).

Surely this is an extremely naive view of the power of sport to overcome deeply entrenched political divisions. Of the case studies explored in this book, much has been made of the positive contribution which has been made by sport in the emergence of the new South Africa. From a situation in which sporting activity was bound up with the politics of division, there emerged what appeared to be a new consensus constructed around the proposition that all South Africans could now identify with all South African sport, epitomised above all by President Mandela's willingness to celebrate the achievements of the Springbok rugby union team, for so long regarded as the sporting representative of Afrikaner nationalism and the apartheid system. Yet, as Adrian Guelke and John Sugden reveal here, there is much work yet to be done if sport is to deserve to be regarded as having played a crucial integrative role. South Africans of different colours are still likely to be involved in separate sporting experiences, either by playing different sports or by playing for teams which do not reflect the country's racial and cultural mix. On the other hand, the situation is now much better than it was and sport may yet achieve what some have already claimed for it. Even if it does so, however, there is little room for complacent reflection on the integrative capacity of sport. As Ian McDonald shows, in India — at times in the past held up as a success story in terms of binding together a multiplicity of ethnic and religious groups — sport, and specifically cricket, is now in the forefront of the politics of communal division. The lesson is always the same. So important is sport as an element in modern society that it will always be contested terrain. That means it possesses the capacity to transcend division but it is just as likely to highlight and exacerbate division and to provide an important forum for the celebration of difference, often with damaging consequences.

It is hoped that this collection will be followed by other studies of sport in divided societies. As the threat of global conflict recedes, civil wars, ethnic strife and cultural antagonism become ever more dangerous to the fabric of modern societies. If we are to fully understand the underlying causes of such friction, it is imperative that we examine every aspect of human life. Sport cannot be ignored in any analysis which is to have real meaning.

References

Bairner, A. (1996) 'Sportive nationalism and nationalist politics: A comparative analysis of Scotland, the Republic of Ireland and Sweden', *Journal of Sport and Social Issues*, Vol. 20, No. 3: pp. 314-334.

Blain, N., Boyle, R. and O'Donnell, H. (1993) *Sport and national identity in the European media*. Leicester: Leicester University Press.

Cronin, M. (1994) 'Sport and a sense of Irishness', *Irish Studies Review*, No. 9: pp. 13-17.

Cronin, M. (1996) 'Defenders of the nation? The Gaelic Athletic Association and Irish nationalist identity', *Irish Political Studies*, Vol. 11: pp. 1-19.

Donnelly, P. (1996) 'The local and the global: Globalization in the sociology of sport', *Journal of Sport and Social Issues*, Vol. 20, No. 3: pp. 239-257.

Duke, V. and Crolley, L. (1996) *Football, nationality and the state*. Harlow, Essex: Longman.

Guttmann, A. (1994) *Games and empires: Modern sports and cultural imperialism*. New York: Columbia University Press.

Harvey, J., Rail, G. and Thibault, L. (1996) 'Globalization and sport: sketching a theoretical model for empirical analyses', *Journal of Sport and Social Issues*, Vol. 20, No. 3: 258-277.

Hill, C. R. (1992) *Olympic politics*. Manchester: Manchester University Press.

Holmes, M. (1994) 'Symbols of national identity and sport: The case of the Irish football team', *Irish Political Studies*, Vol. 9: pp. 81-98.

Houlihan, B. (1994) *Sport and international politics*. Hemel Hempstead, Hertfordshire: Harvester Wheatsheaf.

Jarvie, G. and Walker, G. (eds) (1994) *Scottish sport in the making of the nation: Ninety minute patriots?* Manchester, Manchester University Press.

MacClancy, J. (1996) 'Sport, identity and ethnicity', in J. MacClancy (ed) *Sport, ethnicity and identity*. Oxford: Berg, pp. 1-20.

MacClancy, J. (ed) (1996) *Sport, identity and ethnicity*. Oxford: Berg.

Maguire, J. (1994) 'Sport, identity politics and globalization: diminishing contrasts and increasing varieties', *Sociology of Sport Journal*, Vol. 11, No. 4: pp. 398-427.

Mangan, J. A. (ed) (1996) *Tribal identities. Nationalism, Europe, sport*. London: Frank Cass.

Moorhouse, H. F. (1996) 'One state, several countries: soccer and nationality in a "United" Kingdom', in J. A. Mangan (ed) *Tribal identities. Nationalism, Europe, sport*. London: Frank Cass, pp. 55-74.

Sugden, J. and Bairner, A. (1993) *Sport, sectarianism and society in a divided Ireland*. Leicester: Leicester University Press.

Sugden, J. and Tomlinson, A. (eds) (1994) *Hosts and champions: Soccer cultures, national identities and the USA World Cup*. Aldershot, Hampshire: Arena.

———— (1998) *FIFA and the contest for world football*. Cambridge: Polity Press.

Wagg, S. (ed) (1995) *Giving the game away. Football, politics and culture on five continents*. London: Leicester University Press.

SPAIN DIVIDED: THE BARCELONA OLYMPICS AND CATALAN NATIONALISM

John Hargreaves

University of London, Goldsmith's College

To understand why holding the Olympic Games in Barcelona divided Spain by helping to stimulate Catalan nationalism, we need, first, to employ a clear conception of nationalism and to establish the specific nature of Catalan nationalism in terms of an account of the uneven development of the host state. We can then examine the course of the conflict between Catalonia and Spain over the Games and be in a position to assess its significance.

Nations and nationalism

A sense of national identity, which is what essentially constitutes a nation, may unite or divide states. Modern states attempt to minimize and overcome internal divisions by fostering a sense of national identity so that the state becomes synonymous with the nation, an equation signified by the widespread assumption that we live in a world of 'nation-states'. In reality, the project is by no means always successful: nations may emerge and continue to exist for a long time without states of their own, a large proportion of states are multinational, and increasingly these 'sub-national' elements may be opposed in various ways to their host states. Whether the sense of belonging to a nation is state-induced, or takes the form of opposition to the host state, the nation as the premier symbol of the collectivity and the accompanying sense of national identity, should not simply be equated with nationalism, although, of course, they are in fact, often connected. Nationalism is a form of politics generated where political movements seeking or exercising state power justify their action by attributing a specifically nationalist meaning to the symbol 'nation'. That is to say, nationalist movements typically, posit the existence of a nation with an explicit and peculiar character, and hold that the interests of the nation take priority over all other interests and values, and that this nation should be as independent as possible, that is, it should be politically sovereign (Breuilly, 1993). Such statements are the foundation of all their political claims — they are the central ideological statements deployed by nationalist movements or organisations.

Nationalist movements will tap existing senses of nationhood, but in their absence will readily attempt to construct or invent the character of the nation with any materials at their disposal. Nations and nationalism may take a 'civic' or 'ethnic' form, i.e. membership of the national community may be conceived in terms which include the total population of the territory in question, or membership may be restricted to those with the perceived relevant ethnic characteristics (Greenfeld, 1992). This is an analytical distinction: in fact, some mixture of the two types is usually present with one or other type predominating in given instances. It is important to emphasise that nationalism may be both for or against the state.

Where nationalism against the state is concerned there are, in fact, two foci of conflict: between the 'nationalising' or host state and the national minority, on the one hand, and within the national minority, on the other. Differences in the structure of political competition within the national minority produce different reactions to the central state, ranging from non-cooperation, separatism and violence, to cooperation, flexibility and participation in coalition governments. In the latter case nationalist movements may stop short of demanding complete independence because they perceive the balance of costs and benefits to be unfavourable. A national minority is not a fixed entity or a unitary group but a field of differentiated and competitive positions or stances adopted by different organisations, parties, movements or individual political entrepreneurs, each seeking to represent the minority to its putative members, to the host state, or to the outside world, while trying to monopolize the legitimate representation of the group (Brubaker, 1996).

As far as the policy of the 'nationalising state' is concerned what crucially matters is whether it is perceived as nationalising by representatives of the national minority. A state may or may not pursue a nationalising policy, but it must be perceived as doing so in the field of the national minority for nationalist movements to succeed in mobilising their potential constituencies. The perception and characterisation of the host state is itself a crucial object of struggle within the field of the national minority — a struggle to impose and sustain a vision of the host state as a nationalising or nationally oppressive state.

One can impose and sustain a stance as a mobilised national minority, with its demands for recognition and for rights, only by imposing and sustaining a vision of the host state as a nationalising or nationally oppressive state.

The conditions for ethnic group formation and the generation of ethnically-based nationalism are enhanced where there is relative underdevelopment or overdevelopment of the periphery. A segmental division of labour between centre and periphery concomitantly develops, and peripheral elites monopolise valued niches in the occupational structure and in key institutional spheres (Hechter and Levi, 1979). Uneven development cannot itself explain the nature of individual cases, however, since peripheral nationalisms with such features in common can exhibit very different characteristics, for example, in their propensities to violence. To explain such differences we have to examine the specific nature of the relationship between the centre and peripheral elites and the specific nature of political competition in the periphery. Whether central and peripheral elites are strongly integrated economically and politically, has a strong bearing on the structure of political competition in the periphery and hence on the character of peripheral nationalism. Where they are not integrated, the peripheral elite is likely to be more involved in nationalist movements which are consequently likely to be more variegated (Diez Medrano, 1995). Where the national minority, in addition, is culturally confident and possesses its own political culture and civic institutions, it is likely to be more flexible in its dealings with the host state (Conversi, 1997).

Minority nationalism is generated by the pressures of modernisation, but more often than not it has ethnic roots and origins in the pre-modern 'nation' (Llobera 1994; Armstrong, 1982). The manner in which the state acts vis-a-vis potential or actual opposition in its attempts to manage the modernisation process is a particularly important factor in stimulating and provoking the emergence of nationalist movements (Breuilly, 1993). Once a movement takes off, it often proves capable of sustaining a momentum of its own.

Catalan nationalism

In Spain, where state-induced nation-building has never been a very successful project, nationalism divides the country in the sense that in Catalonia (as well as in the Basque Country) a strong nationalist movement against the state was established by the late 19th century. Its origins lie in the foundation of the Spanish state in the 15th century in the dynastic union between Castile and

Aragon, and thereafter in the protracted, uneven, conflict-ridden process whereby Catalonia was reluctantly integrated into the Spanish state. Prior to the union, from the mid 12th century Catalonia had been an equal partner in a confederal union with Aragon, providing the reigning dynasty of the crown of Aragon at key periods. Through dynastic union or conquest Catalonia expanded its territory to become the dominant military and trading power in much of the Mediterranean from the 13th to the 15th centuries, ruling at various times Languedoc, Majorca, the kingdom of Valencia, Sicily, Sardinia, Naples and Athens. Catalan culture developed apace, notably in the shape of a great literary and philosophical tradition, exemplified in the oeuvre of Ramon Llull. Catalonia had one of the earliest parliaments in Europe, the *Corts*, and a written constitution, the *Usatges* (usages) codifying established customs and practices (Balcells, 1996). Relations between everyone — nobles, burghers, peasants and clerics, as well as between the king and his Catalan subjects were seen as being based upon negotiation. The king could not revoke laws without the *Cort*'s permission, and was not considered legitimate until he had sworn to respect the basic law of the land in the presence of the *Corts*. It became the task of the *Generalitat*, a standing committee of the *Corts*, to defend them, to negotiate grants of money to the king and to manage taxation. Catalan feudalism, in marked contrast to Castile, which was not, properly speaking, a feudal state, is thus the origin of the Catalan practice of political negotiation, of contractualism and of pactism, a tradition which continued long after the union with Castile (Giner, 1994).

At the time of the union with Castile Catalonia had suffered a long period of demographic and economic decline brought about by plague and civil war, so its influence had weakened. While it retained its own independent institutions, currency, customs and tax system — the Spanish crown could not raise taxes without the permission of the *Corts* — and Catalan remained the official language, it was politically subordinate to Castile, the *Corts* met much less frequently, and Castile excluded Catalonia from the economic benefits flowing from Spain's vast empire in the new world.

In the war between France and Spain in 1640 the Catalan peasantry revolted against the expense of maintaining the Spanish army billeted upon them, and the *Generalitat*, supported by France, declared Catalonia's independence. Catalonia was eventually defeated and ironically, lost its northern provinces across the Pyrenees to its ally, France. Although its system of self-government was not dismantled, it was whittled away and weakened. The Spanish king acquired control over nominations to the *Generalitat* and the Barcelona City Council (*Consel de Cent*), and the *Corts* no longing controlling the *Generalitat*, did not meet again until 1701.

The catastrophic loss of autonomy came in 1714 as a result of the War of the Spanish Succession between Britain and its allies against France and Spain. Catalonia took the opportunity to revolt again and take the side of Spain's enemies. Deserted by the latter Catalonia was eventually crushed. Under the Decree of *Nueva Planta* all Catalan political institutions were abolished, Castilian laws, absolutism and centralism were imposed; public use of the Catalan language was prohibited shortly after, and the region was subjected to a heavy burden of taxation.

Catalonia demonstrated its resilience by stepping into the vanguard of Spanish industrialisation and modernisation in the 19th century, when Spain, compared with its main rivals in Western Europe, was a byword for backwardness. State centralisation was clumsy and inefficient: the centre failed to modernise the country economically and politically, and so, regional variations were much more pronounced than in comparable parts of Western Europe. Catalan industrialisation was autocthonous, based on the textile and consumer goods industries, sectors which were small scale and more competitive than the big banking and heavy industry monopolies that emerged later in the Basque Country and were controlled from Madrid. The Catalan bourgeoisie, unlike the Basque oligarchy, was not integrated into the politico-economic regime at the centre and was relatively independent.

Industrial development overlapped with a major revival in Catalan culture from the 1830s, the *Renaixenca*, through which Catalan intellectuals very successfully stimulated a growth in Catalan consciousness. Rural Catalonia, together with the Basque Country, Navarre and Aragon, was also a stronghold of Carlism, a movement which launched three wars against state centralisation between 1833 and 1872. Federalism and republicanism which played an important part in Spanish politics as the century advanced, took hold in Catalonia in particular. Catalan elites were independent, relatively well- educated and were willing and able to play a prominent part in the Catalan nationalist movement. Unlike those elsewhere in Spain, they did not form alliances with elites at the centre and as self-conscious modernisers they increasingly felt themselves to be hamstrung by an inefficient, backward, parasitical centre which did not recognize their region's unique qualities or represent its interests.

From the 1880s these elements coalesced into an increasingly well-organised nationalist political movement which came to dominate Catalan politics at the turn of the century. Under pressure from the nationalists the centre conceded a degree of self-government in 1911 (the *Mancomunitat*), which the nationalists used to such effect that it was abolished and the nationalist movement repressed as a danger to Spain's national integrity, when Primo de Rivera's dictatorship was installed in 1923. Spain's chronic political instability did not permit the dictatorship or the monarchy to survive long and under the Second Republic (1932-39) Catalan nationalists at last realised their ambition when the *Generalitat* and Catalan Parliament were restored. Unfortunately for Catalonia, which, naturally, supported the republican side in the civil war from 1936-39, the Spanish nationalist General Franco won. Franco's nationalising state instituted the most thorough attempt in the history of Spain to subordinate Catalonia to central control at all levels. Any sign of independence, including the use of the Catalan language, was banned and any opposition was brutally suppressed.

With the transition to liberal democracy after Franco's death, the *Generalitat* and Parliament were restored and since the first elections in 1982 the Catalan government has been in the hands of the main nationalist party. Historically, the behaviour of the Spanish state towards Catalonia has been, and still is today, a most significant factor determining the character of Catalan nationalism and today's democratic state is still associated in the minds of Catalan nationalists with centrism and repression. But Catalan nationalism is a function of the interaction between two political fields, that of relations between the Spanish state and Catalonia on the one hand, and that of relations between the different elements within the field of the national minority, on the other.

The contemporary Spanish state's nationalising efforts, in stark contrast to the Franco era, now approximate rather closely to the civic model, but there is no widespread, strong sense of national identity, instead there are fairly widespread feelings of ambiguity about it (Garcia Ferrando, *et al.*, 1994). In the field of the national minority, the governing political party, *Convergencia i Unió* (CiU), i.e. the party commanding the support of the majority of nationalists, is 'inclusive', in the sense that it does not demand compete independence and instead proceeds moderately and pragmatically to obtain the maximum feasible degree of autonomy for the region. The other main nationalist grouping, *Esquerra Republicana* (ERC) is separatist. Both are in competition with a strong, non-nationalist party, the Catalan Socialist Party which is affiliated to the Spanish Socialist Party (PSOE), with the Catalan Communist Party (*Initiativa de*

Catalunya), and with the conservative *Partido Popular* (PP), which is rather weak in Catalonia. The structure of Catalan politics is strongly pluralist and this, combined with Catalonia's contractualist political culture and its pactist strategy, enables it to respond remarkably flexibly and creatively in its relations with the centre. The availability of a wide variety of competing alternatives and the tradition of pactism goes a long way to explaining the absence of violence in Catalan nationalism today.

Catalan nationalism incorporates strong elements of ethnic nationalism. Its claim to the status of a historic nation and its opposition to the host state are rooted in the existence of a culturally distinct community with a very strong sense of its own national identity, which coheres above all, around the Catalan language. Language is the primary ethnic marker distinguishing Catalans from Castilian-speaking Spain and in particular, from that large sector of the region's population which is of immigrant origin from the rest of Spain (Barrera-González, 1995). The Catalan government is officially committed to the notion of civic nationalism, in that it proclaims that Catalans are people who live and work in Catalonia. That ethnic nationalism predominates however, is evidenced by the government policy of 'linguistic normalisation', whereby Castilian native speakers are compelled in a number of ways, to become culturally Catalan, i.e. the school curriculum is taught in Catalan and proficiency in the language is a condition of employment in much of the public sector. The civic emphasis in official Catalan nationalism represents an attempt to avoid major conflict with its own 'national minority' population which is potentially capable of being mobilised by anti-Catalan interests. The ethnic element, i.e. the tendency to exclusiveness and a certain obsessiveness about the vernacular culture, is most evident among the separatists.

Catalan nationalism, having captured political power in the region, also exerts considerable leverage on central government to the extent that the last two governments have relied on CiU support to stay in power. Catalan nationalists are therefore in a position to use state power both directly and indirectly to further their interests. Catalonia is the richest region in Spain and its government commands considerable revenue resources and powers of expenditure. It possess certain powers with respect to law and order, the administration of justice, social welfare, and economic development, and full powers over education and cultural policy. It was this power position which was to prove so crucial in the conflict over the Olympic Games.

The Campaign[1]

The central government saw the Games as a showcase for Spain as a mature, modern democracy, i.e. as an opportunity to enhance Spain's prestige. Catalan nationalists feared that the Games would be used to reinforce the power of the centre at Catalonia's expense and they were determined to oppose this and to Catalanise the Games for their own benefit (Hargreaves, 1994; Hargreaves, 1996; Hargreaves and Ferrando, 1997). With the exception of an insignificant minority, from the start all Catalan interests decided to support the Games, but there were major differences between them over the extent to which they should be Catalanised.

The Catalan government under its President, Jordi Pujol, the main separatist party, ERC and the other separatist groupings, were opposed to the socialists who held in power in the Barcelona City Council under the mayor, Pasqual Maragall (who was also President of the Organising Committee of the Games), and who held power in Madrid as well. The main issues for the nationalists were official status for the Catalan language, the dignified presence of the Catalan flag (*La Senyera*) and national hymn (*Els Segadors*) in the ceremonies, the representation in and around the Olympics of Catalan culture in all its forms, and the right to demonstrate their Catalan identity. The separatists wanted a separate team for Catalonia, or if there was to be an integrated team, that Catalan members be distinguished from the rest.

Early on, a Catalan Olympic Committee (COC), led by a former Minister in the Catalan government, was formed to obtain recognition from the International Olympic Committee (IOC) for a separate Catalan team. Ostensibly a 'non-political' body designed to mobilise support among the Catalan sports federations for this objective, COC in fact, brought together the main elements of the nation-alist movement to Catalanise the Games. The strategy served to focus sustained attention on the Games as a Catalan national issue by articulating the aforemen-tioned demands in one form or other. In May 1989 the Catalan Parliament adopted a resolution to support the COC in its quest for separate recognition. There was a campaign also to have the Games televised in Catalan since Spanish National Television, based in Madrid, controlled Spanish broadcasting rights and was refusing to allow coverage in Catalan. After the Catalan government elections in March 1992 in which the nationalists made gains, *Acció Olímpica* with its 'Freedom For Catalonia' campaign became the main instrument for coordinating the efforts of the more radical activist groups and for launching the campaign on a mass basis (Crexell, 1994)

Up to the opening of the Games the nationalists made the running, pressurising the authorities in every conceivable way short of violence, to Catalanise the Games — threats to disrupt the Games and associated events, actions and demonstrations, public pronouncements and media events, mass meetings, and copious publicity for the cause. It was made clear that if the Games were not Catalanised in a satisfactory manner there would be trouble. Pujol came out in favour of greater Catalanisation. Samaranch, the IOC President, did so as well, and Maragall and the Olympic Games Organising Committee (COOB) were forced to accommodate to the opposition. In mid-June, 1992, six weeks before the Games were due to open, an 'Olympic Pact' (*Pacto Olímpico*) which had been previously approved by the central government, conceding in principle the core nationalist demand that the key Catalan symbols should be included in the Games in a dignified manner, was jointly announced by Pujol and Maragall. By this time the city was covered in Catalan flags and the nationalists were clearly winning the propaganda war over the Town Hall, while the Spanish flag was largely conspicuous by its absence.

Testing the Olympic Pact

For the next six weeks until the opening of the Games, despite the 'Paz Olímpica', (Olympic peace) tension, mutual suspicion and conflict between the nationalists and the authorities continued. The issues were: the civil liberties of the nationalists, Pujol's alleged capitalisation on the Olympics, the relation between Pujol and *Acció Olímpica*'s campaign, and the Catalan government's attempt to marginalise the central government. For the nine days the Olympic Flame was in Catalonia the situation was particularly tense.

At the reception ceremony for the Olympic Flame the Spanish Minister of Education's address was virtually drowned out by the chorus of whistling and shouting. The ceremony was further disrupted by a nationalist militant who suddenly appeared at the centre of the proceedings at the most dramatic moment of the performance, holding aloft a large 'Freedom For Catalonia' banner. Photographs of the incident appeared on the front of the national newspapers.

Central government which was responsible for security, was alarmed and embarrassed by the ease with which security had been breached, offended by the audience's hostile reaction, and by what it regarded as an excessive Catalan-isation of the proceedings. As the Olympic torch carrying the flame traversed Catalonia a well-organised Acció Olímpica preceded the official caravan inundating localities with nationalist flags, banners and other propaganda materials. What was perceived as an oppressive security presence caused strong resentment in certain localities and deep concern among the activists about civil liberties. The Spanish Secretary of State For Security announced his determina-tion to take firm control and the apparently hardening attitudes on both sides contributed to increasing tension. At the nationalist stronghold of Banyoles, an Olympic sub-site of 13,000 inhabitants, the local population and four hundred Guardia Civiles stationed there for the Games, co-existed in a state of cold war, and tanks and helicopters were deployed when the torch went through.

The arrival of the torch in the nationalist shrine of Montserrat, where the nationalists had made their maximum effort to mobilise, witnessed bitter confrontation between them and Maragall. The official welcoming of the flame as a symbol of fraternity and peace by the Abbott of Montserrat, had to compete with a chorus of nationalist slogans, and Maragall was subjected to catcalls and insults. He reacted angrily against those "...whose disproportionate and stupid acts put in jeopardy the spirit of peace, festivity and universality of the Olympic Flame...", and against Pujol, whom he accused of supporting *Acció Olímpica*'s campaign and of acting against the spirit of their accord.

The most serious episode concerning security and civil liberties came on 29th June, when the Guardia Civil detained over thirty suspected members and collaborators of a small, marginalised Catalan terrorist organisation, some of whom were members of legitimate nationalist parties. The majority were eventually not charged and later released, but the arrests immediately fuelled suspicion among nationalists that the state was trying to intimidate them into desisting from their campaign.

The round-up provoked an outcry, particularly because those arrested claimed to have been tortured under interrogation. Catalan Parliament deputies agitated and petitioned the President of the Parliament; the resignation of the Minister of the Interior was called for; Pujol was rumoured to have complained to the King and he accused the socialists of criminalising Catalan nationalism. A telegram campaign ensued to release the detainees and notables formed a support committee. The ERC leader called for an official investigation into the matter, claiming it was a constitutional as well as civil liberties issue, and he presented a formal denunciation of the alleged torture of one of his party's leaders in the Gerona Courts. One alleged torture victim intended to take the matter to the European Court at Strasbourg. A mass meeting rejected the 'Spanish Olympics' and called for the COC to be recognised instead.

A fortnight before the Games the Catalan government provoked a furious reaction in the Madrid press and around the country, against the way it was exploiting the Games and marginalising Spain's contribution. In Spain the Games were being perceived as Catalan and the majority of people thought that the Catalan government was the main financial contributor, whereas in fact the central government was the biggest contributor by far.

At the first of two full dress rehearsals for the Opening Ceremony attended by the public, one week before the Games were due to start, to the consternation of the authorities, loud whistling erupted in the stadium when the Spanish flag appeared and the Spanish national anthem was played. It came from many of the young volunteers, whose presence as an army of helpers was absolutely essential. The authorities on the spot immediately bent over backwards to allay the remaining nationalist suspicions about their intentions and it was not until one day before the opening that the last radical group was persuaded to abandon plans to disrupt the Games.

Meanwhile, the torch had completed its journey around Spain and had finally arrived in Barcelona the evening before the Opening Ceremony. Maragall and Pujol jointly received it in a euphoric atmosphere. Huge crowds in festive mood assembled to watch its passage through the different districts of the city and fireworks, music and dancing went on well into the night.

Catalanisation

The nationalists' campaign paid off handsomely in terms of the extent to which the Games were Catalanised. The first sequence of the Opening Ceremony was followed by the King and Queen's entrance into the Presidential box to the music of the Catalan national hymn, *Els Segadors*, and the parading of the Spanish, Catalan and Barcelona flags together into the stadium. All attention was focused first on the Catalan symbols: the TV cameras, broadcasting the scene to the nation and the whole world, as well as to the stadium audience on the large stadium screen, showed *La Senyera*, the Catalan flag, in close-up, to the stirring music of *Els Segadors*. The Spanish national anthem followed immediately after, this time with the focus on the Spanish flag. The two sets of national symbols were thus accorded equal status in this and all other respects throughout the rest of the Games' proceedings.

Language, being the main marker of Catalan ethnic distinctiveness and identity, figured prominently as one of the four official languages of the Games (Spanish, Catalan, French and English). One of the most significant aspects was the moment when the Games were officially declared open by the King, in which the Catalan language was privileged, for his first words were in Catalan: *"Benvinguts tots a Barcelona"* (welcome everyone to Barcelona).

Catalan culture was plainly on display. The Opening Ceremony began with a strikingly colourful and melodious amalgam of traditional and modern Catalan culture. Eighty musicians sounded the Olympic fanfare on the *tenora*, a reed instrument which accompanies the national dance, the *Sardana*. Catalans are extremely culture conscious and proud of their avant garde reputation in art and design. The Games logotype, designed by a Catalan, evoking Barcelona's important contribution to modern visual art in such work as that of Miró, Dalí, Picasso and Tapies, was formed by eight hundred performers filling the centre of the great arena in the Catalan, Spanish and Mediterranean colours of red, yellow and sky blue. The *Sardana* followed, performed by six hundred dancers dressed in white, accompanied by the Catalan opera singers Montserrat Caballe and Josep Carreras. Its sedate, serious quality is almost the exact opposite of the emotional, passionate *Flamenco* and carefree *Sevillanas*, popular elsewhere in Spain. Dancers link hands at shoulder height and form a circle. Movement is confined mostly to small, intricate steps in unison, requiring mathematical precision and carried out at the direction of a leading dancer. The concentration and discipline it requires is reflected in the usually rather serious facial expressions of the dancers. Catalans like to think of themselves as disciplined, hard-working and efficient, solid and possessed of that quality they call 'seny', meaning something like good commonsense. The orchestra played the *'Cant de La Senyera'* (Song of the National Flag), a popular, strongly emotive, patriotic song with words by the patriot-poet Joan Maragall, the grandfather of the mayor, Pasqual Maragall. Barcelona and Catalonia were foregrounded for fully fifteen minutes in a spectacular epic drama employing one thousand two hundred actors, 'The Mediterranean, Olympic Sea', written and directed by the Catalan theatre group *La Fura dels Baus*. It linked the mythological origins of western civilisation, the Olympic Games and Barcelona in a stunning spectacular, technically brilliant cultural performance. Other spectaculars on the same scale, designed to advertise Catalan flare for design, production and performance, embodying features of Catalan culture, figured in the Opening and Closing Ceremonies.

The elements of Catalanisation above were augmented spontaneously in enthusiastic displays on the part of the spectators. For example, in the main stadium, despite the plethora of flags on display among the foreign visitors, *La Senyera* was easily the predominant flag throughout. Many in the audience during the marchpast of the teams gave an especially warm welcome to small nations that had recently gained their independence from a centralised state. The COC had established relations with the Baltic Republics in order to show solidarity with 'fellow oppressed nations', and its Director General became an official representative of the Lithuanian team in Barcelona. He marched with the Lithuanian team, past the King on the tribune, in front of the world's cameras, waving the only Catalan flag in the whole parade.

Catalan identity found expression also among the Catalan athletes in the Spanish team. When they won a medal they displayed both the Spanish and the Catalan flag and since Catalan athletes won more medals than those from other regions, their flag was relatively prominent in this way.

Españolisation

There was also a strong dose of Españolisation. The torch relay progressed slowly for six and a half weeks around Spain through local communities which usually took the opportunity to stage a fiesta; and in Madrid the King himself received the torch. Thus the relay was turned into a warm celebration of Spanish national unity.

The presence of the King and royal family at the Games and their reactions to the proceedings were a constant focus of attention in the media. The symbolic work centering on the head of state signalled Spanish sovereignty over Catalonia and celebrated their unity. The entry of the Spanish team dressed in the red and gold of Spain, led by the King's son, Felipe, Prince of Asturias, bearing the Spanish national flag, had a delirious effect on the audience. This team contained a greater proportion of members from Catalonia than from any other part of Spain. On the other hand, it was the Spanish team as such, in which they paraded past the tribune before the Spanish head of state and with a Spanish prince at their head. When a Catalan won a gold medal it was celebrated as a Spanish victory, for which the Spanish national anthem was played and the Spanish flag raised in the victory ceremony. Catalonia was thus symbolically subsumed within the greater Spanish nation-state.

The Spanish state was also represented on the tribune throughout by key figures in the government — the President, Felipe González, his deputy Narcis Serra, a Catalan and former mayor of Barcelona, who had been instrumental in putting the bid together and getting the Games for Barcelona, and other ministers and members of the political elite. The presence of Pujol and of Maragall, together with the head of state, the Spanish President, and members of the national government, and all the foreign dignitaries, also strongly signified the harmonious integration of Catalonia within the Spanish state.

Also, in keeping with the organisers' strategy of achieving an acceptable cultural balance to both parties, a familiar image of Spain was projected in certain spectacular sequences of the Opening and Closing Ceremonies — in music, song, costume and dance — at which points the cultural codes switched, interrupting the pronounced Catalanity of the proceedings.

What was also noticeable as the Games progressed was the gradual emergence of the Spanish flag among the crowd — a creeping manifestation of pride in the Spanish flag after years in which it was anathema for any ordinary individual to display it in Catalonia.

Pluralist democracy in process

As the situation developed it became clearer to the contending parties that all of them could gain, provided that they did not overstep mutually agreed limits. Agreement on what constituted these limits emerged out of the process of conflict rather than being stipulated at the outset. All sides came to recognise that it was in their interests to compromise and by the end of the Games each could plausibly claim that they had achieved their objectives and, in a sense, had won.

The central government was unable to fully capitalise on the Games. Public opinion polls show that both during and after the Games the fact that the government was the largest contributor in economic terms was discounted. The Spanish public and even more so, the Catalan public, saw the Games as Catalan, and Felipe González emerged with a low opinion poll rating. Neither did the success of the Games help central government in any way in the general election of the following year, which left González without a majority, and turning to Pujol's Catalan nationalists to sustain himself in power.

Certainly the Spanish state, as opposed to the government, came out well in certain ways. The King and royal family emerged with a very high popularity rating for their contribution and the vast majority of the Spanish public perceived the organisation and the security arrangements as efficacious, and as presenting a good image of Spain, as well as of Catalonia, abroad. This reaction was, no doubt, due to the success of the Spanish team, and it does seem to reflect a new found confidence in Spain and a securer sense of national identity, which is likely to have worked in favour of national integration. Spain as a whole benefited from the impetus the Games gave to the flagging Spanish economy in the period 1987-92. Associated infrastructural investment is estimated to have accounted for between 0.9 and 1.6% growth in GNP (Brunet, 1992).

The conflict over the Games was handled pragmatically and with great skill. The two main protagonists, Maragall and Pujol, are practitioners of the art of 'pactism', a longstanding characteristic of Catalan politics. As members of the Catalan political elite they have something in common. Pujol was sentenced to seven years in prison in the early 60s and served three them for his part in organising a nationalist demonstration against Franco. Maragall declares he is "...a Catalan who claims to be a Catalanist but does not like nationalism." At what the two leaders deemed to be the critical moment, ten days before the torch was due to arrive at Empuries from Greece, they proclaimed their 'Pacto Olímpico'.

Pujol protected his flank against the radical wing within his own party and against the separatists of ERC and other groups, by publicly pressurising Maragall on the question of Catalanisation. Throughout the period when the nationalists were applying the pressure he never repudiated the existence of a pact, although he was himself publicly pressurising the Town Hall and COOB. He was also perfectly capable of speaking out against what he perceived as the excesses of the independistas and of cooling down nationalist tempers if they threatened to get out of hand, or become politically embarrassing. He was prepared to defer the question of gaining recognition for COC until after the Games were over. His reward was a degree of Catalanisation he never originally envisaged. Catalonia was put firmly on the world map and it benefited in economic terms to the tune of ten times the amount of investment there would have been otherwise, reversing trends in unemployment in the region in the period 1986-90 (Brunet, 1992). Pujol's political position was, accordingly, undoubtedly strengthened. It is difficult to see how González could have offered to bring Pujol and his party into a coalition government when he lost his majority in 1993 (Pujol rejected the offer), or came to rely on his support, if the Games had brought about confrontation between them. In this sense Pujol has been a longer term winner, in that the balance of power has shifted in his favour, putting him in a powerful position to extract concessions from the centre which will enhance Catalonia's autonomy.

Maragall responded to the nationalists' and Pujol's provocations by refusing to concede specific demands until it became expedient to do so. He emerged with the highest public opinion poll rating for his contribution to the Games and acquired at the same time an international reputation. He also accomplished his main objective — the modernisation, indeed, transformation of Barcelona. The following municipal elections saw a big national swing against the socialists, with many towns passing into the hands of the opposition, but Maragall and his party retained control of Barcelona due to his achievements with the Olympics.

The separatists also expressed satisfaction with the outcome. The leader of ERC claimed Catalan identity had been strengthened and threw his weight behind Pujol's call for *El Segadors* to have equal status with La Marcha Real whenever the King was received in Catalonia in the future. Although he protested that the medals Spain had won belonged to the athletes and not to Spain, and that the six medals won by Catalan athletes would have gone to COC, he knew very well his party's main objective had been substantially achieved. The separatists had also in the end acted quite pragmatically, accepting concessions on offer and realising they could not achieve all their objectives completely.

Conclusion

This amicable outcome of the Games then, was due to a combination of factors. Although Spain's intervention took a civic form, and Catalonia's took an ethnic form, both were relatively open to each other. The openness to Catalonia on the part of the rest of Spain and the central government, meant that relatively early on, it was accepted that the major benefactors would be Barcelona and Catalonia. Second, the predominant form that Catalan nationalist pressure took was that of 'inclusive' nationalism, i.e. a form of nationalism that was prepared to prag- matically accommodate Spain and which therefore did not threaten the integrity of the Spanish state. The majority of the population of Catalonia does not identify exclusively with Catalonia and want independence from Spain: the biggest proportion identify with both, and the phenomenon of dual identity is more common (García Ferrando *et al.*, 1994). Third, the conduct and the outcome of the struggle around these Games on the Catalan side was orchestrated by 'pactism', a feature of Catalan political culture running across the political spectrum. Unlike Basque or Irish nationalism, with the exception of an insignificant minority, no section of Catalan nationalism espouses violence. The combination of an inclusive nationalism, a policy of democratic, non-violent struggle which is shared by the separatists, and a 'pactist' political cultural tradition take us a good way towards explaining why conflict was fought out largely in symbolic terms and why political and cultural symbols were so important here. This was not mere play acting and it would be a bad mistake to think so. The deployment of political and cultural symbols around the Olympic Games linked the Games to the issue of Catalonia's autonomy and to Spanish and Catalan identity. They were a key element in mobilising public support for the different sides in the conflict. Fourth, the unprecedented success of the Spanish team was perceived as an achievement for the whole of Spain and not for just one region. Had Spain failed to win medals and feelings of national humiliation resulted, tension between Spain and Catalonia would more likely than not have exploded into more serious conflict. Furthermore, the Games were blessed by good fortune in that no terrorist, or other kind of major incident marred them. These last two considerations mean that explanations of nationalism which do not take account of contingency are incomplete. In these circumstances all the main political agents were able to make some significant gains. If this had been a zero-sum game, nationalism could have been an explosive, destabilising force. Here the presence of dual national identities was a stabilising factor contributing to nation-state integration, a timely reminder that a unitary, one-dimensional national identity is not a prerequisite for viable nation-states.

The Games tested the capacity of Spanish democracy to withstand the strains put upon it by tension between Catalonia and the centre. It would be wrong to interpret this success as a reinforcement of Spanish hegemony over Catalonia. If anything, the concessions won by Catalonia in the campaign to Catalanise the Games represent a significant step in the delicate process of negotiating a greater degree of autonomy for Catalonia within the existing democratic constitution.

Notes

[1]   The fieldwork for this research was carried in Catalonia and Barcelona, in particular, from April-May, 1992 with the help of an Economic and Social Research Council Award and a Leverhulme Fellowship.

References

Armstrong, J. A. (1982) *Nations before nationalism*. Chapel Hill: University of North Carolina Press.

Balcells, A. (1996) *Catalan nationalism*. London: Macmillan Press.

Barrera-González, A. (1995) *Language, collective identities and nationalism in Catalonia and Spain in general*. Florence: European University Institute Working Paper No. 95/6.

Breuilly, J. (1993) *Nationalism and the state*. Manchester: Manchester University Press.

Brubaker, R. (1995) *Nationalism reframed*. Cambridge: Cambridge University Press.

Brunet, F. (1992) *The economics of the Barcelona Olympic Games*. Barcelona: Centre d'Estudis Olímpics, Autonomous University of Barcelona.

Conversi, D. (1997) *The Basques, the Catalans and Spain*. London: Hurst and Co.

Crexell, J (1994), *Nacionalisme i Jocs Olímpics del 1992*. Barcelona: Columna.

Diez Medrano, J. (1995.) *Divided nations*. London: Cornell University Press.

Garíia Ferrando, M. *et al.* (1994) *La conciencia nacional y regional en la España de las autonomías*. Madrid: Centro de Investigaciones Sociológicas.

Giner, S. (1984) *The social structure of Catalonia*. London: Anglo-Catalan Society.

Greenfeld, L. (1992) *Nationalism: Five roads to modernity*. London: Harvard University Press.

Hargreaves, J. (1994) *Olympism and nationalism with special reference to the Barcelona Olympic Games*. ESRC Report Ref. No. R.-000.-23.-3970, Swindon, ESRC.

Hargreaves, J. (1996) 'Staat und Nation — Politik auf drei Regierungsebenen', in Luschen, G. and Rutten, A. (eds) *Spanien bei den Olympischen Spielen in Barcelona*. Sportpolitik, Stuttgart: Verlag Stephanie Naglschmid.

Hargreaves, J. and Garcia Ferrando, M. (1997) 'Public opinion, national integration and national identity in Spain: The case of the Barcelona Olympic Games', *Nations and Nationalism*, Vol. 3.: pp 65-87.

Hechter, M. and Levi, M. (1994) 'Ethno-regional movements in the West', in Hutchinson, J. and Smith, A. D. (eds) *Nationalism*. Oxford: Oxford University Press.

Llobera, J. (1994) *The god of modernity*. Oxford: Berg.

SPORT AND QUÉBEC NATIONALISM: ETHNIC OR CIVIC IDENTITY?

Jean Harvey[1]

University of Ottawa

"Québec 2, Canada 0", separatist Québec's Prime Minister René Lévesque was reported to say when speed skater Gaétan Boucher won his two gold medals in Sarajevo in 1984 (Hall *et al.*, 1991: p. 182). Eight years later, at the end of the Lillehammer Games, the leader of the Parti Québécois underlined the number of medals won by athletes originating from Québec, nine out of the 13 of the Canadian team, as an example of the power of the Québec people (Laberge, 1995b: p. 65). These remarks were not isolated incidents. Indeed, since the beginning of its development and of its institutionalization, sport in Canada has been instrumental in the evolution of the national issue debate. In some instances, it has contributed to foster or threaten Canada as a nation, or to foster or threaten Québec as a nation.

Gruneau (1983) in *Sport, Class and Social Development* as well as Metcalfe (1988) have pointed out how some of the first sports clubs created in Montreal in the late nineteenth century became cradles for a Canadian identity different from the British one. Although they took longer to get organized, a modernist and liberal faction of French Canadian community also decided to use sport as a means for the promotion of its nationalist interests with the creation, in 1894, of the Association Athlétique d'Amateurs Le National (AAAN). This later became, La Palestre Nationale. The association wanted to become the French Canadian counterpart of the powerful Montreal Amateur Athletic Association, which was completely dominated by the English. The aim of the AAAN was to demonstrate: "… that our race in sport like in other branches of human activity is not inferior to others" (quoted by Janson, 1995: p. 139) (our translation). One of its leaders, Laurent-Olivier David underlined the "importance for French Canadian

31

youth to register in this essentially nationalist club. We must develop, through gymnastics, the vigour of the growing generations. Almost all English people are involved in sports and French Canadians remain unconcerned. They must get involved in the movement" (quoted by Janson, 1995: pp. 139-140) (our translation).

Ice hockey has played a significant role in the promotion of Canada as a nation in the face of growing American imperialism. Indeed, Gruneau and Whitson (1993) have demonstrated how Hockey Night in Canada, broadcast by the Canadian Broadcasting Corporation every week since the early beginnings of television, has been one of the rare institutions through which Canadians shared a sense of belonging to a unified nation even in the face of increasing threats to that national symbol which is ice hockey. English Canadian media have also fueled pan-Canadian nationalism by the way Olympic Games have been covered (see MacNeill, 1996).

Since the early 1960s, the Canadian state has invested a lot of resources to develop a high performance sport system in order to foster national unity (Harvey and Proulx, 1988; Harvey and Thibault, 1996; Macintosh *et al.*, 1987). In fact, this increasing preoccupation with high performance sport has been motivated by poorer and poorer performances by Canadian teams on the international scene, particularly in ice hockey, 'the national winter sport'. It is for this reason that Pierre Trudeau set up Task Force on Sport for Canadians in 1968 after his election as Prime Minister of Canada. Among other recommendations to strengthen the Canadian sport system, the Task Force recommended the creation of Hockey Canada, an organization charged with dealing with the NHL in order to be able to field competitive teams for international events (see Gruneau and Whitson, 1993: pp. 256-267). With regards to ice hockey, the 1972 Challenge Cup, which brought together a selection of the best Canadian players of the NHL and the powerful Soviet team, was a key event in the construction of Canadian national pride. After several highly unexpected losses against the Soviet team, the Canadians rallied to win the series in a dramatic end to the last game.

Among other initiatives to promote national unity, were the creation of the Canada Games, in which all provinces and territories compete to win the flag of the games and the creation of the Arctic Games, a programme which has been described as a device for the acculturation of native people into the pan-Canadian national project (Parashack, 1997).

However, in some instances, sport has been seen as a threat to Canada as a nation. The impossibility for Canada to field a competitive team in a sport, ice hockey, dominated by a U.S. controlled corporation (Gruneau and Whitson, 1993: p. 265), the recent expansion of NHL in American cities in combination with the moving of the Québec Nordiques and Winnipeg Jets franchises to American cities (Denver and Phoenix respectively), the recent expansion of the American-based NBA to Canadian cities (Toronto and Vancouver), as well as the everlasting financial difficulties of the Canadian Football League, all contributed to a growing sense of an Americanization of Canadian culture (Kidd, 1991) and consequently as a threat to Canada as a nation (Jackson, 1994; Earle 1995; Nauright and White, 1996).

From the pan-Canadian point of view, another set of major threats to Canada are the uncertainties about the relationship with Québec. Inequalities in Canadian sport itself have contributed to the promotion of the idea of Québec as a separate country. Boileau, Landry and Trempe (1976), for example, have discussed the under representation of French Canadians on Canadian national teams. More recently, accusations of discrimination against Québécois athletes were voiced by the Bloc Québécois party in the House of Commons when it was revealed that just one Québécois has been selected on the Canadian ice hockey team to play in the Lillehammer Games. (Canadian Press, 1994)

On some occasions, Canadian and Québécois nationalism have clashed over sport, as was the case with the 1976 Montreal Olympic of Montreal (see, Kidd 1992). In addition, Vicky Paraschak's (1996; 1997) studies on Inuit and other Aboriginal people have underlined how sport has been used, on the one side by the Canadian federal State to promote the national and, on the other side, by Native people to promote their own cultural identity. More recently, Laberge (1995a) has shown how French Canadian members of Canadian national teams are divided between their Québécois and Canadian identities. Finally, Rail *et al.* (1995) have demonstrated how Canadian and Québécois nationalism clashed during the Québec 2002 Olympic bid.

As shown by the examples above, sport has contributed to the promotion of Québec as a nation. The two following additional examples show how the French media in Québec have been involved in this process. First, during the years English Canada was following the performances of the Toronto Maple Leafs on *Hockey Night in Canada*, French Canada was watching the Montreal Canadiens on *La soirée du hockey* where the performances of the French Canadians players have consistently been celebrated.

The most prominent of these 'national heroes' was without any doubt Maurice Richard whose amazing performances and misfortunes were lived out by the

French Canadian people as their own. The events of 1955 provide a telling example. On March 13, the Montreal Canadiens visited the Boston Bruins. As is usually the case, Canadiens' Maurice Richard, then the best player of the league, was constantly harassed on the ice by the opposing players in an attempt to prevent him from scoring. One player hit Richard on the head with his stick. Richard bled and lost control of his temper. He jumped on his opponent and started a fight. A referee tried to separate the two opponents. In the action, Richard pushed the referee and punched him in the face. During the two following days, the entire ice hockey press corps speculated on what kind of suspension would be given to Richard for hitting a referee. On March 16, the decision of the league was made public. Maurice Richard would be suspended for the rest of the regular season as well as for the play-offs: a decision which crippled any chance for the Montreal Canadiens to win the Stanley Cup. Nobody in Montreal was expecting such a tough decision and the French-speaking newspapers were unanimous in condemning it. Clarence Campbell, then President of the League, was asked to resign by several journalists. The following day, Campbell was present in the stands in the Montreal forum for a game against the Detroit Red Wings. Right from the beginning of the game the atmosphere in the Forum was hostile. The fans of Richard and of the Montreal Canadiens were not happy with the presence of Clarence Campbell and a smoke bomb exploded beside his seat before the end of the game. The police immediately jumped into action and evacuated the Forum. The angry and frustrated crowd took to the streets and soon their demonstration turned into a riot. For several days the events were commented on by the local press. In editorials and tributes the fate of Richard was associated with the French Canadian people. Indeed, Richard was depicted as the typical French Canadian unfairly treated by his English boss (personified by Clarence Campbell). Such was the explanation for the riot according to the francophone press. (see Marois, 1993; Bélanger, 1996).

While CTV was promoting Canadian nationalism through their coverage of the Calgary Games, TVA, the French network which teamed up with CTV to form the consortium which won the rights for the retransmission of the games, promoted another nation through an innovative set up. The producer of TVA's coverage wanted a new approach to broadcasting the events which would give Québécois athletes an exposure they never got before through the *Lys d'or* programme ('Golden lily', in reference to the white lily, the flower which appears on the Québec flag). A committee was created which set goals to the Québécois members of the Canadian team, goals that represented an improvement on their personal best performances without any consideration of the fact that these might or not lead to a medal win. The *Lys d'or* were shown on the screen during the performances of the athletes. Underlined Arseneau: "I want absolutely all our Québécois who participate in the games to be seen on TV" (Lemay, 1992, our translation).

The above discussion provides a set of examples of sport being instrumental in the promotion of different forms of nationalism in Canada. This chapter focuses on a specific issue which has become central to the political debates in Canada. What kind of nationalism is being promoted by the nationalist forces in Québec? The aim is to demonstrate how sport which has been always associated with the national issue debates is also closely connected with the more recent ones.

The 1995 referendum in Québec, which resulted in a close decision against Québec separation from Canada (49.3% were in favour, 50.6% against), has created a commotion in the rest of Canada. This is because few Canadians expected such a close call. The referendum is still at the centre of political debates in Canada and will be present for a long time, as the government of Québec is planning another one a few years down the road. Since 1995, the federal government has been painfully trying to promote minimal reforms to the federation in order to satisfy Québec's claims, as well as mounting barriers to the legality of a forthcoming new referendum; the so called plans A and B[2]. The fact is that, in Canada, one can witness three major nations or — to use the term coined by Benedict Anderson (1991) — "imagined communities": Canadian, Québécois and Aboriginal. The latter would also argue that they consist of several autonomous nations themselves. The issue of the national question gets even more complicated in Canada since, during the Trudeau government era (1968-1984), the federal state adopted an official multicultural approach to the definition of the Canadian people, an official bilingual policy for federal institutions, as well as a Charter of Rights and Freedom, which altogether multiply possibilities of clashes between different visions of the nation, as well as cultural (multiculturalism) and specific groups' claims (equality for women, gays, etc.). The pan-Canadian nationalism includes the Québécois as non-distinct individuals within the Canadian nation, although their difference (i.e language and culture) contributes to the definition of Canadian identity, whereas the Québécois consider themselves as a distinct nation. The third nation is formed by the aboriginal people who also see themselves as separate from both the Canadian and Québécois nations (Bourque and Duchastel, 1995; Houle, 1998).

In Canada, the political debates surrounding the possibility of Québec's separation have raised a set of issues concerning, for example, what is a nation, what the different forms of nationalism are, what the Canadian nation is, and is Québec a nation. Moreover, in current social theory, we are witnessing a burgeoning literature on nationalism, democracy, the modern state and national identity. It is our contention that these debates are pertinent to the sociology of sport, as they offer us an opportunity to revisit the literature on sport and nationalism and pose new questions concerning nationalist uses of sport. In the context of this chapter we will discuss an issue that has been central to the Québec referendum and is still being debated, on a day-to-day basis, in opinion newspapers such as *Le Devoir*: namely, is Québec nationalism an ethnic nationalism or a civic nationalism? An ethnic nationalism would be a nation defined exclusively by the culture of a given group, whereas a civic nationalism represents a vision of a nation as the assembliy of autonomous citizens sharing a territory as well as some common values such as democracy and freedom. We will also examine how sport is conceptualized by the promoters of Québec sovereignty and look at how this fits into the general national project. This discussion potentially provides a renewed questioning about sport, nationalism and national identity, specifically with regard to Canada and Québec.

Sport, national identity and nationalism: an overview of the literature

The sociology and history of sport literature on national identity, nationalism and sport is relatively abundant. However, it can be classified under two main headings: 1) nation-state building; 2) promotion of ethnic or national claims.

The first category covers the use of sport for purposes of nation-state building. Sport is used as a platform for promoting a sense of belonging to a specific political community or nation-state. Sport serves to reinforce a national image that ultimately downplays the role of ethnic groups or nations as separate entities. This is achieved though: a) the affirmation of national unity; b) the promotion of a supra ethnic civic nationalism; or c) through acculturation of specific groups or nations to a central state.

a) The building of a nation-state can be achieved through affirmation of national unity. With reference to sport this is exemplified in the development of

Mexican nationalism (1920-1970) where, for example, government officials used popular sports and physical education as a tool for reaffirming national unity and reestablishing Mexican credibility in the international community (Arbena, 1991). In Japan, baseball in the 1980s represented an opportunity to succeed in America's 'national game' and consequently rectify Japan's national image (Roden, 1980). In Germany, the creation of national teams and participation in international competition, since the beginning of this century, has been based on the ideology that international athletic competence is correlated with the superiority of a country (Krüger, 1987). Australia has also embraced the idea that international sport helps the growth and maintenance of a national identity throughout the years 1896-1926 (Jobling, 1988).

b) Sport is also used as a means to promote supra-ethnic civic nationalism. This is depicted in the Caribbean where basketball has been placed in a context in which it is presented as a part of the development of civil society. More specifically, members' interests are advanced independently of the state through the establishment of private, voluntary associations. This consequently helps develop autonomous local organizations and ultimately a new dimension of civil society (Mandle, 1990). This is also exemplified by Caribbean cricket where matches between England (who are considered the former masters) and the West Indies (the former slaves) have focused on national redemption (Yelvington, 1990). West Indian cricket has also been described as "a centralized and artificial authority attempting to meet the psychological doubts and economic jealousies of numerous territories feeling their way towards national identities" (Stoddart, 1988: p. 633). Another example can be seen in Nigeria where sport serves as a means of community identification and integration for the major ethnic groups while simultaneously acting to unify the different cultures (by facilitating their social interaction) in an attempt to enhance national prestige (Olu, 1992). In addition, many leaders in modern African states who are facing ethnic nationalist tensions on the basis of linguistic or tribal loyalties are using sport to encourage national loyalty and ultimately African unity (Monnington, 1986).

c) The building of a nation-state can also be achieved through acculturation of specific ethnic groups and nations to a central state. This is highlighted by North American Indian tribes who, as the result of contact with English speakers, have changed the kinds of games played by their people but have not changed the social processes traditionally promoted by games participation (i.e. group identity and symbolic identification) (Cheska, 1979).

Nations that exist within nation-states also use sport to promote their own claims for sovereignty or the promotion of their interests as ethnic groups within established states. Different forms of communities are solidified or even constructed through sport. Other nations enhance their identity through affirmation or contestation of the hegemonic national model.

In Wales, for example, between the years 1890-1914, success in football fostered local pride and national identity which often took the form of torchlit processions and boisterous celebrations honouring home-coming teams. Jarvie and Walker (1994) have suggested that Scottish sport has emphasized the Scottishness of various different groups whose identities have significantly contributed to Scottish development. In the case of Northern Ireland, sport is a potent social force in the mobilization of political sentiment and used as a vehicle for national and regional identification. ugden and Bairner (1993) maintain that because there is a struggle for the boundaries of this identification, sport ultimately becomes a part of the struggle for self-determination. This is also evident in Australian soccer where the non-Anglo-Celtic soccer clubs of the Illawarra Soccer Association use sport to express different ethnic identities. Clubs maintain that they would prefer to have a player roster consisting of matching ethnic identity (Hallinan and Krotee, 1993).

Finally, nationhood can also be enhanced through contestation of hegemonic nationalism. This is highlighted by the protest against the use of native American mascots by the U.S. state. Davis (1993) argues that through the anti-mascot movement Native groups have ultimately attempted to distance themselves from mythological American hegemonic masculine identity.

Our review of the literature on sport, national identity and nationalism, albeit incomplete, suggests that sport has been used to promote different forms of national projects. We shall now turn to the Québec example to see which type of national project is being promoted there and how sport is related to this project.

The national question in Québec

The central question is: Is contemporary Québécois nationalism a civic or an ethnic nationalism (based on the role assigned to sport by the Parti Québécois, the party currently holding the majority in the Québec National Assembly)?

It is necessary here to discuss definitions of concepts. The current proliferation of literature in social theory concerning nationalism is the result of a renewed interest in the subject during the past 10 years. In 1990, Arnason published a paper which opened by focusing on a complaint about the lack of theoretical progress in the theory and practice of nationalism, a situation which arguably has changed drastically since then. Benedict Anderson's (1991) famous Imagined Communities is among the recent work which has led to a renewed theorization about nationalism. For Anderson and others, nationalism is essentially a modern phenomenon. A nation is "... an imagined community — and imagined as both inherently limited and sovereign" (Anderson, 1991: p. 3). Bouchard adds the following details to Anderson's definition. He argues that a nation is:

> ... a specific mode of collective integration and mental image. This mode is characterized by; a) a sense of belonging expressed in symbols and nourished by a memory; b) elements of a common culture (language, values); c) a consensus on fundamental rules taken in charge by the Law; d) a shared willingness of collective development sustained and refereed by a sovereign state. (Bouchard, 1995: p. 79)(our translation)

As for *nationalism*, Bouchard defines it as:

> ... the ideology aimed at, either, promoting the action of a community with an aspiration to the status of a nation or, defending the attributes of a national community whose status is jeopardized or, stimulating the actions or developmental projects of this community through their inscription into the national thematic. (Bouchard, 1995: p. 79) (our translation)

Some recent works in political philosophy define the notion of civic nationalism as referirng to a de-ethnicized nation, predicated on a civic, rational logic or universal reason. This community is essentially pluralist and respectful of all groups. The definition of this community also implies the primacy of citizenship over any cultural or categorial representation. In other words, it is a liberal view of a nation-state where individual rights take precedence over those of the group. Conversely, ethnic nationalism would be a nationalism essentially promoting the project of a specific cultural group to become sovereign.

Thériault (1994; 1995) argues that this now classic distinction between civic nationalism and ethnic nationalism stems from two specific versions of the origin of the constitution of the nation in modernity: the tradition of the Enlightenment, best exemplified in the French Republic, and the Romantic tradition or the German model. In the first version the nation is constituted by the assembling of autonomous citizens sharing a common territory. "The political generates the community of destiny" (Thériault, 1994: p. 210). Therefore, the nation-state is a constructed reality resulting from the will of individuals to form a society. The second version considers that nations pre-date the state and are pre-political realities. In this version, the nation stems from culture. In other words, a "…shared culture generates the community of destiny" (Thériault, 1994: p. 21).

However, some of the more recent works in political philosophy suggest that, instead of two, there would be three modalities through which a common political identity is generated. As outlined by Houle (1996) they are the following: belonging to an ethnic group, adhesion to a common national culture, or participation in a common political culture. In the first instance, argues Houle (1996), full belonging to the national community is only possible for the descendants of a specific ethnic group. As for the second instance, "associating the definition of the national community not to an ethnic group but to a common national culture allows the foundation of a civic conception of identity" (our translation) (Houle, 1996: p. 152). Houle (1996) argues that in this model all citizens living within a given territory despite their ethnic origin, may belong to the nation and the political community. Finally, Houle (1996) underlines that Habermas considers that it is possible to dissociate cultural and political spaces. This would allow the foundation of a nation only on the ground of individuals sharing the same political culture, despite the absence of any cultural reference.

The classic distinction between civic identity and ethnic identity, albeit seldom presented in these exact terms, has been at the centre of the debates about Canadian and Québécois nationalism since the 1980s. For the opponents of Québécois nationalism, the latter would be essentially an ethnic nationalism, a nationalism dedicated to the defence of the "pure wool" Québécois, those whose ethnic origin would be clearly rooted in the French community from generations past. For these opponents of Québécois nationalism, ethnic nationalism is associated with the worst examples given by human history: Nazi Germany, the former Yougoslavia and Rwanda. Québécois nationalism would be essentially divisive, if not racist, it is argued. More importantly its focus on the preservation and promotion of French language would be contrary to the *Canadian Charter of Rights and Freedoms* which protects individual rights. Pan-Canadian nationalism, therefore, increasingly sees itself as a civic nationalism where all

Canadians, regardless of their ethnic identity, would assemble as individuals to constitute the Canadian nation.

Contrary to its detractors' views, current 'official' Québécois nationalism claims to be a civic nationalism. The so-called civic nationalist project of the current Québec government had been made known in documentation distributed to Québécois constituents before the 1995 referendum. One of the brochures distributed by the Québec Director of Elections included the following statement from the 'yes' side — i.e. the government:

> A YES on the night of October 30 will finally make it possible for Québec to attain the political status its cultural specificity naturally leads to. This initiative is resolutely respective of the identity of the First Nations and the anglophone community. The constitution of a sovereign Québec will recognize the right of the First Nations to self-governement on lands over which they will have full ownership, and their existing constitutional rights will be confirmed. The Constitution also guarantees the anglophone community the preservation of its identity and institutions, notably in the fields of education, health, and social services. (Directeur général des élections du Québec, 1995: p. 23)

The Declaration of sovereignty, included as a foreword to Bill 1, a Law on Québec's Future, underlined the fact that Canadian federalism has led to an undermining of Québec's cultural and institutional characteristics and that jurisdictional fights between the federal government and the provinces have proved federalism to be non functional. The sovereignist project, according to Salée (1995: p. 136), "… stabilizes the tension between citizenship and nation through showing itself as part of a collective will for a common life among all the residents living in Québec's territory, whatever their ethno-cultural origin" (our translation). It is a vision of an ideal supra nation, i.e. above the ethnic groups living in a given territory. Citizenship becomes the common denominator. The decision to create this new country is therefore not a sentimental ethnic one, it is a decision governed by rationality — the functional need of a sovereign state to solve the political and constitutional problems of Québec. As one can read in the 1994 Parti Québécois' political programme:

> Québec follows the road paved by all the nations which, sometimes abruptly, sometimes slowly, have given themselves one by one all the tools to become fully responsible societies. Some even gained their

independence before developing an identity as a people. Such has been the case of the U.S.A. (Parti Québécois, 1994: p. 1) (our translation)

Salée adds that in the Parti Québécois civic nationalist project:

> The primacy of citizenship implies for the individual an allegiance to the State which is above all other allegiances. Liberal citizenship commands individuals to make the state their primary identity basisand all other form of identity (language, ethnicity, culture, etc.) become secondary or complementary. (1995: p. 136) (our translation)

Nevertheless, Québec citizenship as defined in the civic nationalist vision is not completely devoid of a cultural content. Bill 1 specifies that the new constitution will stipulate that Québec is a French country and will hold the government responsible for the protection and development of the Québécois culture (see article 7, our translation). Again, according to Salée (1995), official nationalism sees itself as a civic nationalism, since the project is to:

> ... build a sovereign state, a francophone one for sure, but mainly a democratic state to which all members of society, without any exception or exclusion would rally behind. The nation must not be understood in its restrictive and culturally determined meaning, but as the legal and territorial guarantee which can be given only by a fully constituted state. (1995: p. 127) (our translation)

This leads us to how sport is a part of this Québécois nationalist project, how it has been seen by the sovereignty movement as contributing to the nation-building project and how this vision has evolved over time. To answer these questions, it is necessary to go back to 1976, when the Parti Québécois was first elected to government.

Soon after its election, the government of the Parti Québécois took several initiatives to protect the French language and to promote Québécois culture. The most famous of these initiatives was the controversial Bill 101, an act to protect the French language. Moreover between 1977 and 1979 three major political documents were published in the general area of culture which constituted the government's official policy on related issues, including sport.

It is in the white paper on leisure released in 1978 (Gouvernement du Québec, 1978) that leisure and sport were first assigned a role in the promotion of the Québécois nation.

In essence, recreation was no longer considered only as an area for personal development; it was also assigned a role in the cultural development of the Québécois nation. Recreation became a place for collective emancipation. [...] Accordingly, "... any policy on recreation must first recognize the right of individual and collective expression" (Governement of Québec, 1978: p. 190). State intervention would no longer be confined to the provision of services to individuals. In fact, these services would only be offered to the extent that they were consistent with community interests. [...] In the White Paper on recreation (Charron, 1979), the state's position was made clear. Four categories were laid out: the citizen — the focal point and priority of recreation policy; the municipality — the supervisor of recreation development and organization; the state — the guardian an promoter of collective interests; and national and regional agencies — the partners of the municipality and the state. [...] The Parti Québécois' fierce opposition to intervention by the federal state in the area of recreation and sport was also a major theme in thinking on the subject. (Harvey and Proulx, 1988: pp. 109-110)

More recently, the 1994 electoral programme of the Parti Québécois included three full pages on the leisure and sport policy. The most pertinent parts of this programme are the following;

Leisure is not only necessary for the development of the individual and the family, but is also a privileged moment in community life. Leisure is an expression of a community's cultural identity. It is through leisure that citizens come together and share the advantages of belonging to a more prosperous and humane society. We believe that leisure is part of the values of a society which aspire to a clean environment, to well being and quality of life for all. To reach this goal a government of the Parti Québécois will elaborate a general policy on leisure with the collaboration of all people involved in leisure activities. This policy will make its mark by offering access, universality, equity between men and women and a balance between all sectors of leisure. All Québécois, without any distinction of region, origin, or wealth will have access to leisure. (Parti Québécois, 1994: p. 116)

This programme also provides a long list of initiatives to promote quality of life and democratization of access to leisure, such as financial help to sport cooperatives. The goal of this is to democratize access to sport in villages and neighbourhoods. Finally, the programme includes a set of specific measures to promote high performance sport in which the creation of a national team with considerable financial resources and the creation of national training centres is important.

The chapter of the programme on leisure is not extensive in comparison, for example, to the chapter on the cultural policy, but its elements as outlined here reveal enough about the project. First, the policy reflects the inclusive citizenship of the Parti Québécois' larger nationalist project, as well as underlining the importance of leisure for identity formation. The idea of subsidizing grass roots groups devoted to access to sport is certainly an original proposition. In terms of high performance sport, little precise information is given as to how it will be used to promote national unity within the proposed sovereign state, but the fact that substantial financial resources will be devoted to national training centres and to the national team indicates that high performance sport will be used for national building objectives. Nevertheless the programme's emphasis on access, universality and equity suggests that all forms of leisure (including fitness and non competitive sport) will be promoted within the context of building a non-ethnic, although French speaking, Québécois civic nation. In this regard it is interesting to compare the 1994 political platform with the official policy of 20 years ago. One can see that the promotion of the Québécois as an ethnic group has been somewhat downplayed in the 1994 platform in order to make room for a vision of citizens coming together to share in their belonging to a progressive society.

It is interesting to note that, since the referendum the government of the Parti Québécois has released another leisure policy document (Gouvernement du Québec, 1997). This document does not make a direct reference to the national question. However, it indirectly addresses the issue by recognizing leisure and sport as strong tools for the promotion of a sense of belonging. Several hypotheses may be proposed to explain this evolution, but the most plausible one is that the document emanates more from an extensive consultation with groups involved, than from the political staff of the Ministry. Moreover, it is not impossible that, since the new political direction has been designed within the context of massive cuts in government budgets, it has been judged wiser not to associate the national emancipation project with the issue.

Discussion and conclusion

Our analysis of the past and current Québécois official nationalism has shown that the project has evolved from a more ethnic vision of the nation towards a more civic or even supra- ethnic nation project. In the newer vision, leisure and sport would contribute to citizens' civic identity and sense of belonging to a shared community (inclusive of any cultural and specific group distinction). This is a community whose boundaries are the territory of the Québec state. It is our belief that, besides the extremely stimulating theoretical debates around the notions of nation, nationalism, modernity and the state that have been generated by the 1995 referendum, the Québec case is extremely interesting for both nationalism and sport studies. First, to our knowledge, it is probably the only case where nationalist uses of sport have been so clearly designed in order to contribute to a national project that does not see itself as based only on an ehtnic definition of the nation. In our review of the literature, we have seen several cases, for example in some African countries, where competitive sport is being used for state-building in multicultural states. The difference between these countries and Québec is that the latter does not see the nation as a mix of ethnic communities, but a nation to be built around the existing French culture. Second, the Québec case is interesting in that it underlines the fact that non competitive sport can be used in the promotion of a civic nationalism.

So far as the Québec government and Parti Québécois civic nationalist project itself are concerned, anyone who followed the referendum debates must be aware that the "No" side has made it clear that, in their eyes, this nationalism is indeed an ethnic nationalism. In the context of the referendum, the ethnic nationalist label was even used by some groups within the "No" side in reference to the worst abuses which ethnic nationalism has led to in human history, the most recent examples coming from former Yugoslavia and Rwanda.

It is clear that the official nationalist project is at least partially culturally based, as the promotion of the French language and culture is indeed at its core. First, the nationalist question in Québec has always been closely related to French speaking national aspirations. Second, we live in a world where ethnic or cultural nationalism is indeed burgeoning, not diminishing. However, according to several authors (Thériault, 1995; Taylor, 1997; Finkelkraut, 1997) it may be the case that a pure civic nationalism, the so-called constitutional nationalism à la Habermas, might be impossible to realize and that collective identities will always be a feature of any nation-state. "Some communities are necessary and it is precisely from this point that it would be possible to come back to the idea of a constitutional patriotism which would allow the creation of a sense of identity around certain principles of liberty, diversity and pluralism" (Taylor, 1997: p. 28).

Nevertheless, as a preliminary conclusion to this chapter it may be recalled that sport, being a powerful tool of identity formation, has been used as a vehicle for several forms of nationalism. The Québec example tells us how it can be used for the promotion of both a civic nationalism and an ethnic nationalism, thereby emphasing that sport is a particularly malleable tool for different national projects.

Notes

[1] This chapter is a significantly modified version of a paper presented at the Annual NASSS Conference, Birmingham, Alabama, November 1996. The author acknowledges the help of his colleague François Houle for his comments on a first draft of the paper and the help of Kirsten Tenebaum, research assistant, for a first version of the review of literature and for style editing.

[2] Examples of the Plan A initiatives are the adotion by the House of Commons of a motion recognizing Québec as a distinct society and giving it (as to other provinces) a veto right on forthcoming reforms of the constitution. An example of plan B initiatives is the test before the Supreme Court of Canada of the legality of a referendum on the secession of a province. For a full discussion of the actions of the federal government before and after the referendum, see Houle (1998).

References

Anderson, B. (1991) *Imagined communities*. London: Verso.

Arbena, J. L. (1991) 'Sport, development and Mexican nationalism, 1920-1970', *Journal of Sport History* Vol. 18, No. 3: pp. 350-364.

Arnason, J. P. (1990) 'Nationalism, globalization and modernity', *Theory, Culture and Society* Vol. 7: pp. 207-236.

Baker, W. (1987)'Political games: The meaning of international sport for independent Africa', in W. Baker and J. Mangan (eds) *Sport in Africa. Essays in social history*. New York: Africana Publishing Company, pp. 272-294.

Bélanger, A. (1996) 'Le hockey au Québec, bien plus qu'un jeu: analyse sociologique de la place centrale du hockey dans le projet identitaire des québécois', *Leisure and Society* Vol. 19, No. 2: pp. 539-557.

Boileau, R., Landry, F. and Trempe, V. (1976) 'Les Canadiens français et les grands jeux internationaux', in R. S. Gruneau and J. Albinson (eds) *Canadian Sport: Sociological perspectives*. Don Mills: Addison Wesley: pp. 141-169.

Bouchard, G. (1995) 'La nation au singulier et au pluriel. L'avenir de la culture nationale comme «paradigme» de la société québécoise', *Cahiers de recherche sociologique* No. 25: pp. 79-100.

Bourque, G. and Duchastel, J. (1996) 'Construire une communauté politique', *Le Devoir*. October 26 and 27: p. A13.

Canadian Press (1994) 'Équipe canadienne de hockey aux Jeux: un seul francophone à Lillehammer', *Le Devoir*, January 24.

Cheska, A. (1979) 'Native American games as strategies of societal maintenance', in Edward, Farrer, and Norbeck (eds) *Forms of play of Native North Americans*. St. Paul, Minnesota: West Publishing Company, pp. 227-247.

Dallaire, C. (1995) 'Le projet sportif des franco-ontariens et leurs revendications auprés du gouvernement provincial', *Recherches sociographiques*, Vol. 36, No. 2: pp. 243-263.

Davis, L. (1993) 'Protest against the use of Native American Mascots: A challenge to traditional American identity', *Journal of Sport and Social Issues*, Vol. 17, No. 1: pp. 9-22.

Directeur général des élections du Québec. (1995) *Québec 95 Référendum NON OUI*. Booklet.

Earle, N. (1995) 'Hockey as Canadian popular culture: Team Canada 1972, television and the Canadian identity', *Journal of Canadian Studies* No. 30: pp. 107-123.

Finkelkraut, A. (1997) 'L'archipel identitaire', in M. Ancelovoci et F. Dupuis-Déri (eds) *L'archipel identitaire*. Montréal: Boréal: pp. 37-51.

Fotheringham, R. (1982) 'Sport and nationalism on Australian stage and screen; From Australia Felix to Gallipoli', *Australian Drama Studies* Vol. 1, No. 1: pp. 65-88.

Gouvernement du Québec (1977) *Prendre notre temps: Livre vert sur le loisir au Québec*. Québec: Gouvernement du Québec.

———— (1978) *La politique québécoise du développement culturel*. Québec: Gouvernement du Québec.

———— (1979) *Un monde à récréer: Livre blanc sur le loisir au Québec.* Québec: Gouvernement du Québec.

———— (1997) Towards a renewed partnership: Governemental action framework in the fields of recreation and sport. Québec: Ministére des Affaires Municipales.

Gruneau, R. S. and D. Whitson (1993) *Hockey night in Canada.* Toronto: Garamond.

Gruneau, R. S. (1983) *Sport, class and social development.* Amherst: University of Massachusets Press.

Hall, A., Slack, T., Smith, G. and Whitson, D. (1991) *Sport in Canadian society.* Toronto: McClelland and Stewart.

Hallinan, C. J. and Krotee, M. L. (1993) 'Concepts of nationalism and citizenship among non-Anglo-Celtic soccer clubs in an Australian city', *Journal of Sport and Social Issues* No. 72: pp. 125-133.

Harvey, J. and Proulx, R. (1988) 'Sport and the state in Canada', in Harvey J. and Cantelon, H. (eds) *Not just a game: Essays in Canadian sport sociology.* Ottawa: University of Ottawa Press: pp. 93-119.

Harvey, J. and Thibault, L. (1996) 'Politique du sport et restructuration de l'État-providence au Canada' in Augustin, J.-P. and Sorbets, C. (eds) *La culture du sport au Québec.* Talence: Éditions de la Maison des sciences de l'homme d'Aquitaine: pp. 993-112.

Houle, F. (1996) 'Philosophie politique et minorités nationales: les analyses de Charles Taylor et de Will Kymlicka sur le Canada', *Carrefour* Vol. 18, No. 1: pp. 138-176.

———— (1998) 'La pluralité des identités nationales et l'évolution du nationalisme canadien' in Andrew, C. (ed) *Dislocation et permanence: l'invention du Canada au quotidien.* Ottawa: University of Ottawa Press.

Jackson, S. (1994) 'Gretzky, crisis and Canadian identity in 1988: Rearticulating the Americanization of Culture debate', *Sociology of Sport Journal* Vol. 11, No. 4: pp. 428-446.

Janson, G. (1995) *Emparons-nous du sport.* Montréal: Guérin.

Jarvie, G. and Walker, G. (1994). 'Ninety minute patriots? Scottish sport in the making of the nation', in G. Jarvie and G. Walker (eds) *Ninety minute patriots? Scottish sport in the making of the nation.* Manchester: Manchester University Press.

Jenson, J. (1993) 'Naming nations: Making nationalist claims in Canadian public discourse', *Canadian Review of Sociology and Anthropology* Vol. 30, No. 3: pp. 337-358.

Jobling, I. (1988) 'The making of a nation through sport: Australia and the Olympic Games from Athens to Berlin, 1898-1916', *Australian Journal of Politics and History* Vol. 34, No. 2: pp. 160-172.

Kidd, B. (1991) 'How do we find our voices in the "New World Order"? A Commentary on Americanization', *Sociology of Sport Journal*, Vol. 8, No. 2: pp. 178-184.

—— (1992) 'The culture wars of the Montreal Olympics', *International Review for the Sociology of Sport* Vol. 27, No. 2: 151-163.

Krüger, A. (1987) 'Sieg Heil to the most glorious era of German Sport: Continuity and change in the modern German Sports movement', *International Journal of the History of Sport* Vol. 4, No. 1: pp. 5-20.

Laberge, S. (1995a) 'Sport experience and modes of ethnic belonging', Unpublished paper, NASSS annual meeting, Sacramento, Nov. 4.

—— (1995b) 'Sports et activités physiques: modes d'aliénation et pratiques émancipatoires', *Sociologie et Sociétés* Vol. 27, No. 1: pp. 53-74.

Lemay, D. (1992) 'TVA sur le gros nerf (de la guerre)...', *La Presse*, July 25: p. C4.

Macintosh, D., Bedecki, T. and C. E. S. Franks (1987) *Sport and politics in Canada: Federal government intervention since 1961*. Kingston-Montreal: McGill-Queen's University Press.

MacNeill, M. (1996) 'Networks: Producing Olympic Ice Hockey for a national television audience', *Sociology of Sport Journal* Vol. 13, No. 2: pp. 103-124.

Mandle, J. (1990) 'Basketball, civil society and the post colonial state in the Commonwealth Caribbean', *Journal of Sport and Social Issues* Vol. 14, No. 2: pp. 59-75.

Marois, M. (1993) *Sport, politique et violence: une interpretation des dimentions politiques du sport-spectacle, dela violence des foules aux événements sportifs et de la médiatisation de cette violence*. Montréal: Université de Montréal, Unpublished Ph. D. dissertation in political science.

Metcalfe, A. (1988) 'The growth of organized sport and the development of amateurism in Canada, 1807-1914', in J. Harvey and H. Cantelon (eds) *Not just a game*. Ottawa: University of Ottawa Press: pp. 33-69.

Monnington, T. (1986) 'The politics of Black African sport' in L. Allison (ed) *The politics of sport*. Manchester: Manchester University Press, pp. 149-173.

Moore, K. (1989) Sport and Canadian identity in the 1920s. Unpublished paper.

Nauright, J. and White, P. (1996) 'Nostalgia, community and nation: Professional Hockey and Football in Canada', *Avante* Vol. 2, No. 3: pp. 24-41.

Olu, Akindutire. (1992) 'Sport as a manifestation of cultural heritage in Nigeria', *International Review for the Sociology of Sport* Vol. 27, No. 1: pp. 27-33.

Parti Québécois. (1994) *Des idées pour un pays: programme du parti québécois.* Montréal: Parti Québécois.

Paraschak, V. (1996) 'Racialized spaces: Cultural regulation, Aboriginal agency and powwows', *Avante* Vol. 2, No. 1: pp. 7-18.

———— (1997) 'Variations in race relations: Spoting events for Native people in Canada', *Sociology of Sport Journal* Vol. 14, No. 1: pp. 1-21.

Rail, G., Gaston, V., and Harvey, J. (1995) Québec 2002 and the confrontation of nationalisms. Unpublished conference paper, NASSS annual meeting, Sacramento, Nov. 4.

Roden, D. (1980) 'Baseball and the quest for national dignity in Meiji Japan', *American Historical Review*, Vol. 85, No. 3: pp. 511-534.

Salée, D. (1995) 'Espace public, identité et nation: mythes et méprises du discours souverainiste', Cahiers de recherche sociologique No. 25: pp. 125-154.

Stoddart, B. (1988) 'Caribbean cricket: The role of sport in emerging small-nation politics', *International Journal*, Vol. 43, No. 4: pp. 618-642.

Sugden, J. and Bairner, A. (1993) 'National identity, community relations and the sporting life in Northern Ireland', in L. Allison (ed) *The changing politics of sport*. Manchester: Manchester University Press.

Thériault, J. Y. (1994) 'Entre la nation et l'ethnie. Sociologie, société et communautés minoritaires', *Sociologie and Sociétés* Vol. 26, No. 1: pp. 15-32.

———— (1995) *L'identité à l'épreuve de la modernité*. Moncton: Éditions de l'Acadie.

Taylor, C. (1997) in M. Ancelovoci et F. Dupuis-Déri (eds) *L'archipel identitaire*. Montréal: Boréal: pp. 23-38.

Williams, G. (1985) 'How amateur was my valley: Professional sport and national identity in Wales 1890-1914', *British Journal of Sport History* Vol. 3, No. 2: pp. 248-269.

Yelvington, K. A. (1990) 'Ethnicity "not out": The Indian cricket tour of the West Indies and the 1976 elections in Trinidad and Tobago', *Arena* Vol. 14, No. 1: pp. 1-12.

DIVIDED SPORT IN A DIVIDED SOCIETY: NORTHERN IRELAND

Alan Bairner
University of Ulster at Jordanstown

Paul Darby
Liverpool Hope University College

Introduction

That Northern Ireland is a divided society is undeniable. Of those members of the population of roughly 1.5 million who admit to having a religious affiliation (and they constitute the overwhelming majority), around 60% belong to one or other of the Protestant denominations and approximately 40% are Catholics (Doherty, 1996: p. 201). In addition, most of the former are unionists who wish to maintain the constitutional link between Great Britain and Northern Ireland whilst the majority of the latter are Irish nationalists who seek the unification of Ireland or, at the very least, greater Irish input into the governance of Northern Ireland. Thus, for nationalists, it is the very status of Northern Ireland as a political entity which is in question. Unionists, on the other hand, although by no means constituting a wholly monolithic group, agree that Northern Ireland's status as an integral part of the United Kingdom, supported by a majority of its citizens, supersedes any claims on the part of ethnic nationalism for the unification of the island. This chapter focuses on the six counties of Northern Ireland whilst making no judgements as to the legitimacy or otherwise of their constitutional status.

There is no denying the significant role played by sport in Northern Ireland. Around 8,000 people are in sports-related employment (about the same as in banking and finance). Consumers spend £500,000 each day on sport (more than on alcohol or tobacco). Sport creates £100 million of wealth for the economy per annum, is likely to become the largest growing sector of the leisure industry and has been identified as having huge economic potential (Sports Council for Northern Ireland, 1997: p. 2). It has been suggested that as many as 250,000 are

51

formally involved in sport as participants, coaches, umpires/referees and administrators (Sugden and Harvie, 1995: p. 79). Despite its high profile, however, sport's relationship to politics in this divided society was largely ignored until the mid 1980s since when it has been increasingly well documented (Sugden and Bairner, 1986; Sugden and Bairner, 1992; Sugden and Bairner, 1993a; Sugden and Bairner, 1993b Sugden and Harvie, 1995; Bairner, 1996a).

In general, it has been shown that sport not only reflects the major cleavage in Northern Irish society but also consolidates the main ideologies, thereby exacerbating the political crisis. On the other hand, attempts to use sport for the purposes of improving inter-community relations have also been identified and subjected to analysis (Sugden, 1991; Bairner, 1994). The period since the paramilitary cease-fires of 1994 has continued to provide examples of both the divisive and integrative characteristics of sport in a society whose problems frequently appear more intractable than most.

The chapter begins with a brief summary of the relationship between sport and politics in Northern Ireland. There follows an examination of the ways in which sport has been used for the purposes of creating improved community relations and, in particular, of the latest initiatives which have emanated from the Sports Council for Northern Ireland. Finally, the paper discusses how two major sporting bodies — the Gaelic Athletic Association and the Irish Football Association — are likely to respond to the Sports Council's community relations policy. It is argued that the new strategy will present difficulties for the governing bodies not least because of the serious problems which have affected them in recent times.

Sport and politics in Northern Ireland

According to earlier studies of the relationship between sport and political division in Northern Ireland, it is useful to categorise the main sports played in Northern Ireland under three separate headings (Sugden and Bairner, 1993a: p. 22). First, there are those sports which came to Ireland as a direct consequence of British influence and are still closely linked to Britain, being played primarily in Commonwealth countries or in the case of Ireland by people who either favour the continuation of the constitutional link between Britain and Northern Ireland or who, despite living in the independent Irish Republic, remain influenced by Britain's historic role in Ireland. This category includes cricket, field hockey and rugby union, all of which continued to be organised on an all-Ireland basis even after partition had divided the island into two distinct political entities.

Second, there are sports which also came to Ireland by way of Britain but have become so universally popular as to make a nonsense of suggestions that they are still specifically British in their cultural symbolism. As a result, whilst they continue to be played by people in Northern Ireland who persist in their belief in the political union of Britain and at least one part of Ireland, they are also played throughout the island by adherents to all branches of Irish nationalism. In this category, we find soccer (association football), golf and boxing. Of these, soccer is particularly interesting since it has followed the boundaries established by partition, with separate governing bodies, competitions and national teams for the two parts of Ireland. As a consequence, the game has become one of the most significant cultural identifiers of the presence of two different political entities on the island. By virtue of the fact that soccer is particularly popular with working-class people from each of the two main traditions in Northern Ireland, it also represents contested terrain and an important arena for cultural struggle for those who have been most affected by almost 30 years of political violence.

The third major category of sports played in Ireland, north and south, consists of those games organised and administered by the Gaelic Athletic Association (GAA). Formed in 1884 as an element in the broader cultural struggle mounted to support the political activities aimed at bringing Britain's role in Ireland to an end, the GAA assumed responsibility for revitalising and in some instances virtually inventing games which could be presented as indigenous. The Association continues to advance the cause of Gaelic games — hurling, Gaelic football, camogie and handball — throughout Ireland and in so doing sustains a particular form of Irish sportive nationalism (Hoberman, 1993; Bairner, 1996b). However, since partition, it has been obliged to operate in two different political contexts and has arguably adopted a dual role, both helping to consolidate the independent existence of a 26-county Irish Republic whilst simultaneously acting as an important cultural focus for northern nationalism and its continuing support for Irish unification.

The genesis and early development of sports in Ireland have obvious implications for their contemporary role in Northern Ireland. Traditional 'British' games, like rugby union, continue to betray their cultural origins. Although played throughout Ireland, by Catholics as well as by Protestants, they are essentially a Protestant and Unionist preserve in the north — a situation which is maintained by virtue of the fact that state (grammar) schools are the principal nurseries for these sports. The situation of universal sports like soccer is very different.

Soccer is extremely popular with Catholics and Protestants alike in the north and is played in both state and Catholic schools. At the senior levels of competition, members of the two communities play for the same teams and, even at lower levels, the integrative capacity of soccer, and other universally popular games, has been recognised (Sugden and Harvie, 1995: p. 32: p. 92). Ironically, however, in other crucial respects, soccer is actually more divisive than a manifestly exclusive sport like rugby union. This is highlighted by two separate but related phenomena.

First, support for the Northern Ireland national team, despite the fact that it always includes Catholic players, has become increasingly Protestant and Unionist in character, with a significant minority of the fans expressing their support in highly emotive, anti-Catholic terms. Second, although many Catholics play for senior clubs, most of which have some degree of support from members of the nationalist community, the general ambience of Irish League football is redolent with Unionist rhetoric and symbolism. Most grounds are situated in predominantly Protestant areas. Loyalist songs and chants are frequently heard even when both teams on view are mainly supported by Protestants. Far from there having been any obvious attempt to alter this situation, the involvement of nationalists, other than as players, has decreased over the years with two clubs, supported for the most part by Catholics (Belfast Celtic and Derry City) having been forced to withdraw from the Irish League in 1949 and 1971 respectively.

Like that of British sports, the continuing popularity of Gaelic games in Northern Ireland owes much to a segregated education system with Catholic schools, as well as some of the small number of integrated schools, being the only significant nurseries. Moreover, notwithstanding those Protestant children who may be exposed to Gaelic games at an integrated school, the sports which operate under the aegis of the GAA have had virtually no integrative impact in Northern Ireland. In general terms, the sporting culture of the province has continued to reflect inter-community division and, by playing a significant role in consolidating separate identities, has contributed to the persistence of division. Indeed, it would be futile to simply go over old ground for the sake of illustrating this point. Instead the chapter concentrates on developments which have taken place since the publication of the last major study of sport in Northern Ireland (Sugden and Harvie, 1995). In particular, it outlines the Sports Council for

Northern Ireland's new community relations strategy and considers how the GAA and the Irish Football Association (IFA) might be expected to respond to it in the light of recent problems which have not only affected the normal work of the two bodies but which must also relate to their capacity to respond positively to the Sports Council's proposals.

Sport and community relations

Government agencies as well as non-governmental bodies have long been conscious of the role which sport and leisure might play in subduing inter-community strife and helping to give a semblance of normality to an otherwise abnormal and intermittently violent society. This perception led in the past to two different but related types of strategy. First, there was a massive investment in the provision of leisure facilities aimed at giving those most likely to become involved in civil unrest alternative channels for letting off steam (Sugden and Bairner, 1993a: pp. 115-6). As the political unrest continued and assumed more deadly forms, however, alternative means of utilising sport for the purposes of social control were explored (Sugden, 1991). These belonged to the first phase of community relations policy with its emphasis on seeking ways of bringing members of the two main communities together in a variety of social settings. This had also been an objective behind the expansion of leisure provision but the new approach was far more proactive in seeking to provide integrative experiences. The policy enjoyed some level of success, primarily at the individual level (Sugden, 1991). In general, however, it was faced with enormous obstacles raised by residential and educational segregation as well as an unpredictable but apparently intransigent political situation (Bairner, 1994). Subsequently, community relations moved into a new era with a marked growth of interest in strategies aimed at establishing mutual understanding rather than relatively simple levels of integration which had tended only to scratch the surface of the problem.

In 1990, for example, members of the Cultural Traditions Group of the Community Relations Council discussed sport at their annual conference:

> The group felt it important, firstly, to endorse the inclusion of a discussion on sport in a conference on Cultural Traditions. Many of the participants recognised sport as an important medium through which culture is expressed and all were in agreement that sport was an agent for communication even though it could, at times, be divisive. (Crozier, 1990: p. 107)

During the conference, there was a seminar which focused on "the potential for both producing and reducing division through sport" (*ibid.*). It was recognised in the course of the seminar that there were numerous examples of sport being used to encourage better cross-community relations. But the Group also acknowledged the divisive nature of sport which was described as "an important part of Northern Ireland's problems" (*ibid.*: p. 109). The seminar resulted in the publication of a series of recommendations consisting of a curriculum for comparative sport, greater access to sports facilities for all members of the population, more work by the governing bodies aimed at maximising the cohesive potential of sport within a divided society and recognition of the need for greater concern on the part of public agencies in terms of the sectional effects which their policies might have (*ibid.*: p. 116). By the mid 1990s, although sport's importance was being increasingly recognised, few steps had been taken to translate these recommendations into good practice.

However, the Sports Council for Northern Ireland (SCNI), the central co-ordinating agency for sports development in the region, then took the initiative. In the light of the debate on mutual understanding and mindful of the apparent inadequacy of previous efforts to harness sport to the services of peace-making, social control or a combination of the two, in February, 1996, the SCNI appointed a Sports Development Officer with special responsibility for community relations with a view to devising a new strategy. Aided by a Working Party, the Development Officer drew up a Policy Statement which gained the approval of the Council towards the end of 1996. The formal launch of the new policy initiative took place at the Waterfront Hall in Belfast on Thursday, 29 May, 1997. Significantly, the guest speaker was Mr Mvuzo Mbebe, Chief Executive of the South African National Sports Council.

The aim of the document is "to outline some of the issues regarding the management of sport in a divided society and to consider the future role of the Sports Council for Northern Ireland in directly addressing the issues raised, introducing an anti-sectarianism policy and influencing the work of some of our partners" (SCNI, 1996: p. 2). It identifies three key issues: first, the relationship between sport and the potentially harmful reinforcement of cultural identities; second, the necessity for sport to tackle the problem of bias; third, the need for sports bodies to address problems of sectarianism (*ibid.*: p. 4). The Sports Council's overall objective is " the promotion of equality of opportunity to participate, observe, administrate or develop sport, regardless of religious or political opinion" (*ibid.*). With this in mind, strategic areas have been identified and action plans drawn up.

The SCNI's strategy is directed at everyone involved in local sport — coaches, players, spectators, teachers, leisure centre workers, members of district councils, office bearers of clubs and, of course, the leading figures in governing bodies. All of them are asked to consider whether their practices are in any sense sectarian. Do clubs recruit from both sections of the community? Are all participants treated equally during coaching sessions? Do players and spectators refrain from making sectarian comments during matches? Do district councils have agreed anti-sectarian policies which encompass sport? Do leisure centre managers provide staff equity awareness training? Do schools give pupils the opportunity to sample as wide a variety of sports as possible? It is suggested that anyone who answers no to questions of this sort may be guilty of reinforcing sectarianism through sport. Governing bodies are invited to avail themselves of presentations which will advise them on how best to tackle negative practices and procedures in order to improve the image of their particular sport, enhance community relations and allow their members greater access to socially driven funding. The extent to which the governing bodies responsible for the various sports played in Northern Ireland will be able to sign up to these proposals far less do much to put them into practice remains to be seen. But by looking at two major bodies — the GAA and the IFA — it is possible at least to anticipate some of the problems which are likely to arise.

Gaelic games and community relations

The murder of Séan Brown, the Chairman of the Derry GAA club, Wolfe Tones — Bellaghy, on 12 May, 1997, at the hands of loyalist paramilitaries not only heightened fears that Northern Ireland was on the verge of a return to the pre-cease-fire spiral of sectarian killings but also raised serious questions over whether or not the principles which underpin the SCNI's current community relations drive can be applied to the GAA. Mr. Brown's murder represented yet another example of the sectarian hatred which has plagued Northern Ireland since the late 1960s. At the time of his shooting, his efforts on behalf of both sides of the community in Bellaghy were being publicly commended by the SCNI. In expressing his revulsion and sadness at the death of a man he had known personally for many years, Seamus Heaney, the world renowned poet and Nobel Prize winner, spoke of Séan Brown in the following terms:

> I heard the news in Olympia, just after I had visited the stadium where
> the original games were held, and given Sean Brown's role as Chairman
> of the Gaelic Athletic Club in Bellaghy, I could not help thinking of his
> death as a crime against the ancient Olympic Spirit...He represented
> something better than we have grown used to, something not quite
> covered by the word reconciliation, because that word has become a
> policy word — official and public. (*Irish News*, May 15, 1997)

The widely accepted view that the reason for his killing was none other than that
he was a Catholic and a prominent member of the GAA (Irish Times, May 14,
1997) is not only a horrific illustration of the depth of the sectarianism that
divides Northern Ireland but also serves to compound the difficulties involved
in procuring any meaningful or tangible benefits from the application of a cross-
community initiative to Gaelic sport.

The basic premise upon which the SCNI's promotion of sport as a means of
community reconciliation is based is that "sport should bring people together
regardless of religious background or political persuasion" (SCNI, 1997: p. 2).
Whilst the authors strongly commend any attempts to improve the socio-political
environment in Northern Ireland by drawing on the medium of sport, it is
difficult not to conclude that the sectarian and divisive nature of the climate in
which the GAA operates in the North and the deep-seated perceptions and
sentiments that the Association's history and activities engender within both
communities will seriously restrict its long-term capacity to put all of the SCNI's
proposals into practice. One of the primary barriers to the promotion of cross-
community ideals through the GAA is the fact that its history is intimately tied
up with the development of nationalist politics. This in turn has created strong
hostility and suspicion on the part of the majority loyalist population of the
province and has effectively nullified the potential for Gaelic sport to recruit
participants from 'the other side'. It is within this context that any potential for
the realisation of cross-community objectives, through the medium of Gaelic
sport, must be assessed.

Since its inception, the GAA has come to form a fundamental manifestation
of socio-political and cultural life throughout Ireland. The enormity of the
Association's contribution to contemporary Irish society is such that "its
importance in cultural and social terms can hardly be overstated...it is an intrinsic
element of Ireland's national ethos — much more than just a sporting body"
(Irish News, March 10, 1994). However, when its role in the development of

social life in Northern Ireland is assessed, it becomes clear that, like all other significant aspects of civil society in the province, the GAA is implicated in the politics of sectarian division (Sugden and Bairner, 1993a: pp. 23-45).

Although those who are involved in administering Gaelic games refute all claims that they operate in an overtly political manner, the GAA represents perhaps the clearest manifestation of the linkages between sport and politics in Northern Ireland. The political and cultural history of Ireland since the mid-nineteenth century is reflected, in many ways, in the development of the GAA. The Association was formed during a period of intense opposition to British cultural and political domination which was combined with attempts to revive distinctive Irish cultural forms that would promote a sense of national identity and pride. In view of the political context from which the GAA emerged, it is not surprising that it became a locus for opposition to the diffusion and domination of British sporting and cultural forms and an important forum within which to give expression to Irish nationalist aspirations. Eoghan Corry (1989: p. 12) encapsulates the rationale behind the Association's formation:

It was a national effort to recall a national inheritance, to emancipate a people from an alien, social thraldom: to save them in the practice of their traditional amusements, in the atmosphere of active nationalism and for the ultimate achievement of national independence.

With the partition of Ireland in 1921, the overtly politicised nature of the organisation subsided in the 26 county Free State. However, north of the border, the GAA's continued role in the struggle against British political and cultural control has ensured that its controversial political profile has been maintained. Indeed, within the context of Northern Ireland's deeply divided and sectarian society, a body which has as its basic aim "the strengthening of the national identity in a 32 county Ireland through the preservation and promotion of Gaelic games and pastimes" (GAA, 1991) inevitably finds itself centrally located in the politics of division. The fact that the vast majority of those affiliated to the organisation are Catholic nationalists who, to varying degrees, deny the legitimacy of the Northern Ireland state as a political entity exacerbates the extent to which the GAA is viewed with deep distrust by the loyalist population and their political representatives. The nationalist aims of the GAA combined with certain aspects of the Association's operations within Northern Ireland, parti-cularly the prohibition of members of the British security forces from joining the Association, clearly run counter to the aims and aspirations of constitutional unionism and have served to heighten suspicions that the organisation is not only anti-British, but harbours an anti-Protestant ethos. Indeed, the playing of the Irish national anthem and the flying of the Irish tricolour at matches, as well as the naming of both stadia and clubs after prominent republican heroes, serve to reinforce the image that unionists have of nationalism and its institutions as both exclusive and hostile. John Taylor, the Ulster Unionist MP, has given vent to these sentiments:

> They are a sectarian organisation with political motives. They fly the Irish tricolour, they prohibit certain people from joining it, they pursue only Irish ideals. And, I have to say that until those things change there will be a perception within the majority community that they are biased and bigoted. (Spotlight, BBC Television, September 16, 1993)

Taylor's sentiments were echoed in more sinister terms by Father Seamus Murphy, a Jesuit Priest from Dublin, who described the GAA as politically sectarian. Writing in a religious periodical about what he perceived to be the ambivalence of Catholics to the Irish Republican Army (IRA), Father Murphy argued that "the GAA does not support the IRA, but when it comes to the crunch its policy implies a preference for an IRA victory over a 'Crown forces' victory … the GAA is politically motivated and its political sectarianism lends indirect support to the IRA" (Spotlight, BBC Television, September 16, 1993). Such a perception is particularly prevalent in more hard-line loyalist circles, and the assertion that the GAA acts as a front for the IRA has been cited by loyalist paramilitaries as the reason for the classification of active GAA members as legitimate targets for their terrorist activities.

Indeed, a number of GAA members, in addition to Séan Brown, have been the victims of loyalist violence. As recently as October, 1993, Séan Fox, a former Co. Antrim board official and President of St Enda's Gaelic club in Glengormley, Co. Antrim, was killed at the age of 72 by loyalist paramilitaries who had made previous attempts on his life. Fox's death had been preceded by other similar events. For example, Jack Kielty, the chairman of the Dundrum Gaelic club, was killed by loyalists in January, 1988. The death of Séan Brown indicates that, although the threats to GAA members which were issued in 1992 by the Ulster Freedom Fighters and two years later by the Red Hand Commando may have been lifted as a consequence of the loyalist cease-fire, there are still loyalist terrorists who regard Gaelic administrators, players and supporters as legitimate targets.

All claims of sectarianism or political motivation are emphatically repudiated by leading figures within the GAA. For example, Peter Quinn, speaking a year before he was elected as President of the Association, argued that the divisiveness which Gaelic sport is perceived to encourage is merely a reflection of the divided context in which it operates:

> We cannot be held accountable for the fragmentation of society in this part of our island. To attempt to make sport, especially Gaelic sport, the scapegoat for the failures of politicians and for those paid to manage society and the economy is dangerous, if not hypocritical. (*Belfast Telegraph*, June 30, 1989)

The Association points to the fact that it has no formal links with any political organisation, north or south of the border, as evidence of its apolitical nature. The appointment of Jack Boothman, a southern Protestant, as President of the Association between 1993 and 1996, as well as a number of recent initiatives on the part of Gaelic football clubs in south Belfast aimed at encouraging cross-community participation, are also cited as proof that the GAA does not operate according to a sectarian agenda. Despite these steps, the Association is still opposed by unionists and is regarded as an alien body representing a serious threat to their Protestant heritage. It appears that this will remain the case until such a time as the political situation in Northern Ireland persuades the loyalist population to view Irish cultural institutions in a less parochial fashion and encourages the governing body of Gaelic sport to address some of the more contentious aspects of its operations, particularly its stance over the constitutional position of the Northern Ireland state and its exclusion of the security forces from membership.

In attempting to redress this state of affairs and examine the extent to which the existing sports infrastructure in the province can act as a vehicle for inter-community understanding, the Sports Council has listed criteria which they argue must be adhered to if sports governing bodies are to conduct themselves in a manner conducive to the promotion of community reconciliation. This includes ensuring that their constitution is open and accessible to all, that letterheads and symbols are neutral, as are venues for major tournaments, and that games are played on days and at times which suit the whole community. The difficulties which the GAA would have in conforming to such criteria are manifold. For example, Gaelic games are normally played on a Sunday, a day which a number of the Protestant denominations in Northern Ireland dictate should be observed for religious purposes. Club and inter-county games are often played at venues which are named after popular nationalist or Catholic figures. (The national stadium in Dublin, Croke Park, is named after the Catholic Archbishop who played a central role in the formation of the GAA and the Ulster provincial stadium in west Belfast, Casement Park, is named after the republican hero and British traitor, Sir Roger Casement.) This is unlikely to arouse a desire on the part of a member of the Protestant community to either travel to or participate in sport at such venues. At the same time, few GAA members would agree to having the names of these stadia changed.

There are also problems concerning open access to Gaelic games. Rule 21 of the GAA's statutes bans functionaries of the British security forces from membership. It is perhaps the most problematic issue associated with meeting the challenge of the Sports Council's cross-community initiative and clearly runs counter to the principle of an open and accessible constitution. Although Rule 21 serves no practical purpose given the obvious risks involved in a member of the security forces travelling to and from nationalist areas on a regular basis, all moves aimed at removing the ban from the GAA's handbook have been blocked or voted down at Congress. An appreciation of the rationale behind the continued support for the maintenance of the ban is critical to any understanding of the extent to which the GAA would be prepared to alter its constitution in order to make Gaelic sports more attractive to a community whose primary political motivation is to uphold Britain's foothold in Ireland.

In support of the retention of Rule 21, many GAA members and nationalist politicians have long considered the ban as a legitimate protest against the general historical suppression of Gaelic games and culture and more specifically as a justified response to the continued British security force harassment of those affiliated to the Association. From the time that British imperialism gained control in Ireland, Gaelic games, and, indeed, all manifestations or displays of Irish culture and nationalism, were not only discouraged but were actually prohibited. Prohibition occurred simultaneously with the imperialistic diffusion of Anglophile sports and cultural forms and when this was combined with the ravages of the famine, Gaelic sport almost entirely disappeared (Sugden and Bairner, 1986: p. 92). The suppression and prohibition of Gaelic games has laid the foundations for what many Gaels believe to be a systematic process of oppression of the GAA since its formation. Sensitive to the threat of emergent

Irish nationalism in a period of intense opposition to British rule, the authorities actively sought to limit the potential of the GAA to rekindle the type of distinctively Irish cultural identity upon which the push for political independence could be based. Sugden and Bairner (1986: p. 99) have illustrated that during its early days the Association bore the brunt of severe victimisation from the British and the political defenders of the union. They elaborate on the most violent example of this to date:

> The deep suspicion of the British was made brutally manifest on Sunday 21 November 1920, when, apparently as a reprisal for the assassination earlier that day of a group of secret-service agents, Black and Tans arrived at Croke Park shortly after the start of a hurling match between Tipperary and Dublin and fired repeatedly into the crowd. Thirteen people died as a result of being either shot or crushed and among those shot dead was Michael Hogan, a Tipperary player. 'Bloody Sunday' as it came to be known, was the saddest day in the GAA's history.

With the signing of the partition treaty, the parameters of British suppression of the GAA obviously altered, with those members of the Association in the six counties of Ulster which constitute Northern Ireland becoming the focus for what many believe to be a traditional mistrust of and distaste for anything celebratory of Gaelic-Irishness in the north. Such a belief is not without foundation and, indeed, GAA members in Northern Ireland can point to a catalogue of oppression and attacks on the games by the security forces as clear manifestations of this mistrust. The harassment of GAA members by the Royal Ulster Constabulary (RUC) and the British army and the construction of military barracks on the playing fields of the recent all-Ireland club champions, Crossmaglen Rangers, in south Armagh are examples of how the affairs of the GAA have been disrupted by the security forces. Other incidents have exacerbated the situation. In 1977, William Strathearn, a member of the Bellaghy GAA club, was murdered by an RUC sergeant. In 1988, Aidan McAnespie was shot dead by a British soldier at a border checkpoint in Co. Tyrone on his way to play for his local team just a few hundred yards away in Monaghan. The fact that the soldier accused of the latter shooting had all charges against him dropped after claiming that his hand had slipped further fuels the desire of many Association members to maintain the ban on the British crown forces. Indeed, all of these incidents reinforce nationalist feelings that there has been a campaign on the part of the security forces as well as by loyalist paramilitaries to terrorise GAA members.

In light of the historical opposition and suppression of the British and continued attacks on GAA facilities and members by loyalist paramilitaries, the Association is able to deflect criticisms that its operations north of the border are narrow-minded and exclusive with the argument that it "excludes no-one but some exclude themselves by their activities and by upholding a state which denies parity of treatment to Irish culture" (Irish News, March 10, 1994). Furthermore, the well-catalogued attempts on the part of loyalist politicians to obstruct the development and activities of the Association also limit the extent to which GAA members feel that they should soften their line on nationalism in the north in order to accommodate a proportion of the population whose primary political aspiration is to uphold a state, the political and security apparatus of which has long been associated with oppression of and discrimination against Catholic nationalists. In this respect it is unreasonable and extremely unlikely that the GAA will play down those aspects of its activities which symbolise its connection with Irish nationalism. Even if the GAA were to conduct its affairs in a more 'neutral' manner, as suggested by the SCNI, it is equally unlikely, for the reasons outlined earlier, to expect Ulster Protestants to embrace Gaelic sport in any significant way.

The unwillingness of Ulster Protestants to participate in Gaelic sport as part of a community relations programme is also reinforced by loyalist perceptions of cross-community work in general. In the current political climate, there are significant proportions of the Protestant community which have come to view the British government's role with suspicion. Initiatives such as the Anglo-Irish Agreement and the Downing Street Declaration which were aimed at ending the political impasse in Northern Ireland have been viewed as concessions to Irish nationalism and as part of a broader strategy aimed at devolving increasing powers to the Irish government. It is in a similar light that much of the loyalist population views the recent proliferation of initiatives aimed at facilitating community integration and co-operation.

Whilst such perceptions do not auger well for the implementation of any initiative aimed at utilising Gaelic sport as a vehicle for promoting greater cross-community understanding and respect or acting productively as an agent of reconciliation, it is right and proper that the GAA should involve itself in a process of introspection in order to identify ways in which Gaelic sport could have a positive influence on sectarian divisions in the province. However, there are likely to be many within the organisation who will view the involvement of a British quango in any such process with deep suspicion. Questions will inevitably be raised by some of the more hard-line members of GAA's Ulster branch regarding the motives of governmental involvement in an initiative that would necessitate a dilution of the nationalistic aims of one of the primary cultural institutions in Ireland. Indeed, the experiences of other nations that were colonised indicate that a central strand of British policy in these areas was to utilise sport as a means of facilitating the spread of British cultural values and *mores* and act as a mechanism of social control. Furthermore, in times of political crisis in the colonies, the British Government has become increasingly inter-ventionist in the affairs of civil society in order to reassert its hegemony. The government's massive investment in the provision of sport and leisure facilities in Northern Ireland, particularly Belfast, during a period of intense civil disorder and political unrest clearly illustrates that such a strategy has also been adapted to the circumstances of the province. This can only serve to deepen suspicions within the GAA that the Sports Council's actions in attempting to facilitate community relations through Gaelic sport are underpinned by a strong culturally imperialistic foundation.

The promotion of Irish nationalism, inherent within Gaelic sport, is clearly problematic within the context of the sectarian divisions that characterise socio-political life in the province. Although the organisation's refusal to modify its nationalistic appearance or reappraise some of the more contentious aspects of its statutes are proclaimed as evidence of its intransigence and overt use of sport for political purposes, a transformation of its activities according to the guide-lines published by the SCNI not only runs counter to its *raison d'être* but would also remove the very essence of the Association. In addition, the perception of the GAA within the northern Protestant community further militates against the potential of incorporating Gaelic sport into a broader cross-community framework. The death of Séan Brown provides evidence, if evidence were needed, that until Northern Ireland operates under a broader *political* settlement which encourages understanding and acceptance of the two main cultural traditions, then it is unreasonable to expect Gaelic sport to act as an agent for the promotion of inter-community respect and reconciliation. However, it might be expected that a sport which draws support from both sections of the community would be in a much better position to implement the SCNI's proposals.

Soccer and community relations

Superficially at least, the situation of soccer is very different from that of Gaelic games. As a universally popular sport, it enjoys avid support from both the main communities. In addition, Catholics and Protestants play together as well as in separate teams. Indeed, in the most recent major study of sport in Northern Ireland, the authors wrote that "only association football (soccer) appears to wholeheartedly embrace community relations and this is believed to be paying dividends by increasing the sport's recruitment base and bringing in additional resources" (Sugden and Harvie, 1995: p. 92). It should also be noted that the IFA has responded with some enthusiasm to the SCNI's new policy document. However, in the past twelve months, soccer has also faced problems which have their roots in sectarian division. Although less dramatic and so far less deadly than those problems which have beset the GAA, the difficulties facing the IFA and the Irish League do raise questions about the capacity of soccer's governing bodies to implement in full the SCNI's policy proposals.

As mentioned earlier, the presence of clubs with mainly Catholic, nationalist followers at senior levels of competition has always proved to be problematic for the game's ruling bodies as well as for the security forces. Despite the fact that numerous Catholics play and watch soccer, originally in defiance of the GAA's ambitions that they should shun all foreign games, most senior clubs draw the overwhelming majority of their support from the Protestant community. Inevitably in a society which is deeply divided along sectarian lines, this has led to crowd trouble when clubs representing different sides of the political divide have been in opposition. The remedy in the past has been found in the withdrawal of 'nationalist' clubs from senior competition. One would hesitate to suggest that the demise of Belfast Celtic and the removal of Derry City from the Irish League were the result of a conscious policy on the part of the game's governing bodies. For nationalists, however, the difficulties encountered by these clubs appeared to be symptomatic of the wider discrimination practised by unionists against the Catholic minority. These fears have again been aired with reference to the problems facing Cliftonville FC which became particularly acute during the 1996-7 season.

Since the late 1970s, when Cliftonville first acquired a significant nationalist following, the club's games have been frequently affected by sectarianism tensions. One consequence of this has been that Cliftonville are not allowed to host their 'home' fixtures against Linfield FC at their own ground. Instead, they have been obliged to play at their opponents' Windsor Park stadium. The reason given by soccer authorities for this anomalous situation is that any other arrangement would constitute a more serious security risk. For many Cliftonville supporters and nationalists in general, however, this is a clear example of discrimination. Linfield has long been recognised as a club with an almost exclusively Protestant following and, until fairly recently, a perceived policy of refusing to sign Catholic players. Thus, security arguments could easily be portrayed by nationalists as little more than an attempt to disguise what is, in effect, preferential treatment on behalf of the majority community. Certainly security problems which might result if these matches were to take place at Cliftonville's ground would have at least as much, if not more, to do with the behaviour of visiting Linfield fans as with that of home supporters. However, it is the 'nationalist' club and its followers which are penalised. Controversy about this situation has continued to simmer over many years. Developments during the past season, however, are regarded by nationalists as even more disturbing.

One of the most complex issues to emerge during the recent years of the troubles is that of the marching season and, specifically, the re-routing of parades by the Protestant and unionist Orange Order. The stand-offs which occurred at Drumcree near Portadown between 1995 and 1997 have been the most widely publicised manifestations of this problem but throughout the province there are a number of disputed routes. This issue reached a head as a result of residents of predominantly nationalist areas, in most cases encouraged and organised by Sinn Féin, the political wing of the Provisional Irish Republican Army, objecting to Orange parades entering their areas. For their part, the Order and its political supporters have argued that the parades are following traditional routes and that the security forces, who have taken decisions to re-route parades or even prevent them from taking place, have fallen into a carefully laid republican trap. One curious by-product of this controversial issue was the treatment of Cliftonville supporters during the 1996-7 Irish League season.

Over the years, Cliftonville fans have made their way to most Irish League grounds with a police escort. This has not prevented some of them from proclaiming their political leanings by waving Irish tricolours and singing republican songs. Indeed part of the reason for the security force presence has been to prevent attacks from loyalists living in those areas where most Irish League grounds are situated. Until last season this arrangement worked reasonably well. On 4 September, 1996, however, Cliftonville were scheduled to play an Ulster Cup semi-final game against Crusaders FC at the east Belfast home of Glentoran FC. Apart from a small nationalist enclave, the working-class areas of east Belfast, including the area immediately adjacent to Glentoran's ground, are almost exclusively Protestant. On the night of the match, a group of local loyalists decided to invert the issue of marches by blocking the road and preventing Cliftonville fans from progressing along their 'traditional' route. The police made the decision to turn the Cliftonville fans away and the match went ahead without them. Supporters of the blockade argued that, if nationalists are offended by Orangemen walking through their communities, unionists are entitled to be equally offended by the presence in their midst of republican sympathisers. This argument was to be invoked again the following month when, on 19 October, loyalists gathered outside the home ground of Portadown FC and attacked coaches which were carrying Cliftonville supporters to their team's away fixture. Some fans as well as policemen were injured and once again the Cliftonville supporters were prevented from seeing their team play. On this occasion, however, the Cliftonville players, having heard about what had happened, took the step of refusing to go out for the second half of the match which had to be replayed at a later date.

Loyalist protesters justified their actions at Portadown by referring to attempts by republicans to prevent the Orange Order's church parade at nearby Drumcree and also to the fact that, earlier in the season, Cliftonville supporters, on their way to a game, had laid a wreath in memory of eight IRA volunteers who had been killed by the security forces at Loughgall which is also close to Portadown. The main Cliftonville supporters' clubs dissociated themselves from this act and it was suggested that only three fans had actually been involved. Symbolically, however, in the eyes of certain Portadown loyalists, the entire Cliftonville support was implicated.

Because of these two incidents, concern was expressed that it might prove difficult for Cliftonville fans to attend away fixtures at most Irish League grounds. This in turn was thought to place a question mark against Cliftonville's continued presence in senior competitions. Thankfully, however, the season passed without any other serious incidents of this type. But controversy did surround one other Cliftonville match. On 4 February, after a bottle throwing incident, the County Antrim Shield Final with Ballymena United FC, being played at Windsor Park, was abandoned by the referee, Alan Snoddy. There was no disputing that a Cliftonville fan had thrown the offending bottle. (Indeed, he was immediately subjected to the summary justice of some of his fellow supporters.) What upset Cliftonville followers was that similar incidents involving Linfield had gone unpunished earlier in the season. It appeared to them that here was a glaring example of double standards with one law operating for clubs with mainly Protestant followers and another for the only team with a substantial nationalist support. It is against the backdrop of these episodes and the atmosphere of mutual suspicion which they have helped to fuel that the capacity of soccer's governing bodies to make a meaningful contribution to community relations initiatives should be examined.

It is beyond doubt that the IFA and its constituent bodies have done much to ensure that the game of soccer is open to all. Yet, the feeling persists among many nationalists that, at the highest levels, the game is dominated by Protestant unionists. The Cliftonville saga has given added strength to this view but it is also noted that the overwhelming majority of the game's leading administrators have in the past and continue to come from the unionist community. It is believed, therefore, that the degree of integration in soccer, although massive by comparison with that achieved by the GAA or by British games like rugby union, has come about by accident rather than by any conscious policy on the part of IFA officialdom. Against this, unionists are entitled to argue that northern nationalists have excluded themselves, to some extent, from administering senior soccer not least because of an ambivalent and, at times, positively hostile attitude to the Northern Ireland state. Certainly few nationalists identify with the Northern Ireland team which is the most important international representative of soccer in the province, whereas for unionists themselves the team represents a key identifier of the existence of Northern Ireland as a political entity separate from the rest of the island. Indeed, by their very presence, the IFA and the Irish League bear witness to the distinctiveness of Northern Ireland and, as a consequence, are unlikely to appeal unreservedly to most northern nationalists.

The IFA will almost certainly support the SCNI's proposals and will continue to do valuable work particularly in encouraging young people from both sections of the community to play soccer. As a governing body, however, it is likely to remain an object of suspicion in the eyes of nationalists. Indeed, how the organisation responds to the difficulties facing Cliftonville will have a major impact on how Catholics view its potential for improving community relations. To date, there are few grounds for optimism.

In his report to the Annual General Meeting of the IFA, the General Secretary made reference to "the misbehaviour of spectators and, in particular, bottle throwing incidents" (IFA, 1997). He also drew attention to "the continuing problems of sectarianism, hooliganism and drunken behaviour which continue to confront our sport". His response to these problems was to call for "new legislation which will give greater powers to the police at matches" and "possible new security and stewarding options becoming available to us through special Government or EU funding". It is likely that the IFA will link new security measures to a community relations policy. What is interesting, however, is that in assessing the previous season, the General Secretary chose to refer to the Cliftonville issue only by implication, with his focus being on the bottle throwing incident. There is no mention in his report of the fact that, on two separate occasions in 1996-7, football fans had been prevented by criminal acts from exercising their legitimate right to watch a game. It could be argued that, since the incidents occurred outside football grounds and were only indirectly linked to the games which were to be played, they do not come within the IFA's remit. Nationalists would feel, however, that the governing body should show greater concern for the interests of all soccer fans and that, at the very least, a statement condemning the actions of loyalist demonstrators should have been included in the annual report. At best, one might argue that the IFA has remained fairly insensitive to the feelings of nationalist soccer fans in Northern Ireland. Rabid nationalists themselves suspect a conspiracy. The truth is far less sinister. The leading figures in the IFA and the Irish League are entitled to feel that they have done far more than their GAA counterparts to promote cross-community contacts. The fact remains that their organisations are Northern Irish, not Irish, and that, whilst Catholics are more than welcome to take part in their activities, there can be no place for open displays of republicanism at Irish League games. Indeed, if there is any suggestion that the SCNI's proposals will involve making concessions to the nationalist minority, leading for example to closer cross-border links, it is doubtful if they will be fully implemented by soccer's main governing bodies.

Conclusion

It was always asking too much to expect sport to have a major impact on community relations in the continued absence of a political settlement in Northern Ireland. As has been observed in the past, "the sports which people play are fundamental to the construction of their identities" and, unless and until there is a changed political environment, "it is to underestimate the intensity of feeling engendered by sports to imagine that they can be enthusiastically pursued in a context in which they are freed from the marks of their birth and early development" (Bairner, 1996: pp. 188-9). Moreover, as Jeremy MacClancy observes, "sport and sporting events cannot be comprehended without reference to relations of power: who attempts to control how a sport is to be organised and played, and by whom; how it is to be represented; how it is to be interpreted" (MacClancy, 1996: p. 5). Both the GAA and the IFA are large organisations which wish to maintain control over their own affairs. Instinctively, they are put on the defensive when other bodies, the SCNI included, seek to influence them. Sporting bodies throughout the world would respond in exactly the same way to perceived outside interference. In a divided society like Northern Ireland, however, the nature of the power struggle assumes different and even less tractable forms. For the GAA, the SCNI's community relations policy might seem like an attempt by an agent of the British state to dilute its nationalist credentials. Members of the IFA for their part may feel that the SCNI's proposals, whilst mainly laudable, cannot be allowed to force Northern Irish soccer to abandon its traditional identity in the interests of pandering to a disaffected nationalist minority. Ultimately there will continue to exist within both of these major sporting organisations a large body of opinion which clings to the idea that, because sport is not intrinsically political, it should never be used for the purposes of social engineering and that it is the duty of politicians and not sports people to solve the problems of division. The fact that this represents an exercise in sheer escapism will be ignored by the overwhelming majority of the members of both the Gaelic and soccer fraternities.

References

Bairner, A. (1994) 'The end of pitched battles? The peace process and sport in Northern Ireland', *Causeway* Vol. 1, No. 3: pp. 62-66.

——— (1996a) 'The arts and sport', in A. Aughey and D. Morrow (eds) *Northern Ireland politics*. London: Longman, pp. 181-9.

——— (1996b) 'Sportive nationalism and nationalist politics: A comparative analysis of Scotland, the Republic of Ireland and Sweden', *Journal of Sport and Social Issues,* Vol. 20, No. 3: pp. 314-334.

Corry, E. (1989) *Catch and kick.* Dublin: Poolbeg.

Crozier, M. (ed) (1990) *Cultural traditions in Northern Ireland.* Belfast: Institute of Irish Studies, Queen's University.

Doherty, P. (1996) 'The numbers game: the demographic context of politics', in A. Aughey and D. Morrow (eds) *Northern Ireland politics.* London: Longman, pp. 199-209.

Gaelic Athletic Association (1991) *Rules.* Dublin: GAA.

Hoberman, J. (1993) 'Sport and ideology in the post-communist age', in L. Allison (ed) *The changing politics of sport.* Manchester: Manchester University Press, pp. 15-36.

Irish Football Association (1997) *Annual General Meeting. Notices and enclosures.* Belfast: IFA.

MacClancy, J. (1996) 'Sport, identity and ethnicity', in J. MacClancy (ed) *Sport, ethnicity and identity.* Oxford: Berg, pp. 1-20.

Sports Council for Northern Ireland (1996) *Sports development in the community.* Belfast: SCNI.

——— (1997) *Starting well, staying on course and striving for excellence.* Belfast: SCNI.

Sugden, J. (1991) 'Belfast United: Encouraging cross-community relations through sport in Northern Ireland', *Journal of Sport and Social Issues* Vol. 15, No. 4: pp. 59-80.

Sugden, J. and Bairner, A. (1986) 'Northern Ireland: Sport in a divided society', in L. Allison (ed) *The politics of sport.* Manchester: Manchester University Press, pp. 90-117.

——— (1992) '"Ma there's a helicopter on the pitch": Sport, politics and the state in Northern Ireland', *Sociology of Sport Journal* Vol. 9, No. 2: pp. 154-166.

——— (1993a) *Sport, sectarianism and society in a divided Ireland.* Leicester, London & New York: Leicester University Press.

——— (1993b) 'National identity, community relations and the sporting life in Northern Ireland', in L. Allison (ed) *The changing politics of sport.* Manchester: Manchester University Press, pp. 171-206.

Sugden, J. and Harvie, S. (1995) *Sport and community relations in Northern Ireland.* Coleraine: Centre for the Study of Conflict, University of Ulster.

SPORT AND THE 'NORMALISING' OF THE NEW SOUTH AFRICA

Adrian Guelke
Queen's University, BELFAST

John Sugden
University of Brighton

South Africa has been and continues to be one of the worlds most deeply divided societies. More than anything else, it was the situation there, prior to the end of apartheid, which confirmed to the rest of the world that sport and politics were intimate bedfellows. The significance of sport to white South Africans, particularly Afrikaners, and the fact that an Afrikaner dominated state decreed that sport should be racially segregated, fuelled a situation whereby, first within South Africa itself and then globally, sport became a very important weapon in the arsenal of those opposed to apartheid, not just in sport, but also in South African society at large (Lapchick, 1975).

The use of sport by the ANC (African National Congress), and the anti-apartheid movement in general, as a vehicle for the destabilistaion of the South African state was, in part, made easier by the fact that, for all intents and purposes, non-whites were excluded from the high-profile team sports which meant so much to white South Africa. For instance, persuading the rest of the world not to play rugby or cricket with South Africa had little impact on the daily practice of the vast majority of non-whites who, for generations, had been deprived of opportunities to develop appetites for these games. The special case of soccer will be looked at in some detail later in this chapter. The point to be made is that, not only were sports highly politicised in the old South Africa, but also, through apartheid and longer standing forms of discrimination, patterns of participation in and allegiance to sports were established which reinforced racial and ethnic segregation. This begs the question which is central to this chapter: what is to be the role of sport in the new South Africa?

Judging by policy initiatives and events since the ANC's victory at the polls in 1994, at least rhetorically, sport has been reinvented by the new South African state as a communal resource. In the words of Steve Tshwete, the ANC government's minister for sport, "In our efforts to create a better South Africa, sport could enhance the nation building process, lesson the level of tension and contribute towards creating a healthy and disciplined society" (Tshwete, 1995: p. 36). From the vantage point of the ANC leadership, in a context of simmering cross-community antagonisms and spiralling violent crime, sport is seen as a means of unifying a diverse population behind the fledgling nation and restoring social order.

In these terms, the anti-apartheid slogan 'no normal sport in an abnormal society' could well be rewritten as 'through normal sport to a normal society'. However, to what extent is it possible to take sports, which have been the subject of deep divisions, and clearly implicated in the politics which framed those divisions, and transform them into vehicles for community solidarity? In this chapter we attempt to shed some light on this question by reviewing the political legacy of the two codes of football played in South Africa: rugby union and soccer.

Rainbow rugby?

The game of rugby has been played in the southern part of Africa for longer than South Africa has existed as a political entity. Indeed, the association between the game and the symbol of the Springbok actually pre-dates the formation of the Union of South Africa in 1910. In that time it has had many ups and downs. However, it is easy to identify the game's pinnacle. That was on 24 June 1995 when the President of South Africa, Nelson Mandela, presented the Springbok rugby captain, Francois Pienaar, with the William Webb Ellis trophy after South Africa defeated New Zealand in the final of the rugby world cup. Mandela's commitment to the team was famously underlined by his wearing of a Springbok No. 6 rugby jersey. No. 6 was the shirt number that Pienaar as a flanker wore. The fairy tale nature of the occasion was nicely captured by an Australian publication on the internet, *Global Heroes* (1995) which celebrated Pienaar's feat in not merely leading his team to victory against the odds, but in establishing a special bond with Mandela that drew the whole of South Africa behind the team. It recalled his dedication of the victory not just to the supporters present in the stadium but to 43 million South Africans.

Choice of the nadir of South African rugby is open to argument. Many would say that it was the Springbok tour of the British Isles in 1969-70. One of the worst moments in that demonstration-dominated series of matches was the defeat of the Springboks in the opening match of the tour by Oxford University. However, the events of February 1997 which resulted in the resignation of the Springbok national coach, Andre Markgraaff, represent another nadir, and one more remarkable and interesting in following so close on the heels of South African rugby's greatest triumph. Since the story of the 1969-70 tour is by now rather well known this chapter will focus on the Markgraff affair, not least because of its role in highlighting the problematic relationship of the country's rugby establishment to the new South Africa.

Of all sports, rugby was most closely associated with Afrikaner nationalism. As the sport most closely associated with support for the apartheid regime, rugby and its administrators were slow to adapt to the existence of powerful counter-vailing forces to the Afrikaner nationalist government, despite pockets of popularity for the game in parts of the country among both Coloureds and Africans. Late in the day the two most important figures in rugby administration in the country, Danie Craven and Louis Luyt, entered into negotiations with the ANC. This was in 1989 before the ANC had been unbanned. Such defiance of the government by pillars of the Afrikaner establishment was a sensational development in the context of the country's political development and attracted huge publicity inside and outside the country. That tended to detract attention from the fact that rugby was relatively slow to integrate and to meet the conditions that the ANC had set for all sports for the lifting of the moratorium on international competition. These included the reorganisation of the administration of the sport in a single entity that brought in those who had played the game under the aegis of the anti-apartheid movement within the country.

Re-entry into international competition took place in South Africa against New Zealand — traditionally seen as the country's main rival in the sport with the strongest claim to embody a comparable record of achievement. The Springboks lost narrowly to the All Blacks at Ellis Park in Johannesburg. They also lost the next test against Australia at Newlands in Cape Town. A tour of Europe followed that was only slightly more successful: the Springboks won one test against France but lost the other, and were also defeated by England. In short, the record of the Springbok rugby team on the country's return to international sporting competition was not particularly impressive. As

far as at least some members of the black elite were concerned this was a
rather welcome rebuff to white South African assumptions of their sporting
superiority, including a common belief among white fans that at least part of the
motive for South African exclusion from international sport during the apartheid
years had been envy of the country's sporting achievements and a desire to
exclude a powerful rival from the field.

Blacks derived some pleasure from the anguished discovery among sports
commentators that their team's capacity to win had been adversely affected by
the country's sporting isolation, a point that had constantly been denied
throughout the years of the boycotts. The prospect that it would take some time
for the country to re-establish itself as one of the leading, if not the leading, teams
in the game of rugby was seen as salutary. Also welcome was a further implication that the sport's base would need to be broadened if the country was to
compete successfully against the rest of the world, turning programmes for the
development of the game among blacks into an issue of self-interest and of
survival in the new South Africa, rather than just a paternalistic gesture towards
disadvantaged communities.

Many anti-apartheid whites were also uncertain as to whether it was right to
cheer-on the Springbok rugby team in view of its past association with Afrikaner
nationalism. This was perhaps particularly true of liberal Afrikaners. The novelist
Andre Brink has explained his equivocation over whether to support the
Springboks as follows:

> I grew up in an environment in which rugby was the very emblem of a
> system of values specifically associated with the Afrikaner... Among the
> highlights of my schooldays were Fred Allen's All Blacks tour of South
> Africa in 1949 and Hennie Muller's Springbok tour of Britain in 1951-
> 52. I can remember how pupils and teachers alike fulminated against the
> presence of the "bloody Englishman" Basil Kenyon and the "bloody
> Jew" Cecil Moss in "our" teams. (Brink, 1995)

Once politicised, Brink became "for some 30 years... a fervent supporter of
any foreign team the Springboks played against" and "even during the transition
years since 1991 the chauvinistic arrogance continued to coincide with that of
the political establishment, leaving me unable to root unequivocally for the
Boks" (*ibid.*).

It is easy to guess what episodes Brink had in mind when he referred to 'chauvinistic arrogance'. The test that ended South Africa's isolation coincided with a crisis in the country's transition to democracy. The ANC considered using its influence to have the match cancelled. They decided in the end that it should go ahead but requested that it should not be accompanied by flag-waving which had not been a tradition of the game. Further, the national anthem, *Die Stem*, was played over the ground's loud speakers, drowning out the minute's silence that the ANC had decreed for the victims of the Boipatong massacre. However, there was no repetition of this behaviour at the next test as Newlands in Cape Town, though there was some flag-waving.

In these circumstances, it is hardly surprising that, at the start of the World Cup tournament in 1995, there remained a question mark over whether the team would win support across the country's racial divide. In the light of the Springbok team's record since the ending of isolation, there were no great expectations that the team would win the tournament, even with the advantage of playing at home. The fact that President Mandela threw his full weight unreservedly behind the team was therefore seen as a much needed boost to the Springboks' morale. The crucial point in this process was not the final against New Zealand, but the opening match of the tournament against Australia. The largely white crowd responded to Mandela's display of support for the team by chanting 'Nel-son, Nel-son', laying the basis for the notion of Mandela as an extra member of the team that made all the difference. The scintillating play of the Springboks in their victory over Australia was a further factor in overcoming inhibitions on supporting the Springboks because of their association with the old regime. It was at this point that Andre Brink abandoned his reservations about supporting the team.

The radical newspaper *Weekly Mail and Guardian* was among the converts. On the eve of the final, the paper carried an article by its rugby correspondent, which was headed 'How rugby scored a try for the new South Africa' (Swift, 1995). The article waxed lyrical on the theme of the existence of one team for one country, contrasting the ethic of the Springbok squad that had won "the almost unreserved support of all sectors of the community" with shameful episodes of the past such as the racial clashes between spectators during the 1960 tour of South Africa by the All Blacks. The piece particularly highlighted the leadership role played by Francois Pienaar during the tournament, noting his insistence that all members of the squad should know the words of

Nkosi Sikeli'i Afrika, which formed part of the new South Africa's national anthem. In her book on the South African transition, the *Financial Times* journalist Patti Waldmeir gives a vivid description of the reaction of the country to the team's victory in the final:

> This was pure, non-racial joy of a kind South Africa has never seen in 350 years of shared history. Crowds danced in the streets of Soweto, chanting Viva, Amabokoboko! [the African version of the team name], while black youths waltzed with life-sized replicas of a blond Francois Pienaar in central Johannesburg. (Waldmeir, 1997: p. 270)

The Andre Markgraaff affair is the story of how this vision of a rainbow nation brought together by rugby, which the holding of the rugby world cup in South Africa seemed to have made possible, has since been undermined. When Markgraaff was appointed as the Springbok national coach in 1996, he dropped Francois Pienaar, not just as captain but from the Springbok squad, prompting outrage from fans and sports writers alike. Markgraff had the unfortunate nickname of Saddam Hussein, thanks to this moustache. His sacking of Pienaar was reported under the inevitable headline of 'Coach makes mother of all mistakes' (Swift, 1996).

Adding fuel to the controversy over Pienaar's sacking was the perception of Markgraaf as the choice of the powerful but unpopular boss of South African rugby, the President of the South African Rugby Football Union (SARFU), Louis Luyt. In contrast to Pienaar, Luyt had thoroughly blotted his copybook during the holding of the rugby world cup. At the banquet after the final game, he had suggested that South Africa would have won the cup on the previous occasions when the competition had been held if it had not been excluded for political reasons. Great offence was taken by the New Zealanders at his comments. However, in reality the much greater offence was Luyt's violation of the basis of support for the team in the new South Africa. The rainbow nation version of the Springboks' triumph was of course that the victory had been made possible by the defeat of apartheid both on and off the field. Luyt's commends clearly discounted any role by President Mandela in the victory.

By suggesting continuity with the sport under the old regime, he also re-opened wounds from the battle that had been fought over the team's symbols. In particular, the retention by the team of the Springbok ensignia had been a painful concession for anti-apartheid groups to have made. They had been persuaded to drop their hostility to the use of the Springbok in the interests of the ANC policy on national reconciliation. The argument for change had precisely been based on the need to establish a break with the past and particularly with the period when the award of Springbok colours was confined to whites. Luyt's involvement in the sacking of Pienaar was seen as going beyond the appointment of Markgraaff as national coach. Luyt was suspected of trying to get his own back on Pienaar because of the role that Pienaar had played as an unofficial shop steward for the players over the terms of their contracts after the rugby world cup.

But damaging as the controversy over the sacking of Pienaar was to the image of rugby in South Africa, far worse, was to come. In February 1997 the SABC (South African Broadcasting Corporation) television news got hold of a tape of a private telephone conversation dated from the period of controversy that followed the dropping of Pienaar. SABC television news broadcast it gleefully. The most salient piece of the tape was quoted in the *Weekly Mail and Guardian* ('Verbatim', 21 February 1997) as follows:

Naturally, it is fucking politics with the whole fucking country behind him [i.e. Francois Pienaar]… Now I hear that Mlukeli George also wants to resign on Friday. It's kaffirs man, it's the fucking NSC [i.e. National Sports Congress — the anti-apartheid sports body], the fucking kaffirs.

'Kaffirs' of course is a term of racial abuse for the country's African population, as insulting as the American term 'nigger'. At his inauguration as President of South Africa in 1994, Mandela had made specific reference to the use of such racial epithets, making it clear that they had no place in the new South Africa.

Just before the tape was broadcast, knowing that he was about to be accused of having made racist comments by the media, Markgraaff defended himself with the words "I am a liberal" (*Cape Argus*, 18 February 1997). After the broadcast of the tape, his position became untenable. He made an abject apology and resigned. A few of the players were imprudent enough to say that they wanted him back ('Boks want coach back', *Cape Argus*, 19 February, 1997). That compounded the offence. South African rugby's image was already in decline when this crisis occurred. An editorial in the *Weekly Mail and Guardian* (21 February 1997) conveyed the strength of feeling about the state of the game and the conduct of those who ran it:

The stench arising from the administration of rugby in South Africa is overpowering. If the coaching career of the Springbok coach, Andre Markgraaff, is the immediate casualty of this week's rugby race row, the putrefaction which gives rise to the stink lies with the South African Rugby Football Union (SARFU). It has been obvious for years that something has been seriously amiss with the sport. But Louis Luyt's control of the game at the national level—which might well be described as tyrannical—has kept the lid on it. The Markgraaff affair has given a glimpse of the shenanigans which seemingly go on behind the scenes. The full facts of the scandal are still emerging, but if the central allegations stand—blackmail, rampant racism and a toleration of both by SARFU—it is hardly necessary to call for a clean out at SARFU headquarters, the demand being so obvious.

The perspective of African nationalists, both inside and outside the ANC, was that the Markgraaff affair represented a betrayal of the support given to rugby by Mandela during 1995. There was even an undercurrent that Mandela himself had been at fault in being so trusting of the sport and in having taken at face value its protestations of loyalty to the new South Africa. The Sports Minister, Steve Tshwete, had already launched an inquiry into SARFU over concerns about the organisation's financial dealings, particularly those associated with its President, Louis Luyt. The Markgraaff affair prompted threats of a much wider inquiry into the administration of the game. The problems of South African rugby off the field were compounded by a series of defeats on the field. The Springboks lost a test series to the All Blacks in South Africa for the first time ever in 1996, while in 1997 they suffered the further humiliation of losing a test series in South Africa to the Lions (representing the British Isles). In terms of the latter, it was interesting to note that the games were played in front of crowds which were close to 100% white and that the Lions looked positively multi-racial in comparison with the all-white ranks of the Springboks.

South African rugby's fall from grace needs to be seen in a wider political context. Precisely because of rugby's image as the Afrikaner's game, Mandela's support for the Springbok team during the rugby world cup was seen as a potent symbol of national reconciliation, a policy the ANC saw at the time as essential to securing white acceptance of the new dispensation. Further reassurance was provided by power-sharing with the National Party. This phase ended when parliament reached agreement on the terms of a new constitution in May 1996. At this point the National Party went into opposition, leaving the government so as to be freer to criticise the policies being pursued by the ANC. This move caused little alarm in the country, but rather was presented as a step towards political normality. The new constitution itself made no provision for the continuation of power-sharing. Government would be based in future on the principle of majority rule. The implication for rugby was that there was no reason why it should expect special treatment as the game of a minority the government was seeking to conciliate. In this new situation the association of rugby so clearly with Afrikaners and with Afrikaner nationalism was disadvantageous.

But in fact the story of South African rugby shows that the notion of it as simply a vehicle for Afrikaner nationalism is a gross over-simplification. Many of the symbols associated with the game today, which tend to be perceived as quintessentially Afrikaans, in reality go back to rugby's imperial origins in South Africa. In particular, green jerseys were first worn by a South African representative side in 1903 while the Springbok symbol first appeared during a tour of Britain by a South African representative side in 1906 (Grundlingh, Odendaal and Spies, 1995: p. 67 and p. 74). The green jerseys owed their origin to the colours of the Old Diocesan (OD) Rugby Football Club. These were the old boys of Cape Town's leading Anglican church school, Diocesan College of Bishops, which was modelled on the English public school. ODs made up a majority of the team members of early South African teams and partly as a consequence of that, Bishops as a school has produced more South African internationals than any other school in South Africa. Despite the special place of rugby in Afrikaner life, English-speaking whites have always played a part in the success of Springbok sides. For example, Joel Stransky, Mark Andrews and James Small played a prominent role in the success of the team that won the world cup in 1995.

Also prominent in that team was a Coloured player, Chester Williams. It was perhaps understandable that the outside world has tended to see him as a token figure. The reality is rather different. The game of rugby has enjoyed a following among Coloureds in the Western Cape and among African in the Eastern Caper for well over a hundred years (Grundlingh, Odendaal and Spies, 1995: pp. 24-63). Consequently, it is not surprising that from the base of the game within these communities a player of Springbok standard should have emerged, despite the malign impact of segregation, which also goes back a hundred years and did not originate with the imposition of the policies of apartheid after the election of the National Party government in 1948. SARU (South African Rugby Union) played a leading role in the anti-apartheid sports movement in South Africa in the 1970s and 1980s. It merged with the establishment SARB (South African Rugby Board) to form SARFU (South African Rugby Football Union) in 1992. There is thus an ample liberal basis in the past of the game in South Africa for rugby to change its image to one that is much more representative of the country's population. But it will have to overcome formidable competition for the allegiance of sports fans in the townships from another game, soccer.

Bafana Bafana[1:] Rainbow soccer?

> *Mastermind your craft and tackle them with tact*
> *Up the hills, slopes and valleys*
> *Remember that the nation awaits your resounding victory*
> *Our hopes, our morale, our pride, our reputation,*
> *Our citizenship and country — are all at stake*
> *Shosholoza Bafana Bafana Shosholoza* [shine boys shine]

Who, present in Soccer City, Soweto, on a warm Saturday in February 1996, could not have been swept along with the tide of emotion as, wearing a replica Bafana Bafana shirt, Nelson Mandela handed over the African Cup of Nations to South Africa's captain, Neil Tovey? On the eve of his team's historic achievement, the national soccer coach Clive Barker recognised the relative situation vis-à-vis rugby and cricket (1996: p. 34):

> The feats of these teams (rugby and cricket) should be put into perspective. They were never really isolated whereas we were never exposed. Also football is a much bigger world sport than rugby or cricket which are played by only a handful of countries....

Headline successes, in what were perceived by many as the new South Africa's flagship, 'white' sports, placed added pressure on those charged with playing and promoting soccer, clearly the number one sport of the black population. As the then President of SAFA (South African Football Association) Solomon 'Stix' Morewa put it, "my dream is to win respectability for the South African team. We have to win the cup, whether it is through skill or the grace of God" (Morewa, 1996: p. 9).

That they went on to win the competition is does suggest a degree of divine intervention. The following extracts from the *South African Sunday Times* and *The Economist* sum up the populist view of what this victory was supposed to mean:

One nation, yet another famous victory: South Africa's talisman of victory, President Nelson Mandela, threw up his arms and waved his cap in the air yesterday as substitute striker, Mark Williams scored in the 73 minute... In the 20 months since democratic elections, we have stunned the sporting world, not once, not twice, but three times.., But no sporting contest has been sweeter or done more to unite the nation than Bafana Bafana's moment of Glory. (*South African Sunday Times*, 1996, Feb. 3: p. 1)

Nelson Mandela has used sport to define South Africans' sense of themselves, as he struggles to pull umpteen tongues, groups and faiths into one. Rugby almost did it: blacks surprised themselves, swung behind that Afrikaner secular religion. Victory over England at cricket, with a lone non-white player, helped. But it is the soccer victory that has truly spanned the ethnic divide — and President Mandela, Deputy-President F.W. De Klerk and King Goodwill Zwelithini, Xhosa, Afrikaner and Zulu, were all in the stadium to prove it. (*The Economist*, Feb. 13:1996: p. 43)

Strong and optimistic words, but how ready and/or suitable was soccer in South Africa to assume and progress the mantle of peace-maker for the rainbow nation? Following a world-wide pattern, football had been introduced to South Africa by the British during the latter part of the nineteenth century. The favoured sports of the white elite were those introduced by public school and Oxbridge educated colonial administrators who eschewed (professional) association football, in favour of amateur codes of rugby union and cricket. However, in terms of popular participation, soccer outstripped the development of both of these sports. After being introduced by soldiers and mine-workers, it rapidly became the sport of the white working classes and of a huge black population who were denied access to the pastimes of 'polite society'. "For the African working class, it would not be exaggerated to say that football was sport: no other game showed soccer's remarkable ability to penetrate among the poorest, most exploited group in society" (Archer and Bouillon, 1982: p. 100). Once racial divisions in South Africa became institutionalised, most whites deserted soccer because of its associations with the non-white population. Of course, because the media was controlled by and aimed at 'polite society' the popularity of soccer was ignored by the press, excepting the township newssheets (Bose, 1994: p. 36).

This may partially explain why, in the European and world media, the role of football in the fight against apartheid has tended to take fourth place behind post-1960s protests featuring cricket, rugby and the Olympics. In fact, in 1956 table tennis became the first international sports governing body to recognise the political relationship between apartheid and sport when it severed all sporting links with the all-white South African table tennis federation. The following year, the fledgling African Football Confederation (AFC[2]) suspended the South African Football Federation when it insisted on sending a whites-only team to the first African Nations Cup[3] held in Sudan in 1957.

Ironically, South Africa had been one of CAF's founding fathers along with Egypt, Sudan and Ethiopia — the only 'independent' countries in Africa at that time. South Africa's post-colonial history was clearly distinct from that of CAF's other founder members which, in a variety of ways, after colonialism, were governed by representatives of the indigenous population rather than a residual, white-European elite. Gaining membership of CAF (and through this FIFA) was the cumulative moment when, alongside membership of the Organisation for African Unity and the United Nations, newly independent states took their place on the world stage.

As black Africa threw off the colonial yoke it was unthinkable — in a sport for which they had a strong measure of regional control — that institutionalised racism which characterised South African soccer would be tolerated by the rest of Africa. Nevertheless, there was an initial reluctance to ostracise South African soccer. As Dr. Halim of Sudan, a founder member of CAF, explained in an interview in 1997 with one of the authors, the football administrators in South Africa at that time were English and liberal minded. They agreed to adopt a non-racial approach in their dealings with CAF and to send mixed-race teams to CAF competitions. However, they were overruled by an Afrikaner-dominated political regime which insisted upon absolute segregation in all cultural activities, including football. This left CAF with little choice other than to suspend South Africa, placing football, "at the vanguard of the fight against discrimination and apartheid in sport". CAF's unilateral decision was not well received by FIFA which, at that time, was dominated by white, north Europeans who were yet to see the inherent evil of apartheid. The South Africa issue was indeed a critical one, which, in the long run was to be instrumental in the downfall of the then FIFA President, the Englishman, Stanley Rous. The Rous affair is a neglected episode in the history of the fight against apartheid and is worth dwelling upon.

In the early 1960s the white Football Association of South Africa (FASA) faced a challenge from the non-racial South African Soccer Federation (SASF). In January 1963 Rous and the secretary of the USA Football Federation, Jimmy MaGuire, visited South Africa on a fact-finding mission for FIFA. The two-man commission held interviews with a wide range of sports organisations, and full submissions were received from the two football bodies. The FASA made plain its firm views early on in its submission:

> My Association is certain that FIFA which is entirely non-Political, and will not allow the Federation to adopt the course which it has as its chief aim for a number of reasons, but mainly because the political agitators who are now ruling the Federation behind the scenes, are merely using soccer as a catspaw for their own selfish ends, and they are not in any way interested in what is best for soccer football in Southern Africa, both for Europeans and non-Europeans ... The very large majority of the latter are uneducated, and not fit to assume positions of authority in any sphere of life. I do not desire to enter into any political discussions, as I am aware that your body does not allow politics to enter into any of its deliberations.[4]

Rous and McGuire "unreservedly" recommended that the suspension of the FASA be lifted, and their report gave no credence to the claims of the SASF:

> There is no other body which can take the place of the FASA. The members of the dissident Federation whom we interviewed, would, in our opinion, be quite unsuitable to represent Association Football in South Africa. Their attitude was one of destruction and not construction in any way. We found that they desired to hinder and to act contrary to Government Policy, which clearly indicates their inability to foster and propagate [sic] the game of soccer in that country".

The Rous-McGuire recommendation was supported in the FIFA Executive Committee by 13 votes to 5, Rous referring, in correspondence with Aleck Jaffe of the FASA, to the nature of the vote: "The votes against were all from the left wing and for the first time those members demonstrated their solidarity as a block"[5]. More block voting was to come. By the mid-1960s CAF had more than 30 voting member-nations within FIFA[6]. At its Tokyo Congress in 1964, the Executive Committee decision was overturned, by 48 votes to 15, and FASA was suspended from international football, for, in the formulation of the African Confederation, "the practice of racial discrimination".

For their part, South African sport's white administrators learned a painful lesson with regard to shifting balances of power in world sport. As Dave Marais, then the President of South Africa's white-only soccer body ruefully commented after the Tokyo Congress:

> The tragedy is that most of the important countries are sympathetic. But there is such a large block of African countries, when it comes to one man, one vote, don't have a chance of reversing the decision. I think there should be a qualifying vote. It is absurd for each little country to have the same voting power as countries like England and Italy. (Marais, quoted in Bose, 1994: p. 69)

Rous was either blind to these emergent power dynamics or too 'old school' to admit to the increasing politicisation of sport in the post-colonial era and the impact which this would have on the organisation of which he was head. Either way, the South Africa issue was to haunt Rous throughout his Presidency. At the VIIIth Ordinary General Assembly of the African Football Confederation in Addis Ababa, in January 1968, the FIFA President addressed the assembly, guarding delegates against following the advice of sports politics activists from within South Africa:

> I have noted that you attach undue importance to the SANROC (South African Non-Racial Olympic Committee). In fact you should take no notice of their letter... I know these peoples. I have been in South Africa to meet them... In fact this group is more interested in communist politics than in football.[7]

In response, the Kenyan delegate spoke of "the unwarranted attack of Sir Stanley Rous against the General Secretary and the AFC", on the South Africa question:

> In his declaration we saw the manifestation of old and dying colonialism. It is of no avail of him to say that the Football Association of South Africa has committed no crime because it is the government which is responsible of the apartheid policy. It is the government which controls the affairs of the FASA. We in Kenya wish to see that all means possible are used to bring about a change in South Africa so that our brothers there may enjoy the freedom of sports we have.[8]

Rous' dogged determination to stand by his views on sports politics flew in the face of pan-African sensibilities and eventually was to cost him the presidency. As Oroc Oyo, a former secretary of the Nigerian Football Association recalls:

> I remember the 1974 elections very vividly. There was this struggle (between Rous and Havelange) and I was in the centre of it. Dr. Havelange mounted his campaign in 1971 and he produced a brochure on himself that was circulated around the world. I remember he attended the CAF congress in Egypt 1974. After the congress he invited African delegates to a cocktail party hosted by the ambassador of Brazil in Egypt. All of us were invited. He had a Lebanese-Brazilian who was one of his chief campaigners — in charge of Africa. At that time Africa had a Supreme Council for Sport in Africa, and the secretary general at that time, Jean Claude Ganga. The plank of Havelange's campaign was to ostracise South Africa, because this was the clarion call of African football. This was a carrot which Dr. Havelange brandished before Africa. So Ganga mustered Africa.

Mawad Wade, then the secretary of the Senegal Football Association and now a senior member of FIFA's technical committee, tells a similar story:

> I was one of the men in the CAF who was in charge of making a campaign in our continent for Dr. Havelange. Why? Because it was apartheid in South Africa. I was talking to Sir Stanley Rous in the Sheraton Hotel in Cairo. I told him, if you are elected, can you keep South Africa out of FIFA until apartheid goes down? He says to me, I can't promise you because I follow my country the United Kingdom. I say to him, in this case then we will never vote for you. Also when I meet Havelange in the same Hotel he says to me, okay so long as I am in charge and apartheid still exists, South Africa will never come into FIFA.[9]

Havelange kept his promise and went on to confirm South Africa's isolation from world football in 1976. FIFA's ban was not lifted until July 1992, more than two years after Nelson Mandela's release from prison and, ironically, somewhat later than global sporting links in cricket had been reforged and South Africa had been allowed back into the Olympic movement.

The main reason for the delay was the chaotic state of football administration in South Africa. FIFA's statutes state that membership is accepted only through the offices of a single, viable, and politically independent football association. More than 30 years of isolation had left South African soccer in considerable disarray. Effectively, apartheid racially stratified football in South Africa and over the years a wide variety of governing bodies emerged to administer a segregated game. In an attempt to appease the international community, in 1971 Premier Vorster introduced a 'multi-national' sports policy whereby officially sanctioned racial categories (whites, Indians, Africans and coloureds), under certain circumstances, could play against each other at an 'international level' and, exceptionally, play touring international teams. As Bose states:

> Only a white South African, steeped in the imbecile logic of apartheid could come up with such a tortuous policy. What the international community wanted was normal mixed sport where people of whatever race took part, as they did over the rest of the world. Vortster offered a unique South African Solution: a wonderfully abnormal sporting solution for an abnormal society. (Bose, 1994: p. 97)

A look at soccer in South Africa in the early 1970s reveals separate administrative bodies for Indian Soccer, coloured soccer, African soccer, non-racial soccer and white soccer — as we have seen, with the latter lobbying aggressively to be recognised as the commanding voice for South Africa in the international arena. The Bantuisation of South African football can be viewed as the bizarre zenith of sporting apartheid. At one stage it led to an absurd proposal that South Africa would rotate the racial mix of the national team as it attempted to qualify for successive World Cup Finals. They would enter a black team for England in 1966, a white team for Mexico in 1970, presumably, a coloured team for Germany in 1974 and so on! (Bose, 1994: p. 38).

If soccer in South Africa was forced through apartheid to be split along racial and ethnic lines, it also became quite divided within each segregated group. Divisions in South African society are more than simply black and white. Apart from divisions between Anglos and Afrikaners and among Indians and coloureds, the black community is itself divided along ethno-tribal and political lines. Such divisions find expression through affiliation to different football leagues and clubs. For instance, in the inter-war years Abaqulusi and African Wanderers were representative of different tribes. In response to this, in 1932 a price from the Zulu royal family, formed a team known as the Zulu Royals which became Amazulu in later years.

The notorious Robin Island Prison offered a microcosm of black African sport's internal political divisions. Just as in the wider society sport was one of the few activities which permitted blacks to gather in significant numbers, in Robin Island it was just about the only area wherein the inmates were given relative freedom of association. Steve Tshwete, the ANC's first minister of sport, was incarcerated there in 1964 for his political activity. While in prison he agitated for better conditions, including more exercise and the right to play games. Eventually, under pressure from the International Red Cross, the prison authorities relented and the prisoners were allowed to play football. To his dismay, Tshwete saw the fledgling Robin Island football league fragment into political factions, "with the ANC and the Pan-African Congress each fielding seven teams" (Bose, 1994: p. 171).

These layers of imposed and self-generated racial, tribal and political divisions within soccer led to the emergence of mind-boggling and complex series of competing administrative structures and competing governing bodies (Archer and Bouillon, 1982: p. 250-251). It was this legacy which, more than anything else, caused FIFA to delay South Africa's re admission into international football until 1992, when they were able to identify a single, representative and, apparently, democratic governing body (Oliver, 1992: p. 764).

When Nelson Mandela was released from prison in 1990 he was presented to the people of Soweto at a celebratory rally at FNB (First National Bank) stadium or 'Soccer City' the shared home ground of Kaiser Chiefs and Orlando Pirates. This was more than a matter of crowd capacity. It was, at least in part, recognition of the role that football had played in the fight against apartheid. Debarred from virtually every other area of public office, the football club often became the focus for black-community political activity. Moreover, at a time when the black and coloured population were banned from most other forms of mass-public gatherings, throughout the country, soccer stadia served as venues for mass meetings and political rallies. Six years after his release, in January 1996, it must have been particularly satisfying for Mandela to return to Soccer City, in his capacity of President of South Africa, to present the African Cup of Nations, to Bafana Bafana. However, soccer's anti-apartheid political credentials handicap the sport in the context of community relations.

The national team's distinguished record of achievement suggests that, since the end of isolation, South African football has made rapid progress. However, off the field there are still major problems to contend with. Three are of particular significance: the problem of white identification with South African soccer; the problem of non-white collective identification with the national team; and maladministration and corruption in South African football.

The reports in the newspapers and magazines in the days after South Africa's ACN triumph were misleading. They gave the false impression that during the final, Bafana Bafana were cheered on by a sizeable proportion of white supporters. While no official data has been produced on the racial mixture of the audience at that match, one of the authors was present at the game and can confirm firsthand that, at most, only 5% of the crowd were white. Because of soccer's political history, particularly its association with organisations such as the ANC and the Pan African Congress, the white community continues to distance itself from it. Gary Bailey, formerly the goalkeeper of South Africa and Manchester United, believes that the national team needs, "to be sold to the whites of this country who, at the moment, are dead scared to go to soccer matches. A lot of marketing needs to be done" (Bailey, 1995: p. 21). He goes on to illustrate the extent of white alienation from soccer:

> Whites won't go to the games because soccer is perceived as the black sport. They would prefer to lend their allegiance to psychologically comfortable and time honoured white man's pastimes, such as cricket and rugby. When their attention turns to soccer, the vast majority of them cast their gaze towards teams playing in England and other European Leagues. (*ibid.*: p. 24)

There is a growing view within black South Africa that the National Soccer League should forget about luring back white support and get on with the job of marketing the game within the black community. Former player Jomo Sono puts it this way:

> We have tried our level best and it is obvious that they are not prepared to watch our games. For the past three years we have hosted the United Bank Soccer Festival at which English teams have taken part. They white fans have attended these but soon after these clubs left they (the white fans) go back to their cocoons. (Sono, 1995)

A related problem is the fact that many black South Africans have an underdeveloped sense of South African national identity and very little experience of supporting South African teams in international sport. As we have seen, no international soccer was played for forty years and the achievements of South

Africa in white sports did little or nothing to enhance the sense of national belonging for the rest of the population. Mark Gleeson, writing in a souvenir edition of African Soccer before the ACN, makes the observation that:

> After forty years of isolation, this nation's cup is the chance for the rest of Africa to get to know their lost sons, and for South Africans to learn something about the continent from which they have for so long been alienated. (Gleeson, 1996a: p. 12)

However, Gleeson concludes on a cautionary note:

> It remains to be seen whether the crowds will come out in force to watch the event, however. African soccer is, after all, something of a novelty for a South African audience, and, without the recognition factor there will be very little to attract local fans into the stadium. Sure, South African fans have heard of George Weah (Liberia and AC Milan) and Abidi Pele (Ghana and Marseilles), but few in Johannesburg would recognise them in the street. Most people don't know were Algeria is on the map, and many have never heard of Burkina Faso or Sierra Leone. These are the realities of decades of isolation from the rest of the continent.... (*ibid.*)

These words turned out to be prophetic as, with the exception of the games featuring the host nation, attendance was extremely poor. At certain games, in rugby stadia in Port Elizabeth and Bloomfontein, with capacities upwards of 70,000, the attendances were measured in the 100s. Even when the host team played at its Soweto base, only the opening game and the final attracted close to capacity audiences. There are many reasons for such poor attendances, including the cost of tickets and the poor transport links from black neighbourhoods into the white districts where the rugby grounds can be found. However, it is also the fact that, for generations of blacks who had been brought up to be contemptuous of the notion of the South African nation, to suddenly become loyal, flag-waving South African patriots proved too difficult. As Gary Bailey observes, "most black people in South Africa have no concept of a national team... There is currently nothing like the same support for the national team as there is for the club sides" (Bailey, 1995: p. 21).

Finally, in order for soccer to gain the respect of all segments of South African society, there is a need for some serious house-keeping/clearing. Corruption in its various forms has become one of the most serious problems facing many sub-

Saharan African societies (Bayart, 1993; Leys, 1996). Football has not escaped the attention of those public officials who are as much interested in personal wealth and aggrandisement as they are in sports development. There are signs that South African Soccer has been affected by this trend. As Gleeson put it, "after just four years back on the world stage, revelations of corruption and farcical on-field incidents have threatened to retard this remarkable progress after almost 30 years of apartheid-enforced isolation" (Gleeson, 1996b).

At the centre of these scandals was Solomon 'Stix' Morewa, the President of SAFA and the man who had stood next to Mandela in Soccer City and who had bathed most in the after-glow of the national teams' ACN triumph. It also seems also that he gained much financially. After serious allegations of corruption and mismanagement, Sports Minister, Steve Tshwete, appointed a supreme court judge, Benjamin Pickard, to investigate the affairs of SAFA and related football bodies. According to John Perlman:

> Judge Pickard found that SAFA President ... had sold out to an Irish-based marketing company "virtually every asset it had to earn money". In return for a modest fixed fee, the company which was called Awesome Sports International — you'd think the name might have given some advanced warning — cashed in on all ticket sales, advertising sponsorships and TV rights. One report said that ASI had transferred some R28 million into its European accounts — SAFA's total annual budget rarely tops R10 million". (Pearlman, 1997: p. 39)

In return for his 'co-operation', Morewa received a R500,000 'loan' from ASI as well as accepting from a sponsor a new Mercedes Benz. In addition, Morwea was found to have paid himself a performance bonus of R45,000. This was unlikely to have been checked by the SAFA executive who, after the ACN, voted themselves R15,000 bonuses. Moreover, despite being warned of the dangers of selling out to the multi-nationals by Judge Pickard, SAFA voted to retain ties with ASI and went on to strike a deal with a US based marketing company to promote South Africa's bid for the 2006 World Cup. Morewa is not the only culprit and his graft looks paltry compared with that of former South African league president, Abdul Bhamjee, who was sent to prison in 1992 for embezzling R7.4 million (*ibid.*). The corruption was bad enough, but the more lasting damage done was to the sport's reputation, particularly in the eyes of white South Africans.

Conclusion

At a grass-roots level there are opportunities being taken to develop structures of participation which promote integration, particularly for youth. In soccer there are a number of coaching clinics, which, under the general title of "melting pot development" are designed both to improve basic ball skills and to promote cross-cultural integration amongst children through the medium of soccer. Likewise in rugby and in cricket there is a great deal of development work being done, particularly in the townships, which has a significant community relations emphasis (Mseleku, 1995).

The formation in 1994 of the United School Sports Association of South Africa and its replacement of the separate, racially segregated governing bodies for school sports, has greatly enhanced the opportunities for young South Africans of whatever colour to play the same sports together while at school. Likewise, the implementation of "Education through Sport", a national, cross-curricular initiative designed to accelerate the rehabilitation of a generation of black school children whose education suffered as a direct consequence of apartheid and resistance to it, has had a positive effect upon community morale (*ibid.*: p. 39).

Such initiatives are to be applauded. However, taken alone they stand little prospect of achieving lasting social change. Significantly, when the Sports Council for Northern Ireland launched its policy on community relations in 1997, the guest of honour was the South African Mvuzo Mbebe, Chief Executive, South African National Sports Council. He could have learned much from his visit. As the chapter in this book on Northern Ireland illustrates, it is very difficult to achieve any lasting social reforms merely by tinkering with the sports system. Sport-based community relations programmes can impact on social division, but only if they are part of a wider package of social, political and economic reforms, the goals of which are to remove the generic causes of sectarianism (creed, race or caste). So long as young South Africans continue to live in separate neighbourhoods, go to different schools, speak different languages and have markedly unequal access to economic resources, any mutuality experienced on the playing field will necessarily be ephemeral.

The political legacy of both rugby and soccer and the significance of these sports in the working-up of separate cultural identities present major obstacles for those who would harness them in the service of community relations. We have not ruled out a role for sport in the reconstruction of a new South Africa.

We are suggesting, however, that some of the lavish claims made about the potential of sport to promote universal harmony in a society as deeply divided as South Africa need to be tempered. Once it has been recognised that sports are not experienced in ideological vacuums, that they have socio-cultural and political histories, pragmatic decisions about what can and cannot be achieved through sport can be taken.

Notes

[1] Vernacular nickname of the South African national soccer team, meaning 'boys, boys'. This is an extract from the poem/anthem, *Bafana Bafana*, by Mzwakhe Mbuli, *Soccer News*, February 1996: p. 9.

[2] Although the fact that, after a diplomatic row between Mandela and Abacha of Nigeria over the execution of Ken Saro Wiwa and 8 other Ogoni dissidents, the Nigerian Super Eagles - Africa's strongest national team by some distance - withdrew from the competition, had a lot to do with Bafana Bafana's triumph.

[3] In deference to the increasing number of French speaking countries which joined the association as colonialism receded in Africa, in the 1970s it became conventional to use the French idiom of the *Confederation Africaine de Football* or CAF. This convention will be followed throughout the rest of this chapter.

[4] It was only in 1996, when this competition was hosted by South Africa, that the acronym was changed from ANC to ACN, presumably to avoid any confusion with the African National Congress.

[5] For a detailed discussion of the personalities and political history of FIFA see J. Sugden and A. Tomlinson *FIFA and the Contest for World Football*. Cambridge: Polity, 1998.

[6] FASA report to FIFA Commission, Rous papers, SCAIR.

[7] Report of FIFA Commission to FIFA Executive, Rous papers, SCAIR.

[8] Rous papers, SCAIR.

[9] For congressional decision-making a system of *one member (national federation)—one vote* pertains: meaning, for instance, that the vote of FIFA's newest member is equal to that of the organisation's longest standing affiliate.

[10] Confederation Minutes, p.6 - in Rous papers, SCAIR.

[11] Rous papers, SCAIR.

[12] Interview with authors, Johannesburg, 23 January 1996.

[13] Interview with authors, Johannesburg, 21 January 1996.

[14] For a more general treatment of corruption in African football see the chapter on Africa in J. Sugden and A. Tomlinson, *FIFA and the Contest for World Football*. Cambridge: Polity, 1998.

References

Archer, R. and Bouillon, A. (1982) *The South African Game. Sport and racism.* London: Zed Press.

Bailey, G. (1996) 'For club and country', *The Fixture. South African* Soccer, Issue 1: pp. 19-24.

Barker, C. (1996) *BBC, Focus on Africa*, Jan.: p.34.

Bayart, J. (1993) *The state in Africa. The politics of the belly.* London: Longman.

Bose, M. (1994) *Sporting colours. Sport and politics in South Africa.* London: Robson Books.

Brink, A. (1995) 'South Africa's dirty old habits die hard', *Weekly Mail and Guardian*, 30 June.

Gleeson, M. (1996a) 'Chance of a lifetime', African Soccer. Special souvenir edition: p. 12.

———— (1996b) 'Soccer-corruption haunts South African Soccer', wire service, Reuters Sports Report, Oct. 31.

Global Heroes (1995) at http://www.gwb.com.au/.

Grundlingh, A., Odendaal, A., and Spies, B. (1995) *Beyond the tryline: Rugby and South African society.* Johannesburg: Raven Press.

Lapchick, R. (1975) *The politics of race and international sport. The case of South Africa.* Westport, Connecticut: Greenwood Press.

Leys, C. (1996) *The rise and fall of development theory.* Oxford: James Curry Publishers.

Morewa, S. (1996) Quoted in E. Quansah, 'The cup to surpass all African cups', *Africa Today*, Jan/Feb., Vol. 2, No. 1: pp. 22-30.

Oliver, G (1992) *The Guiness record of world soccer.* London: Guiness Publishing.

Perlman, J. (1997) 'The price of success', *When Saturday Comes*, No. 124, June: pp. 38-39.

SCAIR (Sport Cultures Archive for Investigative Research, University of Brighton) Sir Stanley Rous archive.

Soccer News (1996) 'editorial comment', *Soccer News*, Vol. 61: p. 65.

Sono, J. (1995) interviewed in *The Fixture: South African soccer*, 1995, Issue 1: p. 123

Sugden, J. and Tomlinson, A. (1998) *FIFA and the Contest for World Football*. Cambridge: Polity.

Swift, J. (1995) 'How rugby scored a try for the new South Africa', *Weekly Mail and Guardian*, 23 June.

――― (1996) 'Coach makes the mother of all mistakes', *Weekly Mail and Guardian*, 17 October.

Tshwete, S. (1995) interviewed in *The Fixture, South African soccer*, Issue 1: p. 36.

Waldmeir, P. (1997) *Anatomy of a miracle: The end of Apartheid and the birth of the New South Africa*. London: Viking.

DIVIDED SPORTS IN A DIVIDED BELGIUM

Bart Vanreusel, Roland Renson and Jan Tollenneer

FLOK, Katholieke Universiteit Leuven

Introduction: a complicated nation called Belgium

Although Belgium emerged as a nation-state in 1830 with "l'Union fait la Force" (Unity makes power) as its national motto, several basic causes for the development of a divided society were already there. First, Belgian history is full of linguistic tensions which have polarized political as well as social and cultural life. Starting in 1830, the new nation-state was completely administered in French, by a Francophone power elite. Although the language of the majority of the population was Flemish (which is the same as Dutch), secondary and higher education was in French only, until far into the twentieth century. The language issue has drawn a deeply-rooted language border (see Figure 1, following page) from east to west across the country, dividing the French-speaking south (Wallonia) from the Flemish-speaking north (Flanders). Actually, the language border runs across Belgium as a sharp, political and administrative dividing line. Second, the Belgian language issue is also a relic of traditional cultural influences. The language border appears to coincide with the borderline between Germanic and Romanic culture.

With the rise of industrialization, tensions between the Francophone south and the Flemish-speaking north of Belgium, were increased by economic differences. In the earlier years of the Belgian nation-state, Wallonia became the economic point of gravity, supported by a flourishing heavy industry thriving on the local coal mines. The decline of heavy industry in Wallonia and the rise of technology in Flanders in the second half of the twentieth century gradually caused a shift of the economic centre towards Flanders. In present day Belgium, the linking of these economic tensions with Flemish cultural emancipation has even increased the cleavage.

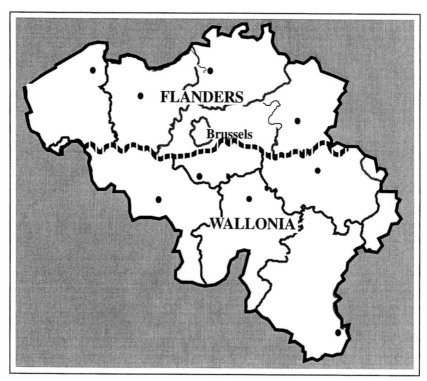

Figure 1   The Belgian language border — a linguistic, administrative, political and socio-economic dividing line

Belgian society has, since its foundation, been strongly divided in terms of three traditional ideologies, commonly called the traditional "pillars" of Belgian society. This refers to the impact that the catholic, the liberal and the socialist "pillars' have had on political, administrative, social, cultural and economic life for generations. Moreover, the ideological division is intertwined with the language division in a special way. Socialist ideology traditionally dominated early industrial Wallonia, whereas the catholic 'pillar', for decades, penetrated most aspects of public and private life in traditional and rural Flanders (Van Isacker, 1978).

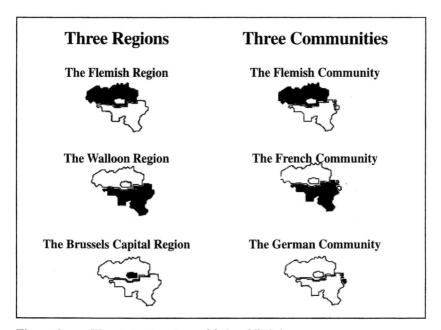

Figure 2:   The state structure of federal Belgium

To sum up, Belgium is a nation divided on more than one issue. The language conflict may be the most colorful and well-known cause of Belgian dissension, but other, major dividing issues have certainly contributed to Belgium's status as a divided nation. The fact that, so far, Belgium has survived these dividing forces and remained a nation-state, is the result of a continuous political balancing act, the constant striving for a subtle sharing of power between Flanders and Wallonia.

The continuous political process of federalization since the nineteen-seventies has now resulted in a complicated, but balanced federal state structure. Today, Belgium is a federal state with a population of about 10 million inhabitants — 60 percent of them Dutch-speaking, 40 percent of them French-speaking and with a small German-speaking community as a third official community. The federal state is divided into three regions (Flanders, Wallonia and Brussels) and into three communities (a Dutch-speaking, a French-speaking and a German-speaking community) (see **Figure 2**).

Six governments, one for each region and one for each community, and a federal government try to run this complicated state structure. Over 70 percent of the total budget is now controlled by the regions and communities and only about 30 percent by the national state. The transfer of power from the federal state to the regions and communities is an ongoing process with a complex and ambiguous nature. On the one hand, this process intends to safeguard the unity of the Belgian nation-state but on the other hand, it widens the gap between the different regions and communities, and it even feeds the aspirations of separatist movements.

Belgium can be called a deeply divided nation but not because of the use of violence to settle its problems, as is the case in many other divided nations. On the contrary, except for some isolated incidents, the dividing issues so far have not led to a major use of violence. We call Belgium a deeply divided nation because of the complicated and accumulative nature of dividing issues, which are still high on the political agenda.

The emergence of a federal state was preceded by a long emancipatory struggle by the down-trodden Flemish majority, led by an intellectual elite, the so-called Flemish Movement. By the end of the nineteenth century, this Flemish resistance against a Francophone power elite was growing and a Flemish Movement was established through three important stages. The first stage consisted of a long-term, grass roots, emancipatory movement which reinforced Flanders' cultural identity and self awareness. The use of the Dutch language at all levels of administration and in education and the expression of a Flemish identity in arts, literature and also in sport were significant markers of a growing "Flemishization" of society, which lasted until the nineteen-sixties. The second stage of the Flemish Movement consisted of legal reform. From the nineteen-seventies on, the different language communities gradually obtained legally based cultural autonomy, with specific authorities and specifically allotted financial powers. This division by legislation initiated in the 1970s the third level of a fundamental, ongoing, political reform from the unitarian state towards a federal state.

Sport, a divided history

Sport has played a remarkable and significant role in Belgium's divided history. On the one hand, developments in sport have followed the encompassing socio-cultural and political process of division. But on the other hand, sport was and is at the same time a remarkably active agent in the continuous conflict between the division and the unity of Belgium. It is indeed surprising to observe that on some occasions, sport represents and reinforces the unitarian state and at other moments, serves as platform and battleground for the actors who seek to split the nation-state. The following part of this chapter focuses on this double-sided role of sport in a divided Belgium.

Renson (1998) analyzed the role of sport in the early Flemish Movement between 1868 and 1914. The first breakthrough of the Flemish Movement on the Belgian sports scene took place already in 1868 in the milieu of gymnastics, which was the most popular physical activity at that time. The importance of the role played by "The real Turnvater of Antwerp", Nicolas Jan Cupérus (1842-1928), was revealed. Cupérus managed to render the Turner movement more and more Flemish by founding De Gymnastischen Volkskring (the People's Gymnastics Society) in 1868. This was the first break through of the Flemish Movement on the Belgian sports scene. Cupérus was a progressive Liberal who was strongly committed both to the social emancipation of the working class and to the cultural liberation of the Flemish population. He was present at the foundation of the International Working Men's Association in 1864 in London. His dream was to bring the benefits of gymnastics within the reach of the working class. The systematic use of the Dutch language was a prerequisite for achieving this aim. He edited a new gymnastics periodical Volksheil (people's Welfare) in Dutch, which appeared from 1873 to 1895; later, the name of the periodical was changed to De Turner (The Gymnast). The importance he attached to language, is revealed by his magnum opus: an extensive Dutch glossary of gymnastics, De Nederlandsche Turnvaktaal of 1886, which also appeared in a French edition, La Terminologie gymnastique, in 1887.

The early awakening cultural identity of the Flemish is also revealed by the following quote from Belgica, the bilingual (French/Dutch) journal issued by the Catholic Gymnastics Federation, from 1895 to 1914. An article contained this typical Flemish complaint:

> The federation is made up of Flemings and Walloons: the former are the architects and founders and they still form the majority. Well, what do we see taking place?... the Walloons have the majority in the administration of the Federation. French has always enjoyed the privileged place and the affiliated Flemish societies are left with only a poor translation... The meetings of the Federation are even worse: there, everything or almost everything takes place in French. (Belgica, 1907, 5: p. 50)

Even more important for the rise of the Flemish Movement was the development of cycling as a sport. The Francophone Fédération Vélocipédique Belge (Belgium Cycling Federation) was founded in 1882. A first attempt by the Flemish members to publish a Flemish edition of the Revue Vélocipédique in 1899 failed and it took several more years before Dutch was accepted as an official language by the Federation. In fact, it was the cyclists themselves who promoted the Flemish Movement most successfully by their performance on the road (Renson, 1998). The cyclist, who would ignite the flame of the enormous popularity of cycling in Flanders, was the legendary Cyrille Van Hauwaert (1883-1974), nicknamed The Lion of Flanders. In 1907, he finished second in Paris-Roubaix and first in Bordeaux-Paris, and in 1908 he won both Milan-San Remo and Paris-Roubaix. Van Hauwaert became a true folk hero, the shy country boy who had beaten the "fine fleur" of the French cyclists. His example inspired many sporting young men to take their chance in a murderous Tour de France rather than to slave as seasonal labourers in the harvest-houses of Northern France. To make a champion a real folk hero, however, you need a minstrel to sing his praises. In the early years of the 20th century, the first generation of Belgian sports journalists started to publish their modern Pindaric odes. The founding father of sports journalism in Flanders was Karel Van Wynendaele (1882-1961). He was the manager of the famous Flandriens, a team of cyclists from the provinces of West and East Flanders. These rustic but strong sportsmen started their impressive list of successes in 1913 (Van Wynendaele, 1943: 109). In the same year, Van Wynendaele published the first issue of his Dutch journal Sportwereld. Again in 1913, he launched his Ronde Van Vlaanderen (Tour of Flanders), still one of the major European Cycling classics.

We elaborate on the actual status of the Ronde Van Vlaanderen further on in this chapter. Renson (1998) concluded that:

> It was the sturdy breed of cyclists, the so-called Flandriens, who put the Flemish Movement on the popular road. Probably more than any poet or writer, they conquered the body and soul of the population at large and provided a muscular answer to the widespread feeling of cultural repression by a long-time hegemonic Francophone Belgian State.

The development and spread of football in Belgium illustrates and confirms the gradual emancipation of the Flemish population from the French-speaking power elite. In an analysis of football and the identity of the Flemish in Belgium,

Tolleneer (1995) noticed that he origins of football in Belgium were amongst the francophone elite. Even those clubs that were founded in Flemish cities such as Bruges and Ghent originally had French names. Only one tenth of football teams founded before 1914 had Flemish names. The title "Union Belge des Sociétés de Football" was not rendered into Dutch until 1913 and even then the Flemish name "Belgische Voetbalbond' was only a token gesture. Meetings, letters and communications — even on the field — were in French. This, of course, was no problem for as long as football remained a socially exclusive sport. But it did not remain so. In Belgium, as elsewhere in Europe, the 1920s saw the rapid democratisation of the game. Football spread from the larger towns and the bourgeoisie to the common people and into the countryside, bringing with it a separate linguistic "regime' for the game.

Tolleneer (1990) also reported that the separate Flemish Football Association, founded in 1930 disappeared completely after 1944 because of the links of its leaders with the German occupying forces during the war. In their remarkable work Playing in the right language Duke and Crolley (1996) also analysed the process of "Flemishization' in Belgian soccer as another indicator of the emergence of a Flemish identity in Belgium. By 1949, the proportion of clubs with Flemish names had risen to about 25 percent. In the early sixties, the gap closed with only a narrow French advantage remaining. Duke and Crolley (1996:54) summarize that these figures reflect both the growing power of the Flemish movement and the shift in economic power to Flanders as more Flemish teams enter the national league. By the 1985-1986 season Flemish clubs were dominant in the Belgian league, which more than reflected the demographic situation in favor of the Flemish, emphasised the economic power of Flanders and indicated that the process of "vervlaamsing' (Flemishization) was virtually complete. The authors conclude that:

> By the time the Belgian state was cemented into a federal system divided along language lines, the process of "vervlaamsing" of football clubs was completed. (Duke and Crolley, 1996: p. 56)

But at the same time, they pointed at the paradox of Belgian football as a national entity in a federal state. Whereas almost all aspects of economic, political, social and cultural life are divided according to language, or at least have felt the pressure to split, Belgian football has remained national in structure until today. So far, all attempts to divide the national Belgian Football Association into a

Flemish and a Walloon division have failed, although major Flemish politicians often allude to it. Since Football as a most popular sport has sufficient private financial resources and is less dependent upon public financial funding, it has remained a bulwark of unitarian Belgicism and has managed to resist the pressure to split in defiance of the law concerning autonomy of the regions.

Divided sport in a divided nation

From this overview, one might conclude that sport has indeed followed and inspired the emergence of a Flemish Movement in Belgium, but that sports organizations and policies now live a settled life in the federalized Belgian state. This however would be a serious underestimation both of the vivid and vigorous Belgian sports culture and of the complexity of divided Belgium.

The actual sports scene in Belgium is characterized by constant tensions in two different ways. First, conflicts in sports-related issues continue to exist between Flanders and Wallonia. Whereas most issues of friction in politics are now settled, sport remains an area of dispute between the language communities. Second, new and rather sharp sports-related conflicts show up between the national state and the regions, particularly the Flemish region. The Belgian nation-state seeks to capitalize on Belgian sports' successes to feed the need for integrative nationalism. The Flemish community, in contrast, seeks to stimulate and express the Flemish image of sport as a major symbol of Flemish identity. We will clarify these double tensions with illustrations from different aspects of sport: (1) public sports policies; (2) elite sports; and (3) a case study on the Tour of Flanders bicycle race.

1.   Public sports policies

A national Belgian Sports Administration (NILOS- INEPS) was founded in 1956. The bilingual NILOS-INEPS was responsible for the promotion and financing of sport and physical education in Belgium. This unitarian administration was split up into a Francophone (ADEPS) and a Flemish (BLOSO) administration in 1969, according to the cultural autonomy policy for the language communities in Belgium. Since then, both administrations have functioned completely independently, developing fully separate policies for the promotion and the organization of sport.

Belgian sports federations were traditionally strong unitarian organizations until 1977. In order to comply with the law on the cultural autonomy of the regions, all sports federations had to split up into an independent Flemish and Francophone federation. Sports federations that refused to split lost their public financial funding. After a few years, the majority of about 90 sports federations had carried out this split, thereby adapting to the divided structure of Belgium. Surprisingly, thirteen sports federations refused to split and preferred to remain unitarian, thus losing entitlement to public funding. Together with some smaller sports federations, the powerful Belgian Football Association, the Belgian Cycling Association and the Belgian Basketball Association stuck to their unitarian nationalist structures. That means that today whereas most federations have a separate competition structure in Flanders and in the Francophone area, some major federations, such as the Belgian Football Association, compete over the entire national Belgian territory.

This odd situation is summarized by Duke and Crolley (1996) as the paradox of Belgian football as a national entity in a federal state. A recent critical comment on this issue by a member of the Flemish High Advisory Council for Sports leaves no doubt about this paradox:

> ...This country would not be called Belgium, if those who do not obey the law, profit the most from public financial support. Unitarian Sports Federations have access to national funds, whereas the Flemish Sports Federations receive limited support.... (De Vis, 1997)

De Vis refers to another Belgian paradox: whereas most of the budget is managed by the Flemish and the Francophone communities, a significant part of the sport-related budget (such as revenues from lottery and gambling) is still in the hands of national institutions. In short, sports policies did not just follow the general trend of a gradual division according to language. On the contrary, sports policies are among the remaining elements of friction, particularly between the national state and the Flemish community.

Two upcoming events illustrate this tension. Belgium, as a nation-state, is co-organising the European Football Championship in the year 2000. But at the same time Flanders, as a region, will host a number of international sports events in 2002, an important commemorative year in Flemish history, being the seven hundreth anniversary of the battle of the Golden Spurs, when a Flemish army beat the fine fleur of the French knighthood near Courtrai in 1302. Although the Belgian cycling Federation is a national institution, the Flemish government itself even sponsors a professional team of cycle racers, again with the highly symbolic name "Flanders 2002', another paradox of Belgian sport, which all reveal tensions between the federal state and the language communities.

2.   Elite sport

The double tension between the language communities on the one hand, and between the communities and the federal state on the other, is sharply illustrated in elite sports. The Belgian Olympic and Interfederal Committee (BOIC) is traditionally a Belgian nationalist stronghold. The BOIC has succeeded in maintaining its national structure and so far has successfully resisted all attempts to split up into a Flemish and a Walloon section. The BOIC also acts as a militant defendant of the unitarian state, thereby adopting Belgium's most outspoken symbols. All issues of "Olympics', the magazine of the Belgian Olympic Committee carry the national colours and show pictures of different members of the Belgian monarchy, socializing with athletes and BOIC members, often on the cover of the magazine. The BOIC uses a subtle nationalist vocabulary and successes by Olympic athletes are strongly praised in a national Belgian context. At the Olympic games in Atlanta, 1996, the Belgian judo and swimming teams won several medals. Almost all the athletes happened to be of Flemish origin. But both, Belgian and Flemish politicians competed in relating these successes either to the image of the national state or to that of the Flemish community. The Flemish coach of the successful judo team who had ongoing conflicts with his Francophone colleagues in the judo federation, was immediately solicited to join the extreme right-wing Flemish nationalist party (which he refused). Since the Atlanta Olympics, Francophone athletes and Francophone federations on their side, have disputed their non-selection for several international competitions such as the Olympics and world championships and they are now defending their cases before a civil court.

The national football team is another bastion of national unity in a divided country. Pledges are held by politicians and by sport leaders for Flemish teams to represent Flanders in several international sports (Echo, 1997)...but not so in football. The national football team can be considered as a solid — and probably unique — symbol of national unity unmatched by other expressions of nationalism. Like the BOIC, the Belgian Football Association and the national team exploit every occasion to show their dedication to the Belgian state and the Belgian monarchy. At crucial games, King Albert is among the audience in the stadium where he personally greets the players of the national team. With regard to the selection of players for the national team, latent disputes continue between Wallonia and Flanders about the proportion of players from each region in the team. The Francophone press deplores the very limited number of francophone players in the national team and even suggests that a coup by a new Flemish power elite is taking place in sport. (La Derniere Heure, 1997). When Belgium qualified for EURO 84 with a team of eleven Flemish players, this was perceived in the Francophone press to be a lack of respect for the linguistic balance (La Dernière Heure, 1996). This argument is acceptable in the Belgian context, where the mere existence of the nation-state fundamentally relies on a subtle linguistic balance and representation.

The newly appointed coach of the national football team, Georges Leekens, was eager to declare to the press "…oh yes, I still shiver when I hear the national anthem, the Brabanconne…' (*Le soir*, 13 January 1997). From an outside point of view, this may sound as an expression of sentimental nationalism. But translated into the Belgian context, this message means that Leekens, as a Flemish coach, agreed not to emphasize the Flemish identity of football, but to comply with the tradition of Belgian football as a matter of national importance.

Sport heroes have played and are still playing a significant role in the divided world of Belgian sport. It already was illustrated how the early cycling heroes of Flanders in the first half of the twentieth century boosted the rise of Flemish identity (Renson, 1998). But other sport heroes increased their popularity by their capacity to be accepted by all linguistic parties in Belgium regardless of the lines of division. The case of Eddy Merckx, Belgium's most popular cyclist ever and the world's best performer in the early seventies, illustrates this point. Born in Flanders but raised in the Brussels area, Merckx was bilingual and throughout his career he managed to be a Flemish among the Flemish, a Francophone among the French community and a true Belgian for the international audience, and at official celebrations at the royal palace. His capacity to speak the language of and to identify with his divided audience by using the popular dialects of his supporters has certainly added to Eddy Merckx' status as Belgian's most popular sports hero. It was only at one occasion that Eddy Merckx caused a serious conflict among his loyal Flemish fans. The wedding ceremony of this popular hero in 1969, a major media event at that time, took place totally in French, which was taken as an insult by his Flemish supporters (Vanwalleghem, 1993). As an undisputable national sport hero in a divided Belgium, Eddy Merckx can be considered as one of 'the last of the Belgicans'.

3.   Divided sport: a case study on the 1997 Tour of Flanders

The Tour of Flanders bicycle race, organized since 1913, is one of Belgium's most popular sports events. It draws over a million supporters along the road on the day of the race. A case study on the identity of this classic sports-event in a Belgian context was carried out on the occasion of the 1997 Tour of Flanders. First, a comparative analysis of content was done on the coverage of the Tour of Flanders in major Flemish (*Het Nieuwsblad*) and major Francophone (*La Dernière Heure*) newspapers, well-known for their extensive coverage of sports events, during the week before the race. Second, an on-site survey was carried out among supporters (N=195) who came to watch the Tour of Flanders. In a short, prepared interview they were asked about their perception of the Tour of Flanders. Respondents had to pick three out of five items which represented the image of the Tour: (1) a Belgian event, (2) a European event, (3) a Flemish event, (4) an international event and (5) a sports event. Next the respondents were asked to put the three selected items in a hierarchical order, the best suited identity label of the Tour of Flanders first.

The results of the analysis revealed a striking difference in the media coverage of the Tour of Flanders. The Flemish paper published major articles on the race daily. On two days these stories made the front page. Several articles contained historical reminders of the Flemish origin of the event and of Flemish victories and heroes. A special issue was printed with a complete road book for supporters. Illustrations portrayed a romantic, idealized picture of the Flemish landscape and several times, the Tour of Flanders was called "a monument of Flemish tradition". The coverage of the same event in the Walloon paper was noticeably limited. La Dernière Heure, the Francophone paper, only paid attention to the race two days of the week before the race. The only historical reminder was about the victory of the Walloon racer in 1987 and most contributions stressed the international character of the race. The articles appeared in the sports section of the paper only and no pictures were printed.

The perception of the Tour of Flanders by its fans along the road is summarized in Figure 3. This table shows the percentage of supporters, for each identity item, who put this item in the first place. Younger (under 50 years) and older (over 50 years) supporters appear to have different perceptions. For almost half of the older supporters, the Tour has a Flemish identity in the first place. Remarkably, one fourth of the older supporters mention the Belgian identity as the most important one. The other labels ('sport', 'international' and 'European')

UNDER 50 YEARS OF AGE		OVER 50 YEARS OF AGE	
1. a sports event	33%	1. a Flemish event	46%
2. a Flemish event	31%	2. a Belgian event	23%
3. an international event	20%	3. a sports event	16%
4. a Belgian event	13%	4. an international event	12%
5. a European event	3%	5. a European event	3%
(N=138	100%)	(N=57	100%)

Figure 3:   The perceived identity of the Tour of Flanders bicycle race 1997. A survey among supporters (N = 195)

are rather marginal, compared to the former ones. For the younger supporters, the Tour is a sports event in the first place. But an almost equal part highlights the Flemish identity. Of this younger generation, only thirteen percent calls the Tour a Belgian event in the first place.

It seems that both, older and younger supporters agree on the Flemish identity of this sports event. But the older supporters manage to harmonize the Flemish with the Belgian identity. As Tolleneer (1995) already pointed out in the case of football, sport appears to them to carry a dual identity: Flemish in Belgium, and Belgian in Flanders.

However, this harmonizing viewpoint is not found among the younger generation of supporters. They emphasize the Flemish identity of the Tour and its Belgian identity is rather marginal to them. Whereas the older generation stresses a harmonious dual identity of the Tour, younger supporters adhere to a more conflicting version of this dual identity.

With some reservation, due to the methodological limitations of the case study, the data indicate a radicalization of the Flemish identity of the event among younger supporters. This is remarkable since the struggle for Flemish awareness, the Flemish Movement, was a core issue of the older generation. and not of the younger. It should be noted that in recent years the Flemish government has been an official sponsor of the Tour of Flanders and has used the event as a promotion opportunity. This campaign may add to the radicalization of the Flemish identity, in contrast to the Belgian identity. But the atmosphere in the media and among the crowd at the day of the race also confirms that the Tour is more a romantic celebration of Flemish identity than it is a militant manifestation of it.

Conclusion

Belgium is a country divided along more than one issue, with the conflict between Dutch-speaking Flanders and French-speaking Wallonia as the traditional, major division line. The even more complicated political and administrative situation of Brussels was deliberately not addressed in this paper. Tensions between the nation-state and its regions however have become more apparent. The realm of sport is as divided as its embedding nation-state. Sport, in its various forms, reflects and highlights both the integrative efforts of those Belgians who wish to maintain the unity of the Belgian nation-state, as well as the striving for separate cultural identity and awareness of the language communities, as was discussed in the case of Flanders. This dual Belgo-Flemish identity of sport is the basis for ongoing disputes and conflicts. Sport not only reflects tensions in this divided country but also serves as a domain of militant activism and romantic celebration as was illustrated by the role of sport in the development of the Flemish Movement. Moreover Belgian sport is often organised and structured in a peculiar, even bloody-minded way, not just following the laws and principles of a divided country. For football, as the most popular sports culture, this has resulted in what Duke and Crolley (1996) have called the paradox of Belgian football as a national entity in a federal state. In a critical analysis of sport and nationalism in Belgium, Govaert (1997) is intrigued by the contradictory fact that Belgian nationalism in sport still prevails in a country where sport organisations, policies, performances and athletes are as divided as the nation itself.

Finally, it should be said again that all these aspects of a divided country, are expressed within the realm of sports as a popular culture. For a country, as politically complicated and divided as Belgium, to have a lucid, transparent and tolerant cultural field such as sport to express unity and diversity, tension and conflict, harmonizing and contrasting identities may, after all, be more a gain than a pain.

References

Belgica (1907) Vol. IV, No. 5 (July/August): p. 50.

De Vis, F. (1997) 'Unitaire sportbonden leven boven hun stand' ('Unitarian sport federations live above their position'), *De Standaard* (newspaper, edition 03. 06. 97).

Duke V, Crolley L. (1996) 'Playing in the right language: football in Belgium', in *Football, nationality and the state* (Chapter 4). Addison Wesley Longman.

Govaert, S. (1997) 'l'hymne national Belge, fait-il encore frisonner?' ('The Belgian national anthem does it still make one shiver?'), *Quasimodo: nationalismes sportifs* (Spring): pp. 117-120.

Het Nieuwsblad (1997) Newspaper issues March 31–April 5.

La Dernière Heure (1997) Newspaper issues March 31–April 5.

Renson R. (1998) 'Sport and the Flemish Movement: Resistance and accommodation 1868-1914', in K. Deprez and L. Vos (eds) *Nationalism in Belgium: Shifting identities 1780-1995*. London: Macmillan

Tolleneer J. (1995) 'Football and the dual identity of the Flemish in Belgium'. Paper presented at the international conference 'Football and Regional identity in Europe', Essen, Germany, November 15-17.

Van Isacker, K. (1978) *Mijn land in de kering* (My country in an era of change) (2 volumes). Antwerpen: De Nederlandsche Boekhandel.

Van Wijnendaele, K. (1943) *Het rijke Vlaamsche Wielerleven*. Gent: Snoeck-Ducaju.

Vanwalleghem, R. (1991) *De Ronde van Vlaanderen* (*The Tour of Flanders*), Gent: Pinguin Productions.

Vanwalleghem, R. (1993) *Eddy Merckx, De Mens achter de Kannibaal* (*Eddy Merckx, the human behind the Cannibal*), Gent: Pinguin Productions.

SPORT, CULTURAL DIVERSITY AND NATIONAL IDENTITY: THE SWISS CASE

Alan Tomlinson

University of Brighton

Introduction

Situated in the heart of Europe, Switzerland is famous for its long-established neutrality in regional and global conflicts, its economic and fiscal independence and strength, its exceptionally striking natural environment, and its institutionalised multi-culturalism. As one drives from the German centre of Zurich in the north of the country to the French-influenced Geneva in the South, passing through a consistently beautiful landscape of lakes and peaks, one travels from *strasse* to *rue*, and from German language place names and motorway signs to their French counterparts. In this high profile linguistic and accompanyingly cultural variety and difference, the Swiss federation is experienced as a society-of-difference, though not necessarily of division. This chapter explores some of these dimensions as they manifest themselves in sport and leisure cultures, and as they have been produced by the specificities and nuances of Swiss political and cultural history.

Stereotypes of Switzerland abound, emphasising the natural beauty of the country's rolling green valleys, the rising snow-capped peaks, and the vast yet unthreatening lakes[1], as well as the administrative and technical efficiency of its service, business and commercial organizations. The Swiss themselves are fiercely defensive of their political, cultural, economic and environmental legacies, resenting the parochialism of the far from untypical visitors from the United States, who glance at the wrong bit of the European map and express surprise that they're not on the road to Stockholm. Swiss sensibility is bound up with a form of self-image which asserts a distinctive and common geographical, historical, and political legacy, alongside the recognition of the cultural and

113

linguistic traditions of the German, French, Italian and Romande constituencies within the country. To be mistaken for Swedes, or anyone else for that matter, is both a joke and an insult, for the Swiss claim that their multi-cultural society based upon negotiation, compromise and reciprocal respect for difference, should be acknowledged more widely. Indeed, the Swiss polity and the multi-linguistic character of the society must be understood before any particular cultural form within that society can be properly assessed.

Swiss made: history, politics and culture

The Swiss Federation has experienced several formative moments in its political constitutional history, a history that, for several reasons (Rappard, 1936: pp. viii-ix), has been of continuing interest to American political scientists. First, Switzerland offers a fascinating long-term history of a relatively stable republic, which was established long before the heroic phase of the republican tradition in the nineteenth century. Second, over five centuries it developed from a loose confederacy of sovereign states into a federal union, and its 1848 constitution was modelled upon (with its bicameral form of central and regional structures) the USA precedent of 1789. The Swiss model therefore inspired and was in turn inspired by the USA model. Democratic institutions such as the referendum also originated in Switzerland. Third, the composite nature of its demography can be linked to the country's policy of neutrality and isolationism with respect to international conflicts, in that the diverse cultural, ethnic and linguistic character of the populace rendered the taking of sides no simple matter. The long-established interest of political scientists in the Swiss polity has consistently recognised the distinctive but complex interplay of politics and culture in a society in which the political imperative has been to provide an all-embracing political ethos which simultaneously respects and preserves the cultural diversity of a multi-cultural and multi-linguistic population. Speaking in Zurich in September 1946, the British politician Winston Churchill could claim that there was a moral to be learned from the Swiss success in "achieving unity based on tolerance" (cited in Thürer, 1970: p. 175), and overcoming differences of race, language and customs. Churchill proclaimed further that in Switzerland politics was a civic task, not a matter of power; and that the Swiss benefit from "an ingrained faith in mutual help and solidarity" (*ibid.*).

    This historical, political and cultural pedigree has created the base for and expectation of a culturally diverse pluralism, and international interest in this accomplishment has been aroused after global crises and conflicts such as the two great world wars of the twentieth century. A former president of the Swiss national council could therefore write, just after the first world war, that Switzerland had as many democracies as it had cantons and demi-cantons and that — as "the oldest of all" examples of "the political system of the future... a federative organization", and along with the USA "the completest" type of this form of political organization — the Swiss Confederation could pride itself on its long tradition of freedom and democracy (Bonjour, 1920: p. 30). The war had provided a threat to the moral unity of the country, with German-French rivalries becoming manifest within its own populace to the extent that in October 1914 the Swiss Federal Council considered it necessary to reaffirm the core values of the confederation: "... to reassert 'the ideal of our country' as a cultural community and as a political idea above the diversity of race and language. 'First and above all are we Swiss, then only Latins and Germans'" (cited in Kohn, 1978: p. 128).

The defining moments of this national ideal were in the thirteenth, sixteenth, eighteenth and nineteenth centuries. Effectively, up until the time of the French Revolution, Switzerland comprised a miniature league of nations, with no national citizenship, representative government or federal structure. For five centuries the 'country' was based upon agreements between separate sovereign states or cantons with differing political characters — at the time of the invasion by French armies in 1798 these numbered thirteen, and included democratic communities, urban aristocracies and oligarchies. Covenants between these bodies, and treaties with contiguous communities, perpetuated core principles of mutual defence against external aggression and peaceful negotiation of internal disputes. These principles had been first documented in an historically recorded treaty in 1291, among men of the Alpine valleys around Lucerne. What bound together this diverse set of interests — despite some tensions such as a civil war throughout the 1430s and 1440s before Zurich renounced its pact with Austria and rejoined the Confederation in 1450 (Thürer, 1970) — was "pressure from without and the cohesive vitality of certain traditions" (Rappard, 1936: p. 16; Codding, 1961: p. 21). These traditions included the *Landsgemeinde*, political assemblies of the mediaeval communities. Neutrality as a principle dates substantially from 1515, when defeat in battle at the hands of Francis I convinced the Swiss that alliances to preserve the status quo, rather than imperialistic expansion, would best guarantee the future of the states and territories, and the stability of the different religious groups within the alliances (Codding, 1961: pp. 152-3).

But the French invasion of its territories shattered this centuries old federal bond. Throughout the Napoleonic period the invention of the French lawyers, the 'one and indivisible Helvetic Republic', was reshaped and disputed in its strong centralism by those close to Swiss traditions. At the Congress of Vienna Swiss majority opinion triumphed, and representative liberal democracies were established in the place of the aristocracies and oligarchies. A short civil war in which seven minority cantons were routed in 1847 was followed by the adoption of the 1848 constitution by means of a constitutional referendum. The revised constitution of April 1874 confirmed the four main objectives of the confederation as national centralization, extended democracy, reinforced anticlericalism and state intervention in social and economic spheres (*ibid.*: p. 25). This was mostly in line with the principles built into the earlier constitution, with the addition of the recognition of the interventionist role of the state. A Catholic, French-speaking minority, however, was clearly less powerful within the newly defined Swiss nation than the Protestant liberal elements. Forms of continuity guaranteed by this constitution could even be noted in the urban topography of the country, with the "dispersed nature of political power which is so typical of Switzerland" working against the formation of any new towns from the middle of the eighteenth century onwards (Phaidon, 1985: p. 27).

The mainstream of Swiss political life was impregnated with more social democratic, and even socialist, principles and influence during and after a general strike in 1918. Alongside the stability produced by the unaltered nature of its international frontiers ever since 1815, this has ensured a continuity and neutrality, and a championing of peace and freedom, the secret of which one commentator has claimed to be maintenance of "a fair balance between all the component elements of its society" (Thürer, 1970: p. 176). Just a few months prior to the end of the first world war, the confederation's president, Calonder, appealed to his country to remain faithful to the national motto of — in the words of the German Swiss poet and patriot Gottfried Keller — "friendship in freedom". Extracts from Calonder's speech warrant extensive citation, embodying as they do the central values of a longlasting Swiss polity. For him, Switzerland's history is one of:

> ... consolidation of the principle of law and peace in internal relationships [through foreign policy].

> [Switzerland] embraces this rich diversity [and has a] profound unity as one people on the basis of mutual respect ... complete confidence can

only be conceived in an atmosphere of full freedom and sincere amity. [Swiss history is one of the] development of international relations in miniature… [its State a] precursor of the future League of Nations. [Switzerland's international mission is] to be the harbinger of concord between all peoples by proving to the world, through its own example, that populations differing in race and language may unite to form a happy commonwealth on the basis of mutual confidence, freedom and equality of rights. (Bonjour, 1920: pp. 206-7).

As most of Europe was plunging towards the tragedy of World War II, the Swiss coined the term 'ideological national defence' for the justification of their own joint principles of liberty and nationalism, and their continuing neutrality. In response to the threat of a totalitarian collectivism prioritising nation, race or class over the individual, the Federal Council issued a message to the nation on the 'meaning and mission of Switzerland', defending 'the dignity of the individual', within the context of federalism and democracy. The author, Philip Etter (cited in Kohn, 1978: p. 129), stressed the importance of the historical longevity and geographical centrality of the country:

For the very reason that we reject the concept of race or descent as the basis of a state and as the factor determining political frontiers, we gain the liberty and strength to remain conscious of our cultural ties with the three great civilizations. The Swiss national idea is not based upon race or biological factors, it rests on a spiritual decision.

The respect for the right and liberty of human personality is so deeply anchored in the Swiss idea, that we can regard it as its basic concept and can claim its defence as an essential task of the nation …. We recognize the individual human personality as the strongest creative force in the life of the spirit, and the state has accordingly limited its own sphere of power.

Such appeals, obviously more widespread in times of threat and international conflict, have nevertheless been typical of the ideals and the rhetoric by which a Swiss politics and culture has been explained and justified throughout its modern history. Some historical realities might appear to refute these claims. Doctrinal deviation in Geneva could not save Spanish anti-trinity scholar Michael Servetus from being burned at the stake in Geneva during the Reformation, occasioning the "charge that Geneva represented a narrow intolerance worse than the papacy" (Johnston and Scribner, 1993: p. 152). During the second world war, trade relations with the Nazis were not halted until 1944-45, and Stalin called the Swiss swine, as Swiss neutrality was squeezed when any access beyond the country became dependent upon some degree of cooperation with the Axis powers (Robertson, 1987: pp. 29-30).

This difficult period for Swiss neutrality has proved a recurrently embarrassing issue for the country, with its "wartime role as bankers to the Nazis" (Jury, 1997: p. 8) coming under increasing scrutiny, culminating in a conference on the issue of the laundering of Nazi gold, in London, England, in December 1997. Around £200 million of Nazi gold — much of it stolen from Jewish victims of Hitler's death camps — poured into Switzerland during the war, and the Swiss were warned by the Allies that much of this was illegally acquired, the spoils of plunder: "but Switzerland thought, and continues to think, that it had to trade with the Nazis as well as the Allies because it was a neutral country" (*ibid.*). This Swiss defence, of course, conveniently ignores the fact that as the war progressed there were no Allies accessible with whom to trade. Surprised by the international furore over the morality of its stance, Switzerland has suspended its bank secrecy laws to help Holocaust victims, released large sums, and established two funds: the Swiss Fund for Needy Victims of the Holocaust (£117 million); and the Swiss Foundation for Solidarity (£3 billion). The first fund made its first payments in December 1997, to Latvian survivors of the Holocaust. The second fund was aimed at making annual awards to victims of catastrophe and poverty. At the same time as recognizing a degree of responsibility in this area, the Swiss have remained indignant at what they see as an unfair singling out of their relations with the Nazis. Countries in Latin America and in Europe — Portugal, Sweden and Spain — are known to have also laundered Nazi assets and gold. But the Swiss case lends itself to suspicion, its principle of neutrality looking like self-serving amorality in the case of the country's relationship with Nazi Germany. Other such issues have haunted the Swiss, its World War Two labour camps for Jews included (Watson-Smyth, 1998: p. 3). The problem for the country is that the ideal of tolerance and respect for the other — if applied to the Nazis, for instance — can amount to a laissez-faire and non-judgemental amorality. Zurich has been home to exiles such as Lenin, writers such as the *Ulysses*-drafting Joyce, but has also provided the perfect basis for laundering $111 billion worth of Citibank bonds — Mafia spoils from a New Jersey warehouse raid in the later 1980s (Honigsbaum, 1997: p. 3). The dispersal of this loot, implicating not just the Italian Mafia but also Swiss lawyers, Russian gangsters, mysterious Croatian militia and even the Vatican, has been traced to the base of Zurich antique-dealer Pietro Zach, long under investigation by the Swiss police and the FBI, but still able to enjoy boasting of his "fairy-tale pink castle in St Moritz ... love of fast cars, beautiful women and fine champagne" (*ibid.*: p. 4); and, presumably, finding enough takers for what has been on offer from his global stings. It is the respect for privacy, banking secrecy and claimed neutrality that can allow a figure like Zach — as well as rock stars such as David Bowie and Tina Turner — to prosper and flourish in Switzerland.

Moreover, the constant celebration of these core values can sound self-righteous, even smug. A literary historian can thus claim that Swiss literature, whilst representing the "different linguistic regions of the country", also shuns any taint of "immoralism". The Swiss "sense of civic-mindedness" produces a "guarantee of morality", even though limiting artistic freedom and lacking imagination (Calgari, 1963: p. 5). Nevertheless, in many of the most prominent spheres of everyday life, comparative autonomy has been important. No Ministry of Education at the federal level has interfered with the educational policies of the different cantons, so that a national *Concordat on School Coordination* in 1970 offered no threat to the separate cantons' authority, and depended upon consultation with all citizens, resulting in an "extremely diversified" but harmoniously developed overall picture of educational policy throughout the confederation (Egger and Blanc, 1974: pp. 46 and 47). The story of Jura separatism also sustains the view that policy developments and political conflicts be settled peacefully. The rugged topography of the Jura region had kept it almost exclusively French-speaking for centuries, but from 1815-1978 Jura was part of the canton of Berne, known as Bernese Jura. In the 1978 referendum 41.5% of electors voted, and of these 82.3% favoured the formation of the new canton. South Jura — 59,000 people in 50 communes — voted for the status quo. Ancestry rather than religious affiliation was found to be the main influence upon those choosing to vote for separatism (Jenkins, 1986). It is striking that, unlike in the cases of Basque separatism or Irish republicanism, violence against human life played no part in the separatists' campaigning. Symbolic violence against objects was employed, but rarely in circumstances endangering human life[2].

Local identity is clearly strongly felt in Switzerland, linguistic and cultural differences having quite as many excluding consequences as integrating effects. But the arguments made for the positive benefits of the Swiss system are that they benefit all sub-sections of the population, producing stable institutional structures. One analyst points to the strong family structure and low divorce rates

— lower only in western Europe's other most linguistically divided nation, Belgium, in 1979; and to the Swiss dedication to "goals of self-sufficiency and social responsibility", in a society which concentrates its resources at the level of the community, and has "little serious disorganization" (Segalman, 1986: pp. 190-91). Segalman also argues (*ibid.*: p. 196) that Switzerland can be seen as a model for the expression of Etzioni's communitarian values. Interestingly, newcomers to the Swiss dream of citizenship and tolerance might tell another story. Community-based welfare organizations, or churches, have been traditionally unresponsive to immigrants, encouraging them to turn for help to official homeland organizations. But it appears too that one immigrant response has been wholly within the spirit of Swiss values: that is, immigrants have "cultivated a regional identity (that is, as Fricelians, Sicilians, Andalusians and the like) that imposed less of a choice between Swiss and homeland identity" (Ireland, 1994: p. 251). Such a choice, stressing locality and language, is entirely consistent with the idea, the polity and diverse cultures of the Swiss model. In a sense, what Walzer (cited in *ibid.*) has called "tyrannical institutional arrangements", offering little support, drive the immigrants into a semblance of self-sufficiency, even though still barred from a full or equal sense of citizenship. This creates a desired form of assimilation, but based upon exclusion, and neutralizes any threatening aspect of the newcomer (*ibid.*: p. 270).

The most specialized analysis on the nature and effects of Swiss multi-lingualism is contained in Macrae's (1983) work. He recognises that the costs of varied languages, political tensions around these and the need for conflict resolution can be high, "ranging from chronic alienation and intergroup hostility to serious political conflict, mass violence, secession or partition, and even civil or international war" (Macrae, 1983: p. ix). The Swiss case is special, he notes, for the tradition of mediation established so early in its history, so that conflicts were usually resolved short of open hostilities (*ibid.*: p. 47). Nevertheless, economic inequalities can sometimes fuel minority sensitivities, and Macrae notes that the French Swiss — once prominent through the financial weight of Geneva — have come to feel a sense of "increasing comparative disadvantage" alongside the industrial strength of the German Swiss. These differences and inequalities remain despite the nature of Swiss development in the second half of the twentieth century; "the multiple, cross-cutting cleavage structure of the postwar period" (*ibid.*: p. 117) (clearly bolstered by the strength of the different language traditions), and the protection of the languages within the constitution.

Three general rules protect and preserve this. First, based directly on Article 116 of the revised constitution of 1874, an absolute equality of all Switzerland's languages is recognised[3]. Second, cantons are sovereign on language-related matters. And third, and relatedly, cantons or linguistic areas can defend their own language against any external threat, the citizen having "to adjust to the linguistic milieu of the canton" (*ibid.*: p. 122). The two consequences of these rules, points out Macrae, are that the federal authorities must deal with the canton in the official language (s) of the canton; and the individual must deal with the canton in the canton's own language, or bear the costs of translation. These consequences guarantee that the federal administration is defined in some of its major functions by the region, and that entrants or newcomers to cantons or areas must communicate in the manner of the canton. This potentially subordinates the centre, and homogenizes the local. In such circumstances, a progressive democratic system can serve the most conservative of interests. Consequently, Macrae can observe that the socialist and catholic gymnastic and sports federations, the "two smaller, ideologically oriented, gymnastic and sports federations have maintained or even improved their relative position since the interwar period" (*ibid.*: p. 116). Again, the delineation of difference at the regional or local level can be claimed as the basis of common political affiliation at the central overarching political level.

One of the potential sources for the expression of this crucial unity-in-difference that is fundamental to the Swiss polity, society and culture, is the terrain of sport, both domestic and international. Sport within the country might be bound up with separate cultural legacies and traditions, whilst the international arena provides a forum for the expression of the nation itself, the political entity. Also, how might the Swiss principles of neutrality and negotiation have contributed to particular aspects of the international sporting scene? The country has a long experience of participation in international organizations, and even if the country has chosen at times not to join certain organizations, such as the United Nations and the European Union, the old League of Nations' buildings in Geneva were nevertheless made available for the United Nations[4]. As a basis for the exploration of these questions, the profile of Swiss sport internationally is reviewed, and broader sport and leisure patterns within the country considered. This provides the basis for an informed and adequate understanding of the place and role of sport within the society.

Swiss sport: its international profile

What, then, is Switzerland known for in international sport? A consideration of its achievements in the arenas of the world's two highest profile sporting events — the Olympic Games, and the football World Cup — provides an answer to this question. First, the summer and the winter Olympics (see Wallechinsky, 1993 and 1996, for medal details). With its ideal location at the heart of the European Alps, Switzerland has produced champions regularly in the winter Olympics. Particularly notable performances were in the Games of St. Moritz (1948, 10 medals, 3rd position), Cortina d'Ampezzo (1956, 6 medals, 4th position), Sapporo (1976, 10 medals, 3rd position), and Calgary (1984, 15 medals, 3rd position). Such achievement and performance at elite level has been achieved in specialist individual sports or small-team sports: 2-man and 4-man bobsled; and the sub-disciplines of alpine skiing, in later years more by men than by women. Medals in the summer Olympics have been harder to come by, particularly since the competitive world of the Olympics became more specialised and profession-alised. In the second modern Olympics in Paris in 1900 Switzerland was fourth in the medals table, with 8 medals, and sixth place was secured in 1906 (Athens, 15 medals), 1924 (Paris, 25 medals), and 1928 (Amsterdam, 15 medals). A ninth position was attained at the 1948 relaunch of the Games after World War Two (London, 20 medals), but since then — apart from a blip in 1984, when 4 gold and 4 bronze medals were won at the Soviet/Communist-boycotted Los Angeles Olympics — the spasmodic Swiss achievements have been based more upon random individual triumphs than upon systematic strategies.

For instance, the Barcelona gold for men's tennis was won by Marc Rossett, ranked only 44th. in the world, in a five hour match against Spain's third-ranked player, Catalan Jordi Arresse from Barcelona itself. Top seeds had tumbled early, beaten by the "brutal heat, the slow clay surface, and the patriotic emotions of their unheralded opponents' (Wallechinsky, 1996: p. 692). Rossett seized his chance, annihilating South African number nine seed Wayne Ferrira in straight sets, and confirming his giant-killing intent with a 6-4, 6-2, 6-1 demolition of number one seed Jim Courier of the USA. Rossett sprang from nowhere and won as an outsider.

Swiss achievements in both the summer and the winter games were based upon a combination of influences. Its excellence in specialist sports which thrived in the country's alpine environment (winter sports and cycling) was bolstered by inherent forms of commercialised professionalism. This generated a sort of topographic determinism so that, as journalist Martin Putter has noted, until the 1980s and 1990s "it was unthinkable that successful skiers would come from outside the Alpine regions" (i.e. the lowlands and the "Jura")[5]. Competence in amateur sports in the earlier phases of Olympic history produced creditable performances and sometimes fairly high rankings, especially when highly competitive nations such as Soviet Union-influenced Eastern European countries did not yet compete, or those such as Germany were excluded from Olympics following on from their defeats in world wars. Otherwise, forms of support could be targeted towards dedicated individuals, home-born or imported, the latter case exemplified in the late 1990s tennis prodigy, Czechoslovakia-born Martina Hingis. There is little evidence of coherent sports development programmes aimed at the production of future champions and, though champions have been respected, they are far from idolized or transformed into national heroes.

Football in Switzerland has a long history[6]. The country was one of the founder members of the world governing body, the Fédération Internationale de Football Association (FIFA) in 1904, and the Swiss Football Association, founded in 1895, is one of the oldest associations in mainland Europe. Internationally, Swiss sides have not been in the top grade, although in 1924 its silver-medal winning side held the champions Uruguay to 3-0 in the Olympic final in Paris; and, in predominantly European fields, in the 1934 and 1938 World Cups in France and Italy respectively, the national sides progressed as far as the quarter-finals; and as hosts in 1954, the Swiss reached that stage again, going down 7-5 to Austria. Outstanding performances seem to have been followed by anti-climactic dips in performance, as in the USA in 1994 when after beating the highly fancied Romanian side 4-1, the Swiss lost 3-0 to Spain in the second stage.

Early British influence upon football in Switzerland is evident from the names of its pioneer clubs — Grasshoppers of Zurich, and Young Boys of Berne, for instance. But it has been argued, by Lanfranchi (1998), that the origins of the game in Switzerland were not just a local affair, and that in the process of the diffusion of football throughout Europe "the Swiss played a role which was essential and which is too often neglected". German Swiss, Britons, Austrians and Italians mixed in early Swiss football clubs in Geneva, and Swiss involvement in international commerce influenced football development in other European countries such as Spain and France. Swiss technical colleges of the 1880s welcomed students from abroad, studying engineering, technology and international banking. Football was in many cases part of their wider cultural education, and was one asset which they returned home with on completion of their training. The founders (in 1900) of the French Mediterranean club, Olympique de Sete, first encountered football during their technical training in Geneva, as did Henry Monnier, a young banker who in 1901 established the Nimes football club. The most renowned of such Swiss "footballer technicians" was Vittorio Pozzo. Initiated into football during his period of study at technical institutes in Winterthur and Zurich, where in 1908 he obtained a diploma in languages and commercial techniques, Pozzo went on, thirty years later, to guide Italy to its two World Cup triumphs of the inter-war period. Lanfranchi lists a number of reasons for this Swiss influence. First, Switzerland favoured English middle-class sports rather than popular and para-military gymnastics, more so than was the case in any other European country, and Swiss private schools adopted English sports, as well as climbing and rambling, as early as the 1860s. The Swiss Alpine Club was formed in 1863, a mere six years after the English original, and football was offered and played in La Chatelaine school in Geneva as early as 1869. Boarding schools established their own sports fields.

Beyond Switzerland itself, the Internazionale club derived its name from the large number of Swiss players. Bari, also in Italy, was founded in 1908 by a Swiss flour and cereal merchant, Gustav Kuhn, along with German, French, Swiss, Spanish and Italian friends. In Naples, Swiss and English international businessmen formed the city's first football teams. In Marseille, le Stade Helvetique (Swiss), three-times national champions between 1909 and 1913, was created at the same time as a Swiss commercial circle. These Swiss internationalists, argues Lanfranchi, expressed in their commitment to football a strongly-felt Anglophilia, the "perfect expression of their conception of modernity". The rational use of spare-time that the games of the British elite represented was consonant with the central tenets, in Zurich liberalism, of the interconnectedness of money and spirit. The Swiss promoted and facilitated the game widely and in varied roles: "In 1912, even, a match between Barcelona FC and the English team Auckland Wanderers was refereed by a Swiss pastor". The sporting sphere could here be seen as part of a wider religious mission, and suited central Protestant values especially. In Switzerland itself sports associations were promoted more in the Protestant community. Lanfranchi describes a sporting culture of a cosmopolitan kind, taking as its inspiration the British team-games and the amateur ethos associated with them. This was not to last. A distancing from the British fair-play model was apparent in the years following on from World War 1, and in 1920, for the first time, the Swiss Football Association was obliged to take up positions: "If the German-Swiss clubs supported a match with the German national side, the Romand-Swiss clubs were unflinchingly opposed". Away from Switzerland, Swiss merchants and businessmen had used football as a uniting force for the international business elite. Back home in Switzerland, football soon became a focus for an everyday politics of cultural identity. The origins of organized sport within Switzerland were characterized by an early prominence of the German gymnastics movement, and a later adoption of the English model of games and sport. Although these, as in many other spheres of a modernizing society, overlapped more fully later in the century, the early tensions between them displayed the schisms that could arise in the sphere of popular culture and sport.

If Switzerland has not been hugely prominent in the international sporting scene, it has drawn upon its traditions of neutrality and international diplomacy in welcoming to its lakeland shores international sports organizations such as the International Olympic Committee (in Lausanne), FIFA (in Zurich), and the Union des associations européennes de football (UEFA, formerly in Berne and now in Nyon, on the edge of Lake Geneva and a short commute from Geneva itself). All of these organizations originated in Paris, but were soon drawn to the advantages offered by the Swiss to international, non-governmental organizations functioning as offshore companies with wide international or global remits. Such benefits could in turn inspire glowing tributes. The founder of the modern Olympic games, the French aristocrat Baron Pierre de Coubertin, could write in 1920 that it was Swiss sporting values that influenced him to locate the IOC's headquarters in Lausanne, and that the future mission of Switzerland could contribute to the popularisation, simplification, facilitation, democratisation and fortification of sport (de Coubertin, 1986). Three quarters of a century later, it was the Gnomes of Zurich and their encouragement of sport's new commercial barons who were confirming the suitability of Switzerland as a site for such international organizations[7].

Sport and leisure cultures in modern Switzerland

Regardless of its relatively limited international impact in sport, Switzerland has been described as "one of the most fully organized countries with respect to sport" (Stamm and Lamprecht, 1996b: p. 1). It has around one sports club for every 250 members of the population, and around 100 national and international sports organizations; and around a quarter to a third of the Swiss population is estimated to be actively involved in a sports club. Tennis, squash, hiking, jogging and skiing may have taken place in other less formal organizational settings, but the most influential strand in the development of Swiss sport has remained the club-based organization.

As in the case of Germany, the gymnastic activity of *Turnen* was prominent in the nineteenth century, the first clubs being founded in Germany in 1819 and, in Zurich, in 1820. These clubs were formed by fugitives from Germany, where the egalitarian, democratic and progressive values of the *Turnbewegung* had led to the movement being banned in 1819. Three points favoured their growth. First, liberal strands in the Swiss polity saw the clubs as models of desirable democratic organization. Second, the Swiss movement saw itself as integrated to the social order, promoting military skills and citizenship. Third, the movement linked with a folk games revival. The Swiss Rifle Association, founded in 1824, also emphasised military skills and Swiss independence. In 1874, sport policy was formally located in the federal military department, where it stayed until 1983, when responsibility for sport was shifted to the department of the interior. Only seven other sport associations were established before the end of the century, the Alpine Club being the first of these, and cycling, rowing, soccer and tennis becoming well-established. All of these were for middle and upper class men, many of whom would also have received compulsory gymnastics at school since this was inaugurated in the revised federal constitution of 1874. Women were for a long time excluded. The women's gymnastic association was not founded until 1920, and though some women participated in gymnastics, cycling and hiking, it was not until 1972 that the provision of physical education for girls was formally included in the constitution.

Whatever the vicissitudes in popularity or profile of a particular sport, and the more individual and commercial settings in which sport is played, the sports clubs have retained an important place in the wider sports culture. Stamm and Lamprecht account for this well, in terms of the framing features of Swiss culture and polity:

> The large number of different sports clubs and sport-related clubs is indicative of a well-known feature of Swiss culture — namely Switzerland's high density of any kind of clubs. With some irony it is sometimes said that wherever three or more people meet regularly in Switzerland, they establish a club. As a consequence there exists a wide variety of clubs encompassing such diverse activities as music, pet care, stamp collecting, sports or political activities. Against this background it is not surprising that most Swiss are members in at least one or two clubs.

Clubs in Switzerland are much more than regular gatherings of people with common interests, however. The term club refers to a specific legal construction that acts as a juridical person and is able to enter contracts etc. in its own right. The Swiss civil code specifies several prerequisites for clubs to attain their legal status. Each club needs written statutes that spell out its goals, means and organizational structure. By law clubs are democratic non-profit organizations whose highest authority is the meeting of all members which votes on important club matters, fixes membership dues, considers new members and elects the president and other executive charges which act as official representatives of the club. (Stamm and Lamprecht, 1996: pp.8- 9)

Clubs also rely extensively upon volunteer labour, which is an economic imperative but also has roots in the values of sport and leisure as special spheres in which involvement and action are based in solidarity and enjoyment.

Beyond these broad common institutional features of the sports club, the historical legacy of the gymnastic and rifle clubs was political, ideological and integrative, with competition relatively marginal; and new clubs based upon an English model prioritised competition and modernity. Although it has been claimed that the politically conservative gymnastic and rifle clubs — *Vereine* — prevailed in the German speaking regions, and the modern clubs — *Klubs* — were stronger in French and Italian parts of the country, the regional distribution of the 28,000 clubs of both types matches the distribution of the population: "three quarters of the clubs [are] in the German speaking part, about a fifth in the French speaking part and the remainder in the Italian speaking part. Thus there is no clear preference of the German speaking population for organized sport" (*ibid.*: p. 10; see, too, Schlagenhauf and Schiffer, 1979). Nevertheless, sports clubs of whatever sort would certainly be identified by separate language traditions. Traditional clubs are only slightly stronger in the German speaking regions, then, but traditional and folk sports vary in the different language regions. German Swiss play tug-of-war, the folk game *Hornussen*, handball and wrestling; whereas *Petanque, Boules* and *Boccia* are restricted to the other two main language communities. French Swiss are comparatively more involved in basketball, water-skiing, weight-lifting and boxing, Italian speakers in basketball, soccer and ice-hockey. The largest clubs have remained the rifle and gymnastic associations (Bose et al., 1994). One hour's shooting a year is prescribed for men under 40 able to do military service, and is organized by local rifle clubs in which eligible males had to be compulsory members up until 1996, thus obviously inflating their membership figures. But it is the gymnastics movement — with almost a third of a million active members — which has remained the strongest organized sport in Switzerland: "Apart from its long tradition and deep roots in Swiss popular culture, the success of the gymnastic movement in terms of membership figures certainly also relates to its ability to integrate people beyond the sphere of "pure" sports into a more encompassing social club" (Stamm and Lamprecht, 1996b: p. 12).

Beyond the formal framework of the club, activities such as hiking, cycling, swimming and skiing are the most popular. Participation rates are reported in the table below:

Most popular sports in Switzerland 1994

Number = 919	
Sport	**% of population regularly participating**
Hiking	31%
Swimming, water gymnastics	29%
Cycling, mountain biking	29%
Downhill skiing	28%
Gymnastics, jazz dance	18%
Jogging	16%
Fitness training, body building	14%
Tennis	10%
Soccer	9%
Cross-country skiing, ski tours	7%
Fitness trails	7%
Basketball, streetball	6%
Table tennis	6%
Volleyball, beach volleyball	5%
Badminton	5%

Source   Swiss Association for Sport, cited in Stamm and Lamprecht
          (1996b: p. 13)

The size of club memberships varies widely, with golf clubs and alpine clubs having large mean memberships of around 800 and 500 respectively; tennis and field hockey clubs around the 200 mark; shooting, soccer, ice skating, swimming and skiing 100 or so; and snow biking, cycling, weight lifting, boxing, motor sports and bobsleigh clubs an active average membership of under ten people.

The only sport associations in which female members form the majority are ice and roller skating, volleyball, dancing and two gymnastic associations. A third or more of the membership comprises women in another nine sports, including sport for disabled people, snowboarding, the academic sport association, another gymnastic association, golf, badminton, horse riding and squash. Male preserves are shooting, ice hockey, soccer and cycling (Stamm and Lamprecht, 1996b: p. 14; and Lamprecht and Stamm, 1996). Organized club-based sports are less conducive to women's participation than are informally generated forms of involvement. So even though frequency of involvement may to some extent have been levelling out between men and women, types of activity and involvement have continued to reflect gendered differences: "A closer examination of the *patterns* [my emphasis] of sport involvement shows that the traditional field of competitive, physically demanding, and club-organized sport remains the preserve of younger men" (Lamprecht and Stamm, 1996: p. 284).

Although an expanding infrastructure for Swiss sport can be identified (Bulletin of Sports Information, 1991), Switzerland has no official sports policy, and there is no federal-level department with responsibility for sport: "Formal independence from political intervention is not only an important feature of organized sport in Switzerland but also applies to other segments of sports" (*ibid.*: p. 15). A federal agency — the Federal Sports Commission — coordinates physical education and youth sport policies, and the educational and communications centre at Macolin acts as a federal sports school and an executive body to the federal agency[8]. It is at the regional level, within the cantons, that sport departments dispense budgets to support a coordinating function, and at which proceeds from the national sports lottery are allocated and distributed. The most important providers are the towns and villages which provide for primary school sport, and can rent facilities, at generously low prices, to independent sports clubs. Across the sports sphere, the Swiss respect for intra-societal independence is translated into a pluralist scenario of self-organization and respect for difference — but one which for obvious reasons might favour tradition and existing inequalities as well as cultural difference and diverse cultural practices and identities.

Some newer and more fashionable sports have challenged traditional practices and structures, and Stamm and Lamprecht (1996b: p. 18) note that gymnastics clubs have failed to adapt, leaving activities such as aerobics out of their programmes, and looking staid and out of touch alongside commercial fitness centres which open all hours and boast high tech facilities and scientific fitness programmes.

Lamprecht and Stamm conclude that traditional norms continue to affect forms of age and gender-based participation in sports; that where women and older people are participating more, it is in areas that organized forms of male-dominated sports do not consider to be 'serious' sports; and that if broadening forms of participation in sport can be seen as contributing to a process of democratization of sport, persisting forms of differentiation in sports lead in an 'opposite direction' (Lamprecht and Stamm, 1996: pp. 284-85). 'Expansion' and apparent 'inclusion' therefore lie alongside a process of 'differentiation and pluralisation', generating outcomes which shore up traditional divisions and inequalities in Swiss society and culture (Lamprecht and Stamm, 1995: p. 1).

Everyday leisure and consumption in Switzerland

The variations in types and structure of clubs and sports involvement may not be as wide as often supposed, but at the turn of the last decade of the century a large-scale national survey could still identify variations in cultural practice on the basis of geographical and linguistic influence[9]. Sporting items in newspaper and television rank as almost important in the weekly free-time schedule of the population as radio music programmes, movies on television and light enter-tainment television programmes. Sports clubs and gymnastics clubs were the types of clubs with most members, "more or less 10% of the population". Almost half of the people interviewed considered that such societies were important social elements in their place of residence, citing especially gymnastic and sports clubs, associations for the protection of nature, orchestras or singing clubs/choirs. One in three of respondents saw pedestrian walkways, cycle routes and sporting facilities as important in their localities. The general participation figures indicate that for physical exercise offering a break from daily routine — such as walking outings, sport, even do-it-yourself — there is minimal variation among the different groups of the population. Nevertheless, detailed figures do indicate some variations which seem to draw upon cultural tradition. German speakers engaged in more do-it-yourself, use of musical instruments, reading of political journals, intensive watching of television game-shows and soap operas, than French-speaking respondents. German speakers also went out drinking less, and took more walks, picnics and excursions, though doing also half as many courses. Big local events such as festivals or sports meetings were attended in greater numbers by French and Italian speakers than Germans. The same was true of village, neighbourhood and society fetes, though German speakers were more likely to be found in orchestras and carnival events.

What is interesting in such variations is the cultural/linguistic legacy, of a kind of German Protestant worthiness in everyday life, and a more hedonistic and communal public culture among the French and Italian speaking, and predominantly Catholic, communities. It is likely therefore that though broad participation figures might suggest few or only small differences in participation, the mode of participation and the meaning of the activity may well in many cases reflect the separate linguistic and cultural tradition.

Sport and the social order in Switzerland: some concluding comments

The task in this chapter has been to explicate the nature of the Swiss polity and culture, and of accepted and respected divisions within the society, and to consider sport's place in the Swiss scheme of things. Whilst there are histories of pedagogic, traditional and international sports organizations and initiatives in Switzerland, these have usually had little to say about the wider values of the Swiss society and culture[10]. It has been emphasised in this chapter that a consideration of sport apart from a fuller appreciation of Swiss values and prevailing ideologies would be a futile task, for reasons that have hopefully become very clear. Where, then, does sport lie in the linguistically divided society of Switzerland?

Whilst sport might appear to be of relatively minor significance in the constitution of Swiss national, regional and cultural identity, it is more important than first meets the eye. The history of its oldest organized ideological sports clubs, blended with some appropriation of a folkloric essence, imbues Swiss cultural history with a longevity and a national robustness that bolsters its centuries-old tradition of political autonomy, cultural separatism and international neutrality. Whereas types of club may be more evenly distributed across the separate language communities than some theorists of division care to admit, mode of participation and the meaning of sports as a cultural practice will express the distinct values of the different constituencies. The deep-rootedness of the regional and local cultures is also such that symbolic and fanatical expressions of national identity seem deeply un-Swiss. Swiss national identity itself is, no more and no less, the multiculturalism of the regions and the politics of consensus. It seems entirely fitting that most national Swiss sports champions are rewarded for their individual labours on the tennis court, the ski slope or the bike saddle, or in small teams of enthusiastic experts such as the bobsleigh champions. Switzerland is a managed diversity too in its community and recreational sports. That such difference can be controlled and administered harmoniously is explained by the constantly reaffirmed principle of social closure, as explicated by Weber. For the language and area-based sub-populations of Switzerland are defined and respected status groups, language being "the common characteristic shared by many people" (Weber, 1978: p. 48). Although Weber could observe, with irony, that his concept could be applied to a 'pure' form of modern 'democratic' society, in "some of the smaller Swiss cities", where "only families belonging to broadly similar taxation groups dance with each other" (*ibid.*: p. 49), it is his notion of social closure that more generally illuminates the Swiss situation. Parkin (1974: p. 3) expands:

> Weber means the process by which social collectivities seek to maximize rewards by restricting access to rewards and opportunities to a limited circle of eligibles. This entails the singling out of certain identifiable social or physical attributes as the justificatory basis of exclusion. Weber suggests that virtually any group attribute — race, language, social origin, descent — may be seized upon provided it can be used for "the monopolization of specific, usually economic opportunities".

This is critical. For inherent to this dynamic of closure and exclusion is the potential for exploitation and, certainly, a lust for tradition. In Switzerland, it is this dynamic with all its potential outcomes that is central to the pluralist political constitution. So difference is not merely tolerated, but encouraged. Homogeneity at the national level is, concomitantly, unwanted and discouraged. Culturally varied, and modern individualist bourgeois sports and physical activities, as well as traditionally conservative *Turnen* based gymnastic clubs and English team games, all fit into the Swiss pluralist jigsaw. It will never be as plain sailing on the inside as it might seem from the perspective of history and an analytical exterior. Pick up a paper in Switzerland and the traveller will soon see that. *The Geneva Post* reported in May 1996 on a proposal to introduce bilingualism in primary education in the canton of Geneva, and raised the question of whether such a second language should be English (the language of global communication) or German. This was front page news:

> The motion comes at a time when the linguistic division of Switzerland is today more than ever straining relations between the Swiss Romande and the German-speaking part of the country. That division has been aggravated by Zurich's economic weight and its ties with Germany, while international Geneva is said to be more of a dollar rather than Deutschemark-oriented area. (*The Geneva Post* [English language] No. 10, May 23-29 1996: p. 1)

No doubt the tradition-steeped German-speaking gymnastic clubs will seem quaint and amusing to more cosmopolitan consumers. But such tensions stand as continuing testimony to the harmony of the wider entity. In the case of sport clubs of any kind, a respect for their differences, for their forms of closure and exclusion, can be both separatist and uniting. That is the paradox at the heart of the Swiss trick. It might not cheer you up if you're French-speaking Swiss on the eve of a national referendum, knowing that if the German-speaking Swiss all turn out and unite on an issue then you might as well stay at home and chew your Camembert. But in the Swiss case, the contribution of sport is not to generate and promote social division, rather it is to celebrate cultural diversity. At local, regional and national levels sport is one of the cultural forms which expresses and symbolizes an authentically felt social harmony and unity-in-difference. Difference and diversity do not, in this sense, constitute division.

Notes

1 Simmel (1991) made interesting observations on Alpinism as an example of the democratization of access to the natural world as an important dimension of modernity.

2 My thanks to Martin Putter for corroboration of this point.

3 This multi-level of provision explains some at-first-glance surprising statistics. For instance, the average amount of broadcast hours of the UEFA Champions' League 1995/96 was forty-eight hours per European country.

But Belgium broadcast 75 hours 40 minutes, and Switzerland 109 hours 33 minutes, for the games had to be simultaneously covered on several different language channels in those two countries (see TEAM, 1997).

4   See Codding (1961: pp. 161-162), for a summary, up to 1961, of Swiss involvement with international organizations. These ranged from the International Red Cross Committee (1864) to technology, communications and financial organizations. Specialized agencies of the United Nations — such as the World Health Organization, and the World Meteorological Organization — were also based in Geneva.

5   Martin Putter was presenting at the *Sport in Divided Societies* symposium, University of Brighton, Sport and Leisure Cultures, at the Sussex Arts Club, Brighton, on 23 May 1997.

6   A summary and a record of Swiss football performance on the international stage can be found in Oliver (1995: pp. 534-546).

7   On the International Olympic Committee, see Simson and Jennings, 1992; and Jennings, 1996; on FIFA, the governing body of world football, see Sugden and Tomlinson, 1998.

8   Research and policy debate is featured in its review, *Macolin*. Stamm and Lamprecht, for instance, debate how to translate the knowledge that all occasional sports participants have of the health benefits of regular sport and exercise, into patterns of more regular forms of commitment and involvement. They suggest targetting groups such as women, particular age groups and men with children, with strategies of encouragement. See Lamprecht and Stamm, 'Qui sont les sportifs occasionnels?'

9   Office fédéral de la statistique, 1990. The data reported in this section are all taken from this source.

10 See Mathys, 1977; Burgener, 1974 and 1981; and Huguenin, Unger and Bare, 1981.

References

Bonjour, F. (1920) *Real democracy in operation — the example of Switzerland* (translated from the French by C. Leonard Leese). London: George Allen and Unwin Ltd.

Bose, S., Sarkar, S. and Chatterjee, A.K. (1994) 'Gymnastics and sport in Switzerland', *Research bi-annual for movement* (Maharashtra State, India), Vol. 10 No. 2, April: pp. 53-57.

Bulletin of Sports Information (1991) 'Suisse: evolution de l'infrastructure sportive de 1963 a 1986', *Bulletin d'Information Sportive*, Vol. 24, March, Brussels: pp. 1815-1816.

Burgener, L. (1974) *Education physique en Suisse: histoire et situation actuelle.* Derendingen-Soleure (Switzerland): Editions Habegger.

———— (1981) 'Games and physical exercises in Switzerland in the 15th. and 16th. centuries', *Olympic Review* No. 162, April: pp. 237-240.

Calgari, G. (1963) *The four literatures of Switzerland.* London: Adam Books.

Codding, G.A. Jnr. (1961) *The Federal Government of Switzerland.* London: George Allen and Unwin Ltd.

de Coubertin, P. (1986) 'Switzerland, Queen of Sports', *Olympic Review* No. 228: pp. 599-603.

Egger, E., and Blanc, E. (1974) *Education in Switzerland*, Geneva, Swiss Educational Documentation Centre (Palais Wilson, Ch 1211, Geneva 14), July.

Honigsbaum, M. (1997) 'The heist meister', *The Observer Review*, Sunday 14 December: pp. 3-4.

Huguenin, A., Unger, B., and Bare, F.L. (1981) '100 years of the international Gymnastics Federation 1881-1981: Essay on the development and the evolution of gymnastics within an international federation', Lyss (Switzerland): International Gymnastics Federation, ii, 143, p. 111.

Ireland, P.R. (1994) *The policy challenge of ethnic diversity — Immigrant politics in France and Switzerland.* Cambridge (Massachusetts): Harvard University Press.

Jenkins, J.R.G. (1986) *Jura separatism in Switzerland.* Oxford: Clarendon Press.

Jennings, A. (1996) *The new Lords of the Rings — How Olympic gold medals are bought and sold.* London: Simon and Schuster.

Johnston, P., and Scribner, B. (1993) *The reformation in Germany and Switzerland.* Cambridge (England): Cambridge University Press.

Jury, L. (1997) 'Swiss stop saying sorry for Nazi gold', *The Independent*, Monday 1 December, p. 8.

Kohn, H. (1978) *Nationalism and liberty — The Swiss example*. Westport (Connecticut): Greenwood Press, (Reprint of 1956 Edition, published by G. Allen and Unwin).

Lamprecht, M., and Stamm, H. (1995) 'Expansion and integration versus differentiation and segregation: The case of recreational sport in Switzerland', short version of paper presented at International Sociological Association Conference, Bielefeld, Germany.

———— (1996) 'Age and gender patterns of sport involvement among the Swiss labour force', *Sociology of Sport Journal*, Vol. 13 No. 3: pp. 274-287.

Lanfranchi, P. (1998) 'Le role de la Suisse dans le développement du Football en Europe', unpublished manuscript, forthcoming, University of Geneva/UEFA.

Macrae, K.D. (1983) *Conflict and compromise in multilingual societies — Switzerland*. Waterloo (Ontario): Wilfred Laurier University Press.

Mathys, F.K. (1977) 'National games in Switzerland and their Relations to other European Games', in Y. Imamura, M. Verhaegen and J. Narita (eds), *History of physical education and sport: Research and studies*. Tokyo, Kodansha Ltd.: pp. 89-101.

Office fédéral de la statistique. (1990) *Loisirs et culture — Microrecensement 1988- Données de base*, Statistique officielle de la Suisse, Numero 305. Berne (Suisse): CP-Institut AG, Zurich.

Oliver, G. (1995) *The Guinness book of world soccer (2nd Edition)* London: Guinness Publishing.

Parkin, F. (1974) 'Strategies of social closure in class formation', in F. Parkin (ed), *The Social Analysis of Class Structure*. London: Tavistock Publications: pp. 1-18.

Phaidon (1985) *Switzerland — A Phaidon cultural guide*. Oxford: Phaidon.

Rappard, W.E. (1936) *The Government of Switzerland*. New York: D. Van Nostrand Company, Inc.

Ridley, I. (1997) 'FA Cup winners turn again to the brown-eyed boy whose bolt from the blue made Wembley history', *Independent on Sunday*, 4 January 1998, p. 9.

Robertson, I. (1987) *Blue guide — Switzerland (4th. Edition)* London. A and C Black.

Schlagenhauf, K., and Schiffer, J. (1976) 'German and the Swiss Club', *International Review of Sport Sociology*, Vol. 14, Nos. 3/4: pp. 87-96.

Segalman, R. (1986) *The Swiss way of welfare — Lessons for the Western world.* New York: Praeger.

Simmel. G. (1991) 'The Alpine journey', *Theory Culture and Society — Explorations in Critical Social Science,* Vol. 8 No. 3, August: pp. 95-98.

Simson, V., and Jennings, A. (1992) *The lords of the rings — Power, money and drugs at the Modern Olympics.* London: Simon and Schuster.

Stamm, H., and Lamprecht, M. (1996a) 'Qui sonts les sportifs occasionnels?', *Macolin — Revue mensuelle de l'EFSM et de Jeunesse + Sport,* 4/96, Avril (April): pp. 7-9.

———— (1996b) 'Sport organizations in Switzerland', *Working paper for the research group "Sport Organizations in Europe"',* unpublished paper.

Sugden, J. and Tomlinson, A. (1998) *FIFA and the contest for world football: Who rules the people's game?.* Cambridge: Polity Press.

Thürer, G. (1970) *Free and Swiss — the story of Switzerland.* London: Oswald Wolff.

TEAM (1996) *UEFA Champions League review 1995/96.* Lucerne, Switzerland: TEAM (Television Event and Media Marketing AG) and UEFA.

Wallechinsky, D. (1993) *The complete book of the Winter Olympics* (1994 Edition). London: Aurum Press.

———— (1996) *The complete book of the Olympics (1996 Edition)* London: Arum Press.

Walzer, M. (1983) *Spheres of justice.* New York: Basic Books.

Watson-Smyth, K. (1998) 'Swiss face fresh scandal after claims of labour camps for Jews', *The Independent,* Tuesday 6 January 1998, p. 3.

Weber, M. (1978) 'Classes, status groups and parties', in W. G. Runciman (ed) *Max Weber — Selections in translation* (translated by E. Matthews). Cambridge (England): Cambridge University Press: pp. 43-56; and 'Postscript: The concepts of status groups and classes': pp. 57-61.

SPORT IN DIVIDED SOCIETIES —
THE CASE OF THE OLD, THE NEW
AND THE 'RE-UNITED' GERMANY

Udo Merkel

University of Brighton

Introduction

In German society not only does sport reflect social and cultural divisions, it also creates them. Although attempts have frequently been made to utilise sport to overcome or to bridge such divisions and to integrate groups with different cultural backgrounds, based on the naive assumption that sport is simply a physical, classless and non-political activity which does not need language to overcome linguistic barriers, the political nature of sport cannot be denied.

The purpose of this chapter is to provide an accessible and balanced account of four selected issues showing significant divisions in German sport. These historical and contemporary examples are not intended to provide a complete overview but to highlight a number of different but nevertheless related forms of division which are not exclusively rooted in sport but rather are associated with the whole of German society and its broader social, economic and political dynamics from which sport derives it significance.

The chapter is organised into two separate parts, each with its own focus. The first section concentrates primarily on historical themes deriving from Germany's late foundation in the second half of the 19th century and the key questions 'What is German?' and 'What is un/non-German?' and thus deals with the issues of nation building and identity formation of the members of a new state. These historical examples confirm that the key agents in these processes are usually the educated and affluent middle classes who in the case of Germany had the most to gain from the replacement of the pre-German Empire social structures. The second part of the chapter considers two contemporary issues, namely the implications for sport of German 're-unification' in 1989, and the impact of ethnic divisions in modern Germany, in particular between Germans and the large Turkish community. Particularly the analysis of the last issue is the product of five years of experience of and research into sport, leisure and ethnic relations in Cologne where the author used to live and work with one of the largest Turkish communities in Germany. The theoretical underpinning of this chapter derives from the affinity between sport and forms of nationalism and ethnocentrism and will be focused upon in the concluding comments.

Historical aspects

In the first half of the 19th century Germany still possessed essentially feudal structures. The aristocracy was the dominant class while the slowly growing middle class had hardly any influence on social life. The vast majority of people lived in rural communities (Fürstenberg, 1972: p. 25). At the beginning of this century Germany as a nation state did not exist. Instead there was a huge number of smaller duchies and a few bigger states assembled on the territory which was later to become the German Empire. Despite attempts to establish a nation state in 1848 and 1849 it was not until 1871 that the first German state was founded. All this happened in an era of dramatic social change which culminated in the publication of Marx and Engels's Communist Manifesto (1848) and in revolutionary outbreaks all over the European continent.

The newly born nation state experienced a number of significant and rapid changes in its infancy, i.e. in the final quarter of the 19th century. It quickly caught up with the industrial capacity of England although the industrialisation process had started about 70 years later. The *Bürgertum*, the German middle class, became gradually the dominant power in society. Its core components were educated persons (*Bildungsbürger*), members of the Civil Service and self-employed qualified artisans. "They distinguished themselves from the aristocracy as well as from the workers and the peasantry by the qualities of *Besitz* and *Bildung*, i.e. by property in the form of inherited money or the ownership of the means of production and/or formal education" (Eisenberg, 1990: 267). The increasing discontent of the growing proletariat was shared by many elements of the middle class. However, the boundaries between the different social classes were drawn very sharply and were almost insurmountable. Since *Bürger* had previously not been admitted to court society (Elias, 1978: pp. 8-12) the social distance between *Bürgertum* and aristocracy was particularly clear cut.

The core-elements of the German *Bürgertum* had pre-industrial origins and, thus, their system of sociability had a long tradition governed by customs and habits. One string in this complex web was the club movement. In terms of their numbers and active participation the most important clubs were the shooting societies and the gymnastics clubs, the *Turnvereine*. "The latter developed as an expression of nationalism and of efforts to restore military strength after the defeat of the Napoleonic Wars" (Eisenberg, 1990: p. 273).

The unsuccessful revolution of 1848 left the German *Bürgertum* in disarray while the aristocracy, initially, retrieved their dominant position and were even able to re-establish their norms and values. Elements of the aristocratic life style, such as fencing, the admiration of the military character of reserve officers, aristocratic attitudes towards the state, power, honour and duty and the high prestige of the military tradition, became widely accepted. It is against this background that the following sporting themes must be understood.

Gymnastics and nation building in 19th century Germany

Turnen, gymnastics, became an essential part of Germany's physical culture in the second half of the eighteenth century when the vast majority of cultural practices in Germany fundamentally imitated French behaviour. The German princes and the slowly emerging middle class copied French architecture, manners and styles. Although *Turnen* is generally perceived to be a uniform, coherent and widely supported set of physical exercises, its development clearly displays a number of divisions within German society between North and South, right-wing and left-wing politics, pro- and anti-clerical politics, as well as attempts to unite a divided people. *Turnen*'s early history, in particular the ban on Turnen (1820-1842), also shows the strict response of a fearful and weak state in apprehensive anticipation of the potential political influence of a sports movement, whilst the 20 year period after the ban shows the most significant political divisions within the *Turnbewegung* (Gymnastics Movement) which led to an important organisational schism which, in turn, contributed to the emergence of the worker sport movement in Germany reflecting an additional, more explicit split along the lines of social class.

The origins of Gymnastics in Germany are usually associated with Johann Christoph GuthsMuths (1759-1839) who identified three different types of physical education: gymnastics, games and manual work. GuthsMuths powerfully promoted the introduction of gymnastic exercises in schools. His major publications repeatedly expressed his concern about the bodily health of human beings. However, the most important figure in the *Turnbewegung* was Friedrich Jahn (1778-1852), who is still referred to as the 'Father of Gymnastics' in Germany.

> In [Guthsmuth's] later years his fame was overshadowed by that of Jahn, who took his new form of education, re-labelled it *'Turnen'*, and made it the instrument of a national movement with profound political and social implications. But though Jahn plucked the fruit, it was Guthsmuths who ripened it. (Dixon, 1986: p. 118)

Jahn included wild and violent and often war-like games in his programme since he "launched his movement with the immediate aim of the physical and moral strengthening of German youth for the liberation of the Fatherland" (Dixon, 1986: p. 121). These objectives led also to a strong emphasis on weapon training as well as on scouting and team games. These games, such as *Räuber und Bürger Spiel* (Brigand and Citizen Game) or *Räuber und Soldaten Spiel* (Brigand and Soldier Game) were fundamentally wrestling competitions between two or more groups which very often ended in rough and violent fights. "Liberation from the 'French yoke' was for Jahn the first step towards the creation of a united Germany, free from feudal class distinctions and with a liberal constitution" (Dixon, 1986: p.122).

In the first half of the 19th century, Germans perceived themselves to be culturally inferior to their French neighbours, admiring and rejecting them at the same time. Jahn tried to fight this inferiority complex and in 1810 published a book, *The German Way of Life*, in which he tries to give evidence of the superiority of everything German over foreign things. When Prussia declared war on France in 1806 the Prussian troops were decisively defeated within three weeks. The successful revenge seven years later was partly attributed to the 'Movement of National Regeneration' in which Jahn played a significant role as he had changed GuthsMuths' concept significantly. His objective was to provide a framework and concept for the training of the entire able-bodied German population for the forthcoming struggle with the French. He saw the united liberated Germany as a country free from class distinctions. Consequently, he promoted a form of egalitarianism which was revolutionary in a country of stiff manners and asked the *Turner* to address each other with the familiar 'Du' instead of the more formal '*Sie*' and also to wear a very simple uniform. However, in 1819, the Gymnastics Movement fell into disgrace, was banned for more than 20 years (1820-1842) and

Jahn spent six years either under house arrest or in prison. "His impact on history is thus confined, in effect, to the years 1811-1819. In this short time he created a movement on a broad social basis, using physical education as a means for the attainment of constitutional reform" (Dixon, 1896: p. 124).

When gymnastic clubs were reinstated in 1842 it soon become clear that 22 years of suppression had made them more radical than ever before. There were fierce arguments and struggles over their motto '*Frisch, frei, fröhlich, fromm*' (Alert, free, cheerful, devout) as the '*fromm*' (devout) became a contested issue which many, particularly in the south of Germany, wished to abandon as it signified an unacceptable closeness to religious ideas. In fact, there was a clear North-South divide emerging as the gymnastics clubs in the South were clearly anti-clerical and democratic in their self-understanding, promoted principles of equality and comradeship, continued to use the familiar '*Du*' and rejected the state's demand to be a non-political movement. In contrast, *Turner* in the North remained religious and pro-clerical, used the more formal 'Sie' to address each other and abandoned all political aims. Consequently, when the desire grew to form a national organisation for all *Turner* the attempt failed miserably due to insurmountable ideological differences. The subsequent emergence of three very different governing bodies for gymnastics (and the lack of representation of a large group of *Turner* who did not want to be associated with any of these three organisations) clearly mirrored the tattered condition of the country. Consequently, during the 1850s the *Turnbewegung* experienced a period of decline and stagnation. However, the war against Denmark (1866) and the Franco-Prussian War (1870-1871) partly re-united the movement as there was some agreement on the objective to attain a free and united Fatherland. In addition, some fractions of the gymnastics movement started to commit themselves to a revival of Romantic nationalism and to the celebration of the mysterious German spirit. They asserted the mystic unity of *Volk und Vaterland* (People and fatherland) and "put national unity before democracy and came to terms with the Prussian-dominated German state of Bismarck after 1871" (Childs, 1981: p. 170). In turn, the authorities recognised the potential value of gymnastics for pre-military training and quickly introduced it to schools.

The decline of the *Turnbewegung* in the second half of the 19th century was partly due to their disunity. On the other hand the emergence of the worker sport movement which regarded the Democratic Turnerbund as its direct ancestor (although there is no evidence that a significant numbers of workers actually participated in it) played an important role. With the industrial rise of Germany in the second half of the 19th century and the increasing division of labour as well as professional differentiation, more and more subdivisions for very specific members, such as students, apprentices, merchants, etc. emerged. At the same time the influence of socialist and social-democratic organisations increased — strongly disliked by the imperial German government who passed the (Anti-) Socialist-Laws (*Sozialistengesetze*) prohibiting all activities of these organisations between 1878 and 1890. However, during this time these illegal organisations used the network of left-wing *Turnvereine* for their political activities which led to a closer association between sport and politics and finally to the foundation of the Worker Turner Association (*Arbeiter Turner Bund*) in 1893. Although the Worker Turner Association lacked a clearly developed ideological basis its political nature derived from the concern about social problems, conflicts and injustice in an increasingly industrial society. Another reason explaining the steady growth of the Worker Turner Association, particularly until 1913, was the very undogmatic and unprejudiced treatment of new sports. Cycling was regarded as emancipatory as it helped to increase workers' geographical mobility. There was, however, also a certain degree of consensus between bourgeois and working class *Turner*. They agreed that physical exercise should foster a culture of well prepared and well rounded athleticism instead of promoting record setting and goal breaking performances. Working class and bourgeois clubs, however, differed and disagreed on some minor but significant details as it was no secret that the Worker Turn Association associated preparedness with the forthcoming class struggle and revolution. Consequently, it is no surprise that bourgeois gymnastics clubs always received public subsidies, particularly by the central and local state, whilst workers' clubs had to put a lot of effort into fund-raising in order to make ends meet (Krüger, 1996: p. 10). However, more fundamental tensions were to come soon.

The conflict between German gymnastics and English sport at the turn of the century

> In Germany with the import of English games there ensued a fierce struggle between the gymnastic 'Turnen' and the new protagonists of 'Athleticism'. (Collins, 1979: p. 102)

Looking at the popularity of football in Germany today it is difficult, indeed almost impossible, to imagine the hostile reception this game (and with it a new concept concerning physical culture) was given when it arrived in Germany. Initially both association football and Rugby football were brought to Germany. The former was usually referred to as *Fußball ohne Aufnahme* (Football without picking-up) whilst the latter was called *Fußball mit Aufnahme* (Football with picking-up). This distinction and the use of explicitly German and long-winded names for these two games already hint at the major reason why these sports struggled to become established in Germany: they were English. The subtitle of a major publication against the introduction of football, 'The English Disease' (Planck, 1898), clearly confirms this. The same publication ridicules English sporting terms and the fashion of using them. All this happened in a historical period of intensive political and economic competition between the major industrial powers in Europe, namely Britain and Germany.

It was not only the Englishness which was generally associated with modern sports and games but also the concept of competitive team sports which caused a public outcry of the sporting, i.e. *Turner,* elite in Germany. In order to understand this resistance it is important to appreciate the nature of *Turnen* which dominated German physical culture for some time. *Turnen* not only consisted of gymnastic exercises and drill but also of games, e.g. 'Circle Football' which was played as follows: All players form a circle holding hands. One player in the middle of the circle with a ball tries to kick the ball through the gaps between the other players' legs. Obviously, their task is to prevent the ball from leaving the circle. Any player who lets the ball through has to leave the circle and move into the middle whilst the successful kicker replaces the player in the circle. In order to avoid arguments about who is responsible for which side within the circle agreement has to be reached prior to the commencement of the game whether players are responsible for covering their right or left side.

There is no doubt that nowadays hardly anybody would describe this as a ball *game* but rather as an exercise or form of practice as it lacks all the significant ingredients of a game: there are no clearly identifiable teams, nor are there losers or winners; there is no time limit nor are there any tactics required; the players do not practise for it, nor does this activity provide much excitement for the participants.

In addition, the nature of gymnastic games, generally, clearly rejected any notion of competitiveness, records and outstanding achievements. Gymnastics and gymnastic games were designed for the physical training of the whole population with the objective of increasing their general fitness levels and contributing to the education of the whole person. German gymnastics consisted of a clearly identifiable set of practices and there were many fierce discussions about what did and did not belong to gymnastics. There was no doubt, however, that football would never belong to German gymnastics.

Consequently, the growing popularity of football "roused the fierce opposition of leading Turner and of others anxious to preserve the purity of the German tradition. They denounced sport as un-German, a symptom of Anglo-Saxon superficiality and materialism, a product of the land without music or metaphysics" (Dixon, 1986: p. 134). English games such as football were considered to be rational, international and Semitic lacking 'higher' values, such as the reference to *Volk und Vaterland*, thereby clearly expressing the strong national feelings of the gymnastics movement. In a nutshell, the *Zeitgeist* of the *Turner* reflects a widespread and deeply rooted anglophobia.

However, this resistance was unsuccessful and English sports soon established themselves in Germany as orthodox Turnen no longer seemed to satisfy the physical and mental demands of the people. The new generation wanted fresh air and play" (Dixon, 1986: p.135). According to Dixon, this was a "natural reaction to new conditions of life" (1986: p. 134) which were caused by the rapid pace of urbanisation, the consolidation of industrial production and the growing fragmentation of everyday life. The modern age's quest for diversion and motion could be met by sport. So the numbers of people participating in some form of physical exercise was constantly growing. There were, however, other factors involved in this development, for example "the failure of the Turnerschaft to keep up a rate of growth comparable with that of the sports associations" (Dixon, 1986: p. 137) shows the general decline of the gymnastics movement and in particular its gradually decreasing degree of power and influence in an emerging differentiated society. Second, since the middle of the nineteenth century, competition and achievement had become the dominant principles of social life. While the English economy was based upon a tradition of commerce and relatively free trade, which could be traced back several hundred years, Germany's economy had traditionally been governed by a high degree of state intervention. "In early and mid nineteenth century Germany contemporaries were just beginning to get used to the growing competition in industry, trade and other parts of their daily lives" (Eisenberg, 1990: p. 274). Third, due to an economic boom in the 1880s and 1890s the standard of living in many European societies had risen; therefore the material preconditions were very positive. Industrialists, particularly those involved in the production of consumption goods, came to recognise the importance of sport. In time, these commercial interests fostered sport. Since it was essential for the newly emerging sports equipment industry to advertise its products, sports "exhibitions were held in Berlin (1882) and other cities, showing the equipment for every kind of sport from horse-racing to billiards" (Dixon, 1986: p. 134). Fourth, the "foundation of the International Olympic Committee in Paris in 1894 at the instigation of Baron de Coubertin gave a further stimulus to public interest in sport" (Dixon, 1986: p. 135). Although the *Turner* opposed the modern Olympic Games which they regarded as an 'invented tradition', the fact that they were staged in Athens in 1896 and in Paris in 1900 also contributed to a boost of modern sports. Fifth, since the newspapers discovered very soon that sport provided an opportunity to increase their circulation by sports reporting they, in turn, helped sport to gain more public attention. In addition, one influential state agency promoted the introduction of football for very political reasons as this game was expected to cross class divisions and to undermine the growing influence of the Social Democracy movement. Finally, clubs and national associations in England had already established working organisational structures which could be taken over without any time lapse. This meant, that after a brief introduction to the new English sports, clubs were founded, followed only a few years later by the principal sports associations, such as "the German Rowing Association (1883), the German Cycling Association (1884), the German Swimming Association (1887), the German Skating Association (1888), the Reich Association for Athletics (1891), the German Fencing Association (1897), the German Sport Authority for Light Athletics (1898)" (Dixon, 1986: p. 135).

Altogether, these were very powerful factors behind the acceptance of the new English sports though this happened very slowly and in the first instance was confined to only a few places. The final breakthrough of modern sports and in particular for football as a part of a mass culture did not occur until the First World War.

According to Hopf (1979), three reasons were responsible for the introduction and spread of football instead of Rugby, the other well known game among the early sport enthusiasts in Germany. Football appeared to be less dangerous than Rugby. On the other hand it was still wild enough to attract boys and men to participate. A soccer team needs fewer players than a Rugby team — an important consideration in the initial phase of its introduction. Politically important was the fact that soccer could be declared to be German football while Rugby was considered to be English football. Since the supporters of the game were aware of the resentments the introduction of an English game would provoke, they tried to give evidence that football also had a long tradition in Continental Europe and that it was already played in 'Germany' in the Middle Ages.

It must be stressed that, in fact, the rivalry between sport and the Gymnastics movement was very much a rivalry between the bourgeois elements of the *Turnbewegung* and sport. The Worker Turn Association had no such reservations, accommodated the introduction of English sports and even decided to change their name to 'Worker Turn and Sport Association' after the First World War (Krüger, 1996) although some of its members, particularly those who were involved in the German labour movement, opposed the professionalisation of the game which happened parallel to the increasing popularity of football as a spectator sport. These left wing activists feared that soccer would become the new opiate of the people and thus distract their attention from the forthcoming class struggle. However, such pleas remained fairly unsuccessful as the declining popularity of working class leisure and sport organisations clearly indicate (Gehrman, 1988). However, it was not until after the First World War that football became a working class sport (Lindner and Breuer, 1982), whilst at the end of the 19th and beginning of the 20th century this sport was dominated by the involvement of young middle class men.

Nowadays, football is the most popular spectator sport in Germany and for many the embodiment of 'Germanness' — a concept many Germans would still struggle to define due to the relatively short and extremely varied history of this nation state. It is this fundamental dilemma combined with some major socio-demographic changes in the composition of German society over the last decade (Bade, 1994) which contributes significantly to various forms of boundary setting and, thus, to a polarisation between 'us' and 'them'. Consequently, in the 1990s clearly identifiable characteristics, such as skin colour, certain cultural practices and linguistic differences, have increased in importance as a means of distinction. The following two examples which outline the social, political and cultural divisions between East and West Germany despite the 're-unification' and analyse the relationship between Germans and the large Turkish community will demonstrate major practical implications of this debate.

Contemporary issues

The end of the Cold War and increasing levels of human migration in the late 1980s and early 1990s have affected Germany more than any other country in Europe.

First, the divided post World-War II Germany was 'reunited' which meant an increase of its population by 17 million people. At the same time the Federal Republic inherited an inefficient and out of date economy but also a sporting system which was commonly known as the "Sporting Miracle" as it constantly produced disproportionately large numbers of outstanding athletes and teams (Gratton, 1990). Second, the Federal Republic has been the destination of approximately 7 million migrants since the 1960s with more than 2 million people arriving in the first half of the 1990s, particularly from politically unstable countries such as the former Yugoslavia but also including German repatriates from Eastern Europe (Merkel, 1996). In this context sport plays an ambiguous role. On one hand it is used by the state to promote unity but it is also implicated in the promotion of cultural distinctiveness as well as nationalist, racist and xenophobic ideas.

Sport in the 're-united' but still divided Germany

The modern democratic Germany is one of the fifteen member states of the European Union, home to almost 88 million people. Of these, 17 million are so called "*Ossis*" (a fairly derogatory and patronising term for East Germans used by the West Germans) whilst the other 64 million are the so called "*Besser-Wessis*" (the West-Germans knowing it all better, used by the East Germans).

In sporting terms Germany, both divided and united, has always done well despite the very reluctant and slow process of accepting the concept of sport. After World War II the defeated nations were excluded from the Olympic Games in London in 1948. When Germany was readmitted to the Olympic family it competed as a united country from 1952 to 1964, representing both West and East Germany. However, due to the size of the West German population, the political influence of the West German government and the achievements of West German athletes the East-German David demanded separation from the West-German Goliath so that from 1964 onwards the German states sent two separate teams to the Olympic Games. They competed not only against the rest of the world but more importantly against each other. For both the Federal Republic of Germany (FRG) and the German Democratic Republic (GDR), international sporting success had become a significant means by which to pursue political objectives. Three major aims can be clearly identified. Sporting success was meant to:

- reflect the superiority of their political system;
- provide and consolidate a distinct national identity;
- establish and increase a positive international reputation and recognition.

The latter objective was vital for the political future of the GDR due to the world-wide political isolation caused by the political and economic power and influence of the FRG. The 'Hallstein Doctrine', a key policy of the Foreign Office, meant that West Germany would have no economic or diplomatic relationships with countries which acknowledged the political existence and sovereignty of the East German state.

Both states certainly established themselves as sporting powers in the international arena and achieved international recognition for this sporting success. However, there is no doubt that the sporting success of the GDR was more substantial, e.g. in Olympic Games, than that of the FRG, particularly when we consider its international sporting success in relation to the size of the population of 17 million people (compared to 71 million in the West), the Gross National Product and the industrial output. The following four ingredients were the core elements in the recipe for success and clearly explain the East German 'sporting miracle':

1. The scientifically organised and rational selection of boys and girls in their early childhood.

2. The best possible facilities and a highly structured approach to coaching and training of potential gold medal athletes.

3. Sophisticated and institutionalised networks of support from highly qualified scientists from all relevant specialisms.

4. Efforts in a very restricted range of sports, particularly the Olympic sports, and those where there was some kind of evidence of a "German tradition" (Merkel, 1995).

However, as Houlihan clearly points out:

> The political collapse of the GDR was so sudden and the willingness of the Germans to vote for the staunchly anti-communist Christian Democrat Party of Helmut Kohl so apparent that it must call into question the success of the GDR policy of using sport to contribute to the development of a new socialist national identity. (Houlihan, 1991: 48)

On the other hand, more recent electoral evidence suggests a revival of support for radical left wing ideas and ideologies in East Germany as the growing support for and the continual success of the PDS (Party of Democratic Socialism), the modern successor of the old SED (Socialist Unity Party) in regional elections show. This unexpected development must certainly be seen in conjunction with the rediscovery of a distinctive Eastern identity which will be discussed later and is fundamentally an expression of dissatisfaction with the current socio-economic situation in East Germany.

Despite the sporting successes it was obvious to all GDR citizens that there were a number of fundamental problems. People experienced constant shortages in the workplace. Production plans had to be adjusted downward annually. The supply of consumer goods was unsatisfactory. The housing situation, too, became ever more critical in the 1980s. At the same time Christian groups and environmental movements sensitised the population to new issues ranging from refusal to serve in the armed forces to the obvious contradiction between the commitment to environmental protection anchored in the constitution and the actual situation. Dissatisfaction and disillusionment came to a head when in the summer 1989 tens of thousands of GDR citizens voted with their feet and escaped from the socialist regime via Austria and Hungary. Those East Germans who intended to stay in their country also took action and initiated the "Monday Demonstrations" in Leipzig which later spread to the entire country and forced the government to discuss citizens' demands openly. On 9 November the time had come for the implementation of a policy with unpredictable consequences: the opening of the borders to the West which could be crossed without visa, compulsory exchange, an identity card or a stamped passport. In the middle of the night enormous crowds brought the car traffic to a standstill. Additional border crossings were opened in order to relieve the congestion at the existing checkpoints, underground stations — shut down for years — suddenly bustled with new life and buses commuted from East to West and back again (Schwartau *et al.*, 1990).

Only 11 months later, on 2 October 1990, the two German states officially merged. Already before this date, due to the high number of sportsmen and women migrating to the West, many East German clubs ceased to exist or had to cancel scheduled competitions due to the lack of competitors. Consequently, some sport organisations were among the first to call for ''re-unification'' in order to stop the mass exodus of top-level athletes. What they did not realise was that 're-unification' would mean for sport the destruction and dismantling of the established sporting structures.

Although in the years immediately after the wall came down an average of about 40% of the sporting budget of the Home Office was designated to go into the five new regional states, the sporting structures of the former GDR which made top-level sport so successful have ceased to exist (Merkel, 1995). The Unification Treaty paved the way for this development since it clearly stated that the new regional states of the former German Democratic Republic had to adopt the political structures of the FRG in all areas of social life, including sport and culture. Consequently:

• the *Deutscher Turn- und Sport-Bund* (the German Gymnastics and Sports Union), the administrative and organisational heart of the East German sport system, was dissolved and all its staff made redundant;

• most of the relevant research centres and sport institutes were either closed down or could continue their work only on a very reduced scale in terms of staffing and budget;

• more than 90% of the about 10,000 highly qualified coaches were made redundant;

• over 80% of the 12,000 support staff were made redundant within the first year after the Unification treaty came into force;

• top-level athletes were left without any state support (which in the "good old times" of the German Democratic Republic included monthly grants, equipment, total access to sport facilities and support staff, travel expenses, etc.);

• the majority of sport boarding schools were privatised and almost all centres for excellence closed down.

In addition, the majority of the remaining administrative and management positions in East German sport were taken over by Western staff, whilst athletes and coaches are East-German, thus creating a great deal of tension (Brettschneider, 1994; Damklaer, 1994).

This dramatic transformation of the East German sports miracle was caused by the lack of willingness of the Federal government to keep up payments for this complex system, i.e. the central government in Bonn did not refuse to support sport in the five new regional states but argued that sport — like all other cultural institutions — is under the administration of the regional states and, thus, it is they who should provide the necessary funds. In fact, there is a clear division of labour and responsibilities in German sport: top-level sport in Germany is organised and looked after at the Federal level with the responsibility lying with the Home Office, whilst the regional states are in charge of Sport for All.

During this destruction process the focus of the public and political discourse of the East German sport system shifted and primarily focused upon issues such as the privileged status of top-level athletes, sportsmen and women serving as (informal) informers of the Ministry of Security [*Staatssicherheitsdienst* ('Stasi')], unethical training and selection procedures, the exploitation of children, and the development and (ab)use of drugs. These discussions obviously helped to justify the dismantling of the sporting structures, although the major argument was clearly that, in the process of reconstruction, scarce resources need to be allocated to solve the most important and pressing problems.

Critical commentators have argued that there is a sense that the destruction of the East German sports miracle was much more an act of revenge for all the humiliating defeats West German athletes (and with them politicians) had suffered in the past, combined with an inability to appreciate the merits of the sporting system and thus it reflects and illuminates the arrogance and ignorance of the Conservative West German government and its attitudes towards the achievements of the former East Germany.

However, some features of the East German sporting system have in fact survived and have been extensively exploited and promoted by the all-German government in order to enhance its sporting system despite some public protests about their unethical nature. As a number of different newspapers reported independently, these include the principle of sporting soldiers as well as the early and systematic selection of talented children based on anthropometric measurements.

The latter was introduced in the Centre for Excellence in Hamburg in 1992 by a successful former East German swimming coach. Initially he had to overcome some fierce resistance before his plan to measure the body composition of children in primary schools in order to predict their final physical shape was accepted. It was not only the ethically sensitive nature of this approach but also the fact that in Germany two authoritarian systems in this century have used physical characteristics for selection purposes that caused the initial resistance. However, systematic anthropometric measurements ("Made in the GDR") have now been introduced and are now frequently used, in particular by swim coaches.

The other policy has a much longer tradition as the German Armed Forces have been home to top-level international athletes since 1964. Today there are 25 sporting units which provide specialist training facilities for about 600 male and 100 female athletes. Eighty-eight out of the 479 participants of the Atlanta Games were sport soldiers. Twenty-two returned with a medal. These "soldiers" go through a three month basic training like all other soldiers in the German forces but are then relieved to train in one of the 25 units. Many perceive the German forces to be the most significant sponsor of top-level achievements. Only recently, the Ministry of Defence decided to expand this programme and publicly admitted to a preference to buy one tank less rather than cut the funding of the training of top-level athletes. Considering the end of the Cold War, this is certainly a plausible but also a hypocritical approach as the same politicians regularly accused East German (and other Eastern European) athletes of 'shamateurism' due to their military background.

In the meantime, the all-German government has initiated the development of two strategy papers, the 'Golden Plan East' and 'Rebuild the East' — both dealing with the future of sport in East Germany, the investments needed to upgrade old and build new facilities and the promotion of the club as the core unit for community. The central government in Bonn is supporting these plans but has repeatedly stressed that it is not prepared to provide any additional finances. The governments of the regional states, however, have started to allocate funds to sport, but (due to other problems they have to tackle, e.g. the disproportionately high unemployment in the East) in a very modest way. Consequently, due to the lack of sufficient and attractive facilities and the absence of successful athletes as role models — the majority have moved to the West to compete for the (financially) stronger clubs there — general levels of participation are at an all time low and will remain so if the Western propaganda machine continues to constantly associate the sporting success of the former German Democratic Republic with doping, exploitation of children, athletes serving as informers to the Ministry of Security, etc.

However, during the last two years, many East Germans have started to acknowledge and to appreciate the numerous merits of their old Socialist system. Obviously, there is more than a touch of nostalgia involved when some now organise Trabant-meetings, prefer to purchase products made in the East, visit museums and galleries displaying everyday objects of the Socialist era, and refuse to turn in their old passports.

At the same time, sport clubs are in the process of overcoming the spectator crisis which hit them hard immediately after the wall came down. Sport, in general, it seems, provides excitement in times of stagnating economic depression, offers the newly emerging middle-class a forum to celebrate nostalgic moods and allows many others to publicly display a (re-)emerging self-confidence which is clearly based on the celebration of East-West divisions. In some grounds the old GDR flag has become part of the standard equipment of fans. Chants at football matches, such as "We don't want any Western swines", refer to Western opponents, players, supporters and even the referee. This is frequently accompanied by the request to "Put up the wall again". There is no doubt that the terraces of sports grounds have become meeting places for both the winners and the losers of the 're-unifica-tion'. What they share is the desire to publicly express their feelings and moods. Although many clubs and teams have changed their names and colours, their fans have started to use the old (i.e. pre-1989) names and colour combinations again. When they refer to Berlin, many add 'East' to demonstrate their distinctive sense of belonging. On several occasions, particularly when top West German sides play East German underdogs, chants referring to the 1974 World Cup match between East and West Germany in Hamburg (which the East German team won 1-0) can be heard. These unusual and unexpected developments have, in turn, attracted the attention of the mass media (despite the weak performances of many East German teams) and subsequently the attention of sponsors whose money has predominantly been used to buy in new players from all over the world. Only a tiny minority of football, handball or ice hockey players in East German clubs are native East Germans. Consequently, it is no surprise that the members of many management teams of professional clubs have Western origins. As the fans can hardly afford to regularly buy new kits with the name of recently purchased stars on the back many have started to wear kits with simply the word 'Ossi' on the back.

Although immediately after the dramatic political change hardly anybody went to see sports like football, handball or ice hockey, sport events appear to offer amongst the few remaining opportunities to provide a frame of reference for East Germans. Political parties, the unions, the German-Cuban Friendship Society and other institutionalised GDR meeting places did not survive the changes. In addition, sporting success has become a valuable marketing feature for East German regions. Therefore, local governments have started to invest heavily in prestigious sporting facilities such as multi-functional sport halls.

Needless to say all former citizens of the GDR became automatically citizens of the FRG in October 1990 and were thus entitled to all citizenship rights. However, for many West Germans their 'brothers and sisters in the East' appear to be more alien than for example the Turkish community of whom the vast majority have been living in the FRG for more than ten years without having all citizenship rights. The next example concentrates on this group and outlines ethnic divisions in German society and sport which will clearly show that the concept of German nationality remains — even in the second half of the 1990s — closely bound up with ethnicity and language as well as cultural history and heritage and thus ignores the reality of a multi-cultural immigration society.

Ethnic divisions and sport in contemporary Germany

There are about 6.8 million 'foreigners'[1] living in Germany; 97% in the territory of what was the Federal Republic of Germany before 1990, the other 3% living in the territory of the former German Democratic Republic. 1.92 million people of these 'foreigners' (27.9%) are Turkish, many Germans still refer to them as "*Gastarbeiter*" (guest workers) although many of these have been living in Germany for more than 30 years returning *home* only for the summer vacation.

Without doubt Germany has become one of the most popular immigration destinations in the last quarter of the 20th century despite the fact that the complex legal system (which treats different groups of migrants differently) discriminates against all migrants. In addition, particularly in the late 1980s and early 1990s, migrants have increasingly become the victims of violent attacks by offenders with a right-wing, racist and/or xenophobic background. This most recent period in German history has clearly shown that the 'foreign' community in Germany functions for many as a scapegoat, apparently being responsible for a number of social and economic problems. It is no surprise that critical commentators have repeatedly hinted at parallels to Hitler Fascism when the Jewish community became the scapegoat for a number of problems. However, none of the post war governments can be accused of exploiting sport for the promotion and demonstration of the national and racial superiority of the German people.

Nevertheless, there has been a marked increase in racist and xenophobic manifestations; the majority are verbal and symbolic but a small number consists of physical attacks. The main targets are athletes who are involved at top level in the most popular sports and who are visibly different, such as black football players in the German *Bundesliga*. However, these only constitute the tip of an iceberg whilst the vast majority of discriminatory practices, racist and xenophobic attitudes, hostilities between Germans and migrants in the world of sport as well as coping strategies developed by those concerned are usually hidden from the public eye. A prime example is the situation of Turkish athletes and sport enthusiasts who have hardly been considered in the past when the problem of racism or xenophobia has been analysed in the German context.

As the largest single group of immigrants in Germany, the Turks clearly require particular attention. Labour migration to Germany started about 10 years after the end of World War II and was driven by economic considerations. Despite the recruitment ending in 1973, there has been a steady influx of migrants over the last 25 years. Currently, there are for example about 30,000 Turks arriving each year either due to 'family reunion' or 'family formation', i.e. a Turkish person resident in Germany marries a partner from Turkey who is then, after a waiting period, allowed to migrate to Germany. As the unsuccessful attempts to reduce the migrant population through remigration incentives have clearly shown the majority of Turks in Germany do not wish to return to Turkey. Although there are opportunities for naturalisation only a tiny minority uses this opportunity as the German law on citizenship disallows holding dual nationality.

People of Turkish descent are not as visible in German sport as for example black athletes from Africa or certain regions of South America. This has two reasons: first, Turkish athletes do not necessarily stand out because of visible physical characteristics; and second, they are clearly underrepresented in the vast majority of sports with the notable exceptions of wrestling and weight lifting. Although the Turkish community is evident in everyday life there are hardly any Turkish players in the German *Bundesliga*. If they do take part, however, racism at institutional and individual levels is apparent in sport involvement by Turkish migrant workers and their families, as with members of other minority ethnic groups. At an individual level there is evidence that Turks experience racist abuse in sport clubs, in schools and whilst watching sports. The few Turkish players who were with German *Bundesliga* clubs in the 1970s and 1980s were very often the first to be abused by racist and xenophobic chants, in many cases by their own supporters who used these Turkish players as scapegoats if things went wrong. This scapegoating practice can also be seen in the wider socio-economic context. Weeks before a match against Turkey in 1983 in Berlin, a political leaflet was distributed at a number of German football stadia accusing the Turkish community of stealing German jobs, exploiting the social security system and flooding the country. The same flyer openly threatened the Turkish migrants with violent attacks. Although many German trade unions and political parties (particularly those on the Left) expressed their disgust at this message and at the same time their solidarity with the Turkish community and despite the fact that 5,000 police officers turned the football ground in Berlin into Fort Knox only 35,000 people attended the match. The half-empty football stadium in Berlin clearly reflected both the vulnerability and the fear of the Turkish community whose male members are very interested in and enthusiastic about sport, in particular football. However, this enthusiasm happens very often behind the closed doors of Turkish bars which typically comprise basic furniture and are usually populated only by men talking, playing cards or watching television, particularly sports programmes. Whilst some years ago it was predominantly German sports programmes, it is now due to cable and satellite TV, Turkish broadcasts which these middle-aged and older men watch (which, in turn, excludes younger men as their linguistic skills are in many cases not sufficient to follow these programmes as they were born and brought up in Germany with German their first language and Turkish the 'foreign' language). Outside these bars, cars are often decorated with the pennants of two football clubs, one that of a top-level First Division club in Turkey and the other referring to the local or regional semi-professional Turkish club. Women's "leisure" is much more home-bound than that of men whose leisure can be described as semi-public as it is not entirely open and very often not accessible for outsiders, i.e. for non-members of the Turkish community. Consequently, due to this degree of seclusion, at an institutional level, there is evidence of stereotypical assumptions about Turkish youth in schools as being not interested in sport or too frail for contact sports as well as lacking stamina. Turkish girls hardly participate in sport at all. First, they are expected by their families to take on major domestic responsibilities in the home. Second, culturally prescribed gender appropriate behaviour is widely accepted by (PE) teachers who in turn do not encourage Turkish girls to take part in sport and are more lenient concerning their absence than with other young people. However, it is interesting to note that Turkish girls tend to sign up for more extra-curricular activities than boys as these provide them with an opportunity to flee from the constraints of home.

Due to the size and the length of stay of the Turkish community in Germany there exists a network of (almost) exclusively Turkish clubs which are very popular among Turkish migrants, attracting large audiences and having financial backing from Turkish businesses. Whilst initially these clubs formed their own leagues and were comprised only of Turkish migrants, nowadays they play in the major local and regional leagues and, thus, compete against predominantly German teams. In addition, these clubs are not any longer exclusively Turkish as members of other minority ethnic groups as well as German players have joined them. However, these clubs remain explicitly Turkish institutions with Turkish names, supporters and having their headquarters and meeting points in areas dominated by Turkish migrants. Such clubs are seen by one of the chairmen (in a recent interview) as valuable social institutions which can help prepare young Turkish children for the difficulties they are very likely to encounter in their lives as well as providing them with a stable cultural background within their native community. They are expected to help boys to develop self-confidence and to express themselves through sport in ways that will be beneficial in other realms of life. They are also about distinctive cultural assertiveness, a pride in being Turkish. The motives of the organisers are certainly admirable but such initiatives hardly challenge the social context and thus the roots of some of the problems. However, this cultural separatism combined with a certain degree of openness is certainly more helpful than the dogmatic stance of the German Sport Association which repeatedly stressed that only individual membership of migrants in German clubs can finally lead to full integration of minorities. For the German Sport Association 'foreign' or 'ethnic' clubs are only an interim step on the way to full integration. Those involved in the running of ethnic clubs very often express a less dogmatic view as they are more interested in playing a sport and doing it well as this could lead among other things to a professional career in Turkish football.

As research into this field is still very limited it might be useful to compare the role and meaning of football for Turks in Germany with the historical example of the Polish community in order to explain the enthusiasm for organised football. For both ethnic minorities the sporting activity provides the potential to revive and express communal relationships in a highly differentiated society which Germany became at the beginning of this century. Looking at the history of the Ruhr area, the industrial heartland of Germany, it becomes apparent that at the turn of this century its inhabitants had to face two dilemmas, the rapidity of social change and the lack of a common cultural tradition. Due to the emergence and expansion of industrial production in this region there was an enormous demand for additional workers who came from all over central Europe, particularly from areas which once had been Prussia. "While in 1861 there were altogether 16 (!) Polish living in the counties of Rheinland and Westfalen, this number increased to more than 30,000 in 1910. In 1907, in many mines the proportion of workers from the old German eastern areas and from Poland was higher than 50%" (Lindner and Breuer, 1982: pp. 35-7).

So, the vast majority of people living in the Ruhr area at the beginning of this century were migrants. Therefore it is no surprise that these people lacked a common cultural tradition. However, they utilised a sporting activity as a framework to perform cultural practices which were borrowed from their traditional life in rural communities which they had left. Putting it in Toennies' terms one could conclude that due to the emergence of *Gesellschaft*, an increasingly complex and differentiated German society, those people affected kept up Gemeinschaft-like patterns of life in certain enclaves which enabled them to self-locate and identify their place in society. So, football and the active participation in the club became for those people an experience of particular depth and intensity.

Conclusion

Germany is one of the youngest nation states in Europe as it was only founded in the second half of the last century. The composition of German society has always been less homogenous than other European nations. However, particularly at the end of the 20th century Germany has become one of the most popular destinations for migrants — a fact with which many Germans struggle to come to terms with. In addition, Germans still insist on defining themselves in ethnic terms. Any attempts to explain these contradictions must make reference to the fragile sense of identity of the German people. This, again, has been challenged and requires yet another new definition due to the merger of East and West Germany after the political collapse of the German Democratic Republic in 1989. Although 'ethnicity' is one significant element in securing the Germans' sense of themselves, in general, expressions of anti-migrant, racist and xenophobic attitudes clearly display a focus on cultural and religious differences as well as scapegoating practices.

An analysis of the world of sport leads to very similar observations. This chapter has attempted to show the magnitude and complexity of divisions in the world of sport using historical as well as contemporary examples. However, it needs to be stressed that these divisions do not only reflect wider social, political and ethnic divisions but can also contribute to their emergence and help to sustain such divisions. It was also intended to outline the links between the realm of sport and regional and national identities and thus to locate the discussion in the wider theoretical framework of issues related to nationalism. Benedict Anderson (1991) provides a very useful differentiation between ethnic and civic nationalism; the latter referring to the assembly of autonomous citizens in an identifiable territory sharing a certain set of norms and values, whilst the former stresses the strong devotion to one's own nation based on the cultural traditions of an imagined community. As the exclusion of the Turkish community from citizenship rights clearly shows, the German state has adopted the notion of ethnic nationalism as a guiding principle. These two forms of nationalism clearly correlate with the two most common underlying principles of naturalisation in Europe, the principle of *jus sanguinis* (blood right) and *jus soli* (soil right). In the German context this has always meant that only a person with at least one German parent can be German. Only in recent years has it became possible to acquire German nationality without having German parents, a policy which clearly reflected a dogmatic and out-of-date German approach to citizenship and nationality. In this sense, nationalism can best be understood in the light of the origins of the German nation state and its varied history which is one of instability due to several fundamental, significant social, cultural, political and geographical changes over the last 120 years. Consequently, to provide an answer to the question "what is (a) German?" is still a difficult task. There is no doubt that despite a few moments when sporting success actually united the West German people (Merkel, 1994a), efforts to use sport as a means to create stability, coherence and distinctive national identities have failed as e.g. the political collapse of East Germany and the willingness of the East Germans to accept a conservative social order have clearly shown.

Divisions in sport have a long tradition in Germany. The first historical example intended to demonstrate a number of different divisions in German society: regional, political as well as religious divisions, all fought out in the gymnasia and exercise grounds. Furthermore, it shows how, initially, gymnastics were feared as a form of popular culture and at a later stage used for pre-military training in order to liberate and unite the German people against their arch rival, France. When the German Empire was founded the lowest common denominator was that the German people could easily identify their enemy but certainly did not have a national identity going beyond a definition of who they were united against.

The second example highlights how philosophical discussions about the nature of physically active forms of recreation and exercises were linked to the emerging new class structure, particularly to the formation of a new middle class, in the modern industrial Germany. When soccer was introduced in Germany, educationalists saw the potential educational value of this English game although the spirit of team sports and the philosophy of competition were counter to the concept and apparently inherent values of gymnastics. As Eisenberg (1990) has explained in much greater detail, the initial resistance to the introduction of soccer in Germany must be seen in conjunction with the formation and consolidation of the German middle class at the end of the 19th century: "While modern sports contributed to the English middle class' attempts at class formation, they could hardly serve this function for the German *Bürgertum* (i.e. middle class). With regard to the latter identity sports played at most an ambivalent, but mainly a disintegrating, role" (p. 266).

Equally ambivalent is the contemporary perception of the German nation state and its political role and responsibilities in the global context, particularly as Germany rose like a Phoenix from the ashes after it recovered from the defeat in and the destruction caused by the Second World War. Having been (literally in geographical terms) at the forefront of the Cold War between East and West, capitalism and socialism, for almost half a century, the breakdown of the Warsaw Pact came for many as a big surprise. Even more astonishment caused the rushed 're-unification' process between the Federal Republic of Germany and the German Democratic Republic. It took less than a year to formally legitimise the take over of East Germany. Subsequently, what in the past was usually referred to as the East-German 'sporting miracle' was systematically destroyed. This development has all the characteristics of a hegemonic process as it finds widespread public support, particularly in the West, due to orchestrated public discourses which focus on drug abuse by East German athletes, their roles as spies, their privileged status in East German society, unethical training and selection procedures, the exploitation of children, and disregard for the concept of amateurism. However, many people in the East have now realised that they are the losers of this 're-unification' process and have started to express their dissatisfaction in a number of imaginative ways. Whilst the central government in Bonn hoped to be able to use sport to create national German identity, many East Germans use sport for the celebration of regional differences. Cultural practices of this sort as described above are more than passive reflections of political and social divisions between East and West Germany. By its very nature, sporting events provide a focus for regional identification and a forum for symbolic confrontation with — in this case — the central (Western) state, represented by Western teams and athletes, which exacerbates conflict, at least in a symbolic way.

Less symbolically important but all the more obvious are the numerous and varied forms of discrimination in everyday life to which the Turkish community is subjected to. However, Turkish people do not appear to constitute a problem in the vast majority of sports in Germany — simply because they are usually absent both as players and spectators which is in stark contrast to the popularity of modern sports, in particular football, in Turkey. Anecdotal evidence suggests that the few

Turkish players and spectators in the *Bundesliga* have regularly been subjected to blunt anti-Turkish abuse. Therefore it is no surprise that the Turkish community in Germany, particularly in large conurbations like Berlin and Cologne, have established their own network of ethnic football clubs which have found widespread support and financial backing. Although in the wider German debate about integration these clubs are often accused of cultural separatism there is no doubt that they fulfil important functions in an ethnically divided society as these clubs can help the Turkish community to build self-confidence, gain recognition, fight prejudices and assert their cultural distinctiveness although they do not challenge the wider social context which generates the problem in the first place.

Note

[1] The German Aliens Act provides a precise definition of *foreigners*. However, in reality the division between Germans and *foreigners* has become increasingly unclear. Therefore the use of inverted commas in association with the term *foreigner* is meant to highlight the problematic nature of the term. Whenever possible the term *migrant* will be used in this section.

References

Abrams, L.(1992) *Workers' culture in Imperial Germany — Leisure and recreation in the Rhineland and Westphalia*. London and New York: Routledge.

Allison, L. (ed) (1986) *The politics of sport*. Manchester: Manchester University Press.

Anderson, B. (1991) *Imagined communities*. London/New York: Verso.

Bade, K.J. (1994) *Homo migrans-Wanderungen aus und nach Deutschland*. Essen: Klartext.

Brettschneider, W. D. (1994) 'Unity of the nation-Unity in sports?', in R. C. Wilcox (ed) *Sport in the global village*. Morgantown: Fitness Information Technology, pp. 251-259.

Childs, D. (1978) 'The German Democratic Republic', in J. Riordan (ed) *Sport under Communism*. London: Hurst & Co, pp. 67-101.

Collins, L. (1979) 'A comparative study of the development of sport in Great Britain and West Germany', *Physical Education Review*, Vol. 2, No. 2: pp. 101-114.

Critcher, C. (1982) 'Football since the War', in B. Waites, T. Bennett and G.Martin (eds) *Popular culture: Past and present*. London: Croom Helm, pp. 194-218.

Dixon, J.G. (1986) 'Prussia, politics and physical education' in P.C. McIntosh, J.G. Dixon, A.D. Munrow and R.F. Willetts (eds) *Landmarks in the history of physical education*. London: RKP, pp. 112-155.

Damklaer, S. (1994) 'The unification of German sports systems' in R. C. Wilcox (ed.) *Sport in the global village*. Morgantown: Fitness Information Technology, pp. 261-268.

Dunning, E. (1979) *Soccer: The social origins of the sport and its development as a spectacle and profession*. London: Sports Council/ SSRC.

Duke, V. and Crolley, L. (1996) *Football, nationality and the state*. New York: Longman.

Elias, N. (1978) *Über den Prozeß der Zivilisation*. Frankfurt: Suhrkamp.

Eisenberg, C. (1990) 'The middle class and competition: Some considerations of the beginnings of modern sport in England and Germany', *The International Journal of the History of Sport*, Vol. 7, No. 2 (September): pp. 265-282.

Fürstenberg, F. (1972) *Die Sozialstruktur der Bundesrepublik Deutschland-ein soziologischer Überblick*. Opladen: Westdeutscher Verlag.

Gehrmann, S. (1988) *Fußball-Vereine-Politik. Zur Sportgeschichte des Reviers*. Essen: Reimar Hobbing Verlag.

Gratton, P. (1990) 'The production of Olympic champions: International comparisons', in A. Tomlinson (ed) *Sport in society: Policy, politics and culture* (LSA Publication No. 43). Eastbourne: Leisure Studies Association, pp. 50-67.

Hopf, W. (ed) (1979) *Fußball-Soziologie und Sozialgeschichte einer populären Sportart*. Bensheim: Päd Extra.

Houlihan, B. (1991) *The Government and Politics of Sport*. London, RKP.

Huck, G. (1980) *Sozialgeschichte der Freizeit*. Wuppertal: Peter Hammer Verlag.

Koch, K. (1900) *Die Erziehung zum Mute*. Berlin.

Kothy, J. and Blecking, D. (1990) 'Migranten im Sport". K. Zieschang and W. Buchmeier (eds) *Sport zwischen Tradition und Zukunft*. Schorndorf: Verlag Karl Hofmann.

Krüger, A. (ed) (1984) *Forum für Sportgeschichte. Die Entwicklung der Turn- und Sportvereine*. Berlin.

Krüger, A. (1996) 'The German way of worker sport', in A. Krüger and J. Riordan (eds) *The Story of Worker Sport*. Urbana/Champaign (Illinois): Human Kinetics, pp. 1-26.

Lindner, R. and Breuer, H.T. (1982) *"Sind doch nicht alles Beckenbauers"*. Frankfurt: Syndicat.

Loose, F. (1904) *Die geschichtliche Entwicklung der Leibesübungen in Deutschland. Der Kampf zwischen Turnen und Sport.* Erlangen: PhD thesis.

Mason, T. (1986) 'Some Englishmen and Scotsmen abroad: The spread of world football', in A. Tomlinson and G. Whannel (eds) *Off the Ball*. London: Pluto Press, pp. 67-82.

Merkel, U. (1994 a) 'Germany and the World Cup: solid, reliable, often undramatic-but successful', in J. Sugden and A. Tomlinson (eds) *Hosts and Champions*. Aldershot: Arena, pp. 93-118.

——— (1994 b) 'Fremdenfeindlichkeit und Rassismus im europäischen Sport als Spiegelbild gesellschaftlicher Realität', in W. Tokarski, K. Petry and N. Schultz (eds) *Brennpunkte der Sportwissenschaft*, Köln, No. 8: pp 54-69.

——— (1995) 'The German Government and the politics of sport and leisure in the 1990s: An interim report', in A. Tomlinson, M. Talbot, and S. Fleming, (eds) *Policy and politics in sport, physical education and leisure*. Eastbourne: Leisure Studies Association Publication, pp. 95-108.

Merkel, U. and Tokarski W. (eds) (1996) *Racism and xenophobia in European Football*. Aachen: Meyer&Meyer Verlag.

Pflaum, M. (1967) 'Die Kultur-Zivilisations-Antithese im Deutschen' in J. Knobloch (ed) *Europäische Schlüsselworter. Wortvergleiche und wortgeschichtliche Studien*. Munich, pp. 288-427.

Planck, K. (1898) *Fußlümmelei. Über Stauchballspiel und englische Krankheit*. Stuttgart.

Schwartau, A., Schwartau, C. and Steinberg, R. (1990) *Berlin im November*. Berlin: Nicolaische Verlagsbuchhandlung.

Tomlinson, A. and Whannel, G. (eds) (1986) *Off the ball*. London: Pluto Press.

Waites, B., Bennett, T. and Martin, G. (eds) (1982) *Popular culture: Past and present*. London: Croom Helm Ltd..

Verlag Die Werkstatt (ed) (1993) *Fußball und Rassismus*. Göttingen: Verlag Die Werkstatt.

Weber-Klüwer, K. (1993): '"Neger Raus" gegen "Zeugen Yeboahs" — Fußball und Rassismus in Deutschland', in Verlag Die Werkstatt (ed), *Fußball und Rassismus*. Göttingen: Verlag Die Werkstatt.

Whannel, G. (1983) *Blowing the whistle — The politics of sport*. London: Pluto Press.

SPORT AMONG THE SOVIET RUINS:
THE REPUBLIC OF GEORGIA

Lincoln Allison

University of Warwick

Georgia presents a very different case from South Africa and Northern Ireland: in those countries sport is recognised as at least a reasonably important dimension of the ethno-political conflict occurring and in the South African case most people would accept that sport has played a crucial part in the political development of the country. It is obvious that Georgia is 'divided' beyond the normal and in several respects, but it is not obvious that sport has played any significant part in that division. Indeed, this author has often been met with incredulity in Georgia when he has asked questions about sport in the midst of national tragedy! Yet, of course, sport is a dimension of the collapse and division of Georgia. It is not just that Georgian sport exemplifies and 'reflects' what has happened to Georgian society; there are also interesting questions arising out of the nature of the collapse of Georgian sport and important ones about its route to revival. But these cannot be examined without a prior account of the situation in which the Republic of Georgia has found itself in the 1990s.

Georgia was one of the smallest of the fifteen constituent republics of the Soviet Union: its territorial size and population are both very similar to those of Scotland. That is, it has about five million people on about 30,000 square miles (75,000 square hectometres) of territory. Greater accuracy would be spurious at this stage, because it depends which territories exactly one assumes that the Georgian government controls and how many people remain after a period of unprecedented emigration during the economic collapse of the 1990s. Most geographical accounts of Georgia place it in the Caucasus — the area of land between the Black and Caspian Seas — but it is more useful to describe Georgia's location by the more old-fashioned term the 'Transcaucasus' because

Georgia is divided from the Russian Federation by the Caucasus mountains which rise to 6,000 metres in height. Even in modern conditions this is a formidable obstacle and it has often been the case during the 1990s that all the roads from Georgia to Russia have been impassable owing to weather or civil disorder. Georgia is much more naturally connected to Turkey than to Russia and by 1994, within five years of the Russian-Georgian schism, Turkey had become Georgia's principal trading partner (see Coppieters *et al.,* 1997). However, it should be added as a kind of warning about the ethnic implications of geo-graphical terms, that even even moderate Georgian nationalists dislike the term 'Transcaucasus' as it is only 'across' the mountains when seen from Russia. They prefer the use of the term 'South Caucasus'.

The identity of Georgia is complex in a number of respects which are parallel to the complexities of identity of most southern and eastern states within Europe. Indeed, although a very ancient nation, Georgia has always been thought of as more than one place. Modern Georgia is based on the kingdom of Kartli-Kakheti which is principally Eastern Georgia. In Georgian, the people are the Kartvelebi and their land is Sakartvelo, both more limited than modern Georgia. In Russian the name *Gruzia* does apply to the whole as the western name Georgia does. Under Soviet arrangements Georgia was recognised as possessing the greatest ethnic complexity outside the Russian Federation with two autonomous republics, Abkhazia and Adjara, and an autonomous region, South Ossetia.

The extent to which these areas are regarded as 'Georgia' by their inhabitants and by other Georgians differs markedly. The South Ossetians do not regard themselves as Georgian and are not regarded as such by Georgians. The Ossetes are a people of Persian extraction and North Ossetia is part of the Russian Federation on the other side of the Caucasus mountains. 'South Ossetia' is a valley north of Tbilisi, inhabited by about eighty thousand people two thirds of whom were Ossetian in the late Soviet period. (Probably this figure is much higher now since the area has been effectively autonomous during the post-Soviet period.) It is widely believed that the Ossetian population was tiny in the pre-Soviet period and was deliberately built up by the Bolsheviks. By contrast, Adjara, bordering the Black Sea and Turkey, is considered fully part of Georgia, despite being predominantly Muslim and having operated as the semi-independent fiefdom of Aslan Abashidze since the collapse of the Soviet Union. This perception has always seemed to fit strangely with the centrality of Christianity to Georgian identity, but the construction of national identities never was a matter of logic. By contrast, the whole issue of Abkhazia, on the Black Sea coast bordering Russia, has been debilitating and bloody since the Soviet Union collapsed. It is not within the scope of this paper to examine the complex and emotive question of Abkhazian identity and rights, but three points must be clarified. First, Abkhazians were a minority within their own country and Georgians a majority at the time of Soviet collapse. Second, this was at least partly the consequence of Georgian or Soviet policy under the short-lived Georgian Republic and, more importantly, under Stalin. Third, Abkhazians and Georgians disagree on the nature of Abkhazian identity, with Georgians insisting that to be Abkhazian is also to be Georgian, much as the English might assume that being Cornish means that one is also English. Thus Georgians have tended to blame Abkhazian secession on the agency of Russians[1].

Finally, although it had no separate status under Soviet arrangements, there is also a sense of separateness about Megrelia (Mingrelia in Georgian) the inland province bordering Abkhazia. Megrelians speak their own language and have many of their own customs, certainly their own *cuisine*. They do not share the distinctive family names normally ending in -*vili* or -*ze* of the Kartli-Kakhetians. Megrelians, though distinct, are normally regarded as Georgians: Zviad Gamsakhurdi, the ultra-Georgian nationalist, was a Megrelian, though he also had a long-term vision of Caucasian Federation[2]. Laventi Beria, Stalin's chief of secret police, was also a Megrelian. Some Caucasian experts, however, insist on categorising Megrelians as non-Georgians[3].

Despite these complexities, Georgians identify with a very long history and see themselves as having occupied their land for thousands of years and possessing cultural attributes, including a language and a tradition of viticulture, which go back three millenia. (There is dispute about the origins of the Georgian alphabet, but it certainly dates back to the early Christian era.) For most of that history the land has been under threat: between the rise of Islam (by which time Georgia had already been an officially Christian country for over three centuries) to the eighteenth century, the country was invaded twenty seven times by Persian, Arab and Turkish armies. In 1783 Kartli-Kakheti became a protectorate of the Russian Empire and, after a particularly brutal Persian invasion at the end of the eighteenth century, Tsar Paul I annexed the country to the Russian Empire, abolishing all vestiges of independence the following year. Russia succeeded in annexing the whole of what is now Georgia over the next generation and for a century the country was under the direct rule of a Russian governor.

After the Russian Revolutions of 1917 Georgia was an independent country for less than four years until incorporated into the Soviet Union by the Red Army in 1921. The country had an elected Social Democratic (or 'Menshevik') government and a democratic constitution which was never finally ratified. In the Soviet period Georgian antipathy to Russian domination was muted by a number of factors including the outstanding success of leaders such as Stalin and Beria, but also a wide variety of career opportunities for Georgians. Soviet nationalities policy (which was, after all, designed by Stalin) also favoured Georgian interests in many respects, protecting the Georgian language and folk culture and securing huge markets for Georgian agricultural goods. However, hostility to Soviet dominance increased after Stalin's death in 1953 and particularly after Khruschev's 'secret speech' in 1956 denouncing Stalin. There were demonstrations and repression in Tbilisi: these feature much more prominently in contemporary Georgian mythology than in official Soviet accounts and it would be impossible here to make an accurate judgement between the two versions of history. It is important to note that after Stalin Georgia remained almost an extreme example of the paradoxes inherent in the Soviet conception of the "problem of the nationalities" (Stalin, 1947). In terms of the bases of political power it was a totally dependent country, militarily and economically so completely integrated into Russia that the industrial economy has since collapsed more than any other. On the other hand, Georgia remained a Georgian-speaking country whose folk traditions, utterly separate from those of Russia, were preserved in their entirety. Indeed, I have argued elsewhere that Georgian culture was better preserved under the Soviet Union than it would have been if western influences had been permitted (Allison, 1997). The intra-Soviet tourist industry helped encourage Georgian separateness in some ways and Eduard Shevardnadze, as General Secretary of the Georgian Communist Party in the 1970s, evolved policies which appealed to a certain kind of nationalist sentiment by, for example, devoting large resources to the conservation of Old Tbilisi. Occasionally, there was official Soviet objection to the cultural independence of Georgia: for example, in 1978 the "leading ideologist" of the Politburo, Yegor Ligachev, on a visit to the State University of Tbilisi, expressed the view that the university ought to increase the number of its courses in Russian and decrease the requirements of Georgian language and history. In their usual way the Georgian university officials nodded and took him to lunch. The demographic context of Soviet Georgia is also significant from that of many other republics. The proportion of Russians in the population never rose above 7%, which is a lower percentage than the English in Scotland or of Protestants in the Republic of Ireland. Unlike the Baltic States, Ukraine or Kazakhstan, for example, Russian-Georgian relations were never shaped by a colonising Russian population.

The recent history of Georgia has been nothing less than a disaster. On 9 April 1989, Soviet troops crushed nationalist demonstrations in Tbilisi, killing twenty people. In some ways this was an event parallel to the Easter Rising in Dublin in 1916 in that it converted many people to the nationalist cause and convinced many that it would ultimately succeed. As Soviet authority faded multi-party elections were held in October 1990 resulting in the victory of the nationalist leader Zviad Gamsakhurdia. In April 1991 the Georgian parliament formally declared national independence[4]. However, Gamsakhurdia's vindictiveness and economic ignorance, combined with the effects of the disintegration of the Soviet economic system caused a wild reversal of Gamsakhurdia's support and he was overthrown in January 1992 after an uprising in December 1991. The former Communist leader Eduard Shevardnadze was invited back to head a provisional government, a position which was confirmed by an election in October 1992.

Georgia entered a period of decline and chaos. Shevardnadze was only able to rule with the aid of gangsters, in particular the Mkhedrioni ("cavaliers") led by Djaba Ioseliani, who became deputy leader. Crime ruled the countryside, corruption the city; the war in Abkhazia was lost when Sukhumi fell in September 1993. An attempt to introduce a provisional currency (the "coupon") collapsed into hyper-inflation. By 1995 the economy had declined to 17% of its 1989 size (European Bank, 1995)[5]. Ghia Nodia, emerging as the leading Georgian intellectual interpreting his country to the outside world, commented "nobody else has ruined their own country as much as we ruined ours" (Nodia, 1995). However, since the failed attempt to assassinate Shevardnadze in August 1995 and his subsequent election, this time as President, in November, things have begun to improve steadily. Crime has reduced dramatically, small businesses has begun to revive and there is a reasonably stable currency, the *lari*.

Let me try to draw together some of the main strands of Georgian history as a prolegomenon to discussing Georgian sport. First, relations with Russia are deeply ambivalent. Historically, Russia has been a genuine protector of Georgia as well as an imperialist oppressor and the Soviet Union was naturally a source of Georgian pride. It was, after all, the vehicle which allowed a Georgian, Josef

Stalin (né Djugashvili) to become one of the most powerful men in the world. Georgians will curse Russians with one glass of wine and bristle with pride over the next because their fathers fought at Stalingrad. At some level, all Georgians except the very young are nostalgic for the Soviet Union, particularly for the "years of stagnation" under Brezhnev, when economic growth was 5% p.a., Georgia was a relaxed and ordered place, one of the most prosperous parts of the Union, when hunger did not even happen in nightmares and legions of Russian blondes arrived in summer with the specific objectives of a sun tan and a better acquaintance with Georgian men. Russia was never seen as a threat to Georgian culture and the continued existence of a Georgian society as it was to the societies of the Baltic states.

Second, Georgia has been in an abyss. Most people in Georgia will remember the nineties as a time when they were hijacked by gangsters, endured long winters without heat, put children to bed hungry, lost relatives to war, emigration and ethnic cleansing and saw their jobs destroyed. Given those experiences many things come to seem trivial and sport is one of them.

Third, Georgia has no real tradition of independence. Unlike the Baltic and former COMECON states, there was no legacy of pre-Russian institutions on which to draw. Thus, as I have argued elsewhere, Georgian civil society is profoundly weak (Allison, 1998). I have been surprised and fascinated, in a number of different contexts, about how important the flimsy legacy of the republic of 1917-21 is to Georgians: they seek precedents in it for the constitution, for property rights and for defining ethnic relations.

In what senses is Georgia a "divided society"? It is, first, an ethnically divided society, the proportion of 'Georgians' within the Georgian republic at the end of the Soviet period being estimated at 70-73% (rather less than the 77% black Africans in the 'rainbow nation' of South Africa.) In any case, we should be careful about what 'Georgian' means in this context. Some of the minorities who compose the remainder, including the Armenians, Azeris, Jews and even Russians have been welcome 'guests' in Georgia for a long time and their existence does not indicate 'division' in most of its implications. Old Tbilisi with its mosques, synagogues and three national varieties of orthodox church has been divided more like multi-cultural London than the long-term hatred of Belfast. Georgians really do believe that "the guest comes from God" and are rightly proud of their ancient multi-culturalism. Yet, at the same time, the conflict in Abkhazia has been played out with Balkan savagery typified by the statement of the Georgian general Karkarashvili that he was personally ready to send 100,000 Georgians to their deaths in order to kill 80,000 Abkhazians (that being the official Georgian figure for the total number of Abkhazians). The other great division has several different dimensions, including the cultural and the geo-political: it concerns Georgia's relations with Russia. It has already suggested that Georgian attitudes to a country which has been their protector and oppressor, their opportunity and obstacle to appearance on the world stage, are deeply ambivalent. That level of ambivalence is overlaid with disagreement as to how Georgia should pursue its interests with regard to Russia in the post-Soviet period. Russia has been politically meddlesome and economically unco-operative; forcing Georgia to rejoin the CIS in return for military help to Shevardnadze's government in defeating the Zviadist forces in 1993 was part of a short, sharp and horrible period in which Georgia within months faced both the loss of Abkhazia and the necessity of a formal climb-down in its aspirations to complete independence. Bruno Coppieters has detailed how the West has disappointed Georgian expectations of "rejoining" the mainstream of Europe (Coppieters, 1997); my own experiences of young Georgians in the early post-Soviet years were of hopelessly exaggerated expectations of what Georgia meant to Westerners, of western eagerness to buy Georgian goods and of the imminence of the arrival of NATO troops to protect Georgia. Since that time, the U.S. State Department has let out subtle but clear messages that Georgia is within a Russian sphere of influence and must secure a constructive accommodation with the Russian Federation. But Georgians are politically divided in quite complex ways about the future role and identity of their nation.

Yet these divisions must be understood in the context of a profound and powerful sense of Georgian unity. Georgians have a very strong sense of ancient lineage and a clear identity. Few cultures show such clear and distinct traits in everyday life, as when two or three Georgians are gathered together for a meal they will ritually toast their country, peace, women, parents and so on. This shared sense of Georgianness has been articulated to the extreme by nationalist writers, especially Gamsakhurdia whose curious account of Georgian legend and philology generates a sense of national "mission". It is difficult to explain such a powerful sense of identity, which is capable of over-riding other senses of division such as class and region. A sense like this is more present in small Western European nations such as Norway and Ireland then it is in the larger ones like France and England but it is, nevertheless, much weaker in those cases.

In terms of theories of nationalism, there is a strong sense of the kind of *ethnie* which is posited as the ancient origins of modern nations by Anthony Smith (1983, 1986). It is more difficult to cast the state in the role of ideologising the nation, as, for example, Ernest Gellner (1983) did, since twentieth century Georgia's experience of the state has principally been of the Soviet State, proselytising doctrines of 'internationalism' and a loyalty to the Soviet Motherland which coexisted with, but was supposedly more profound than, Georgian patriotism.

The consequences for Georgian sport

This has been a long prolegomenon, but I have been anxious to clarify some of the historical complexities which provide the context for Georgian sport. The most important aspect is negative: as of 1989 Georgian sport had no pre-Soviet or extra-Soviet existence. Georgia was still a rural backwater when the Red Army took it over in 1921 and the situation of Georgian sports authorities was not like that of the Czechs or Hungarians, with existing and successful national associations which had to accept Communist domination, but continued to run a national association and field national teams. Georgian sport was an entirely Soviet creation. Thus Georgian national sports associations were not able to act as vehicles for patriotism or nationalism as those in Scotland, Ireland and Wales have done (in different and complex ways) within the United Kingdom. Georgian national teams, unlike Hungarian footballers and Czechoslovak ice hockey players, never served as a focus for anti-Soviet feeling. Instead, Georgian sportsmen aspired to win medals at the Olympics for the Soviet Union and Georgian footballers aspired to play for the Soviet national team. At the height of the success of Georgian football in the late 1970s and early 1980s as many as seven Georgians took the field in the Soviet team.

I have often been curious as to the psychological realities of Soviet sports policy. The official rationale of the heavy Soviet investment in sport was that it, like the space race, was a rare opportunity to demonstrate the success of the Soviet system to the outside world, many other opportunities being denied by the conditions of the cold war (see Riordan, 1991). It always seemed more likely that the more effective role of the policy was in the 'near-abroad', demonstrating to the 'hundred nations' in the Russian Federation and fourteen other republics the strength and success of the 'one people of the Soviet Motherland'. Indeed, despite rumours of jealousies and ins and outs of favour of Russians and non-

Russians in Soviet teams, all the evidence suggests that it was an effective policy in this way. Asking Georgians in the 1990s, when they had every reason to resent Russians, whether they had felt pride in the "Soviet Motherland" when, for example, Soviet athletes mounted an Olympic rostrum, they have always admitted that they did, at least to some degree, though there is some evidence of hostility from the Tbilisi crowd to the Soviet football team, which played there in 1986. In the end, the story of Georgian reaction to Soviet sport seems to be a complex tale about a deep ambivalence. Sports-minded Georgian intellectuals are keen to qualify the apparent enthusiasm for Soviet representative sport with a number of riders. For example, support was much greater among working class people and the rural population than among educated people. It was also partly determined by the Georgian connections of the sport concerned; thus Georgians were much more likely to cheer for the Soviet football team if there were compatriots playing and highly likely to take an anti-Soviet stance in sports which had no Georgian connections at all (supporting Canada or Czechoslovakia against the USSR at ice hockey, for example). In any case the situation changed over time with pro-Soviet enthusiasm probably peaking in the period 1945-56, between the end of the 'Great Patriotic War' and the condemnation of Stalin, began to decline more rapidly with *glasnost* and the rise of nationalist propaganda in 1985 and was replaced by overt hostility in 1989. In this context, as in many others, we know that we are not faced with a situation of levels of support which might be arranged along a continuum, but of covert and contradictory emotional affiliations. I can, as they say, relate to this as a Eurosceptic who nevertheless passionately supports Europe in golf's Ryder Cup against the United States. In any case, Georgian teams face some attitudes of scepticism and ambivalence, as they are bound to from people whom the state once asked to identify with the world's mightiest sports machine and are obliged to support a small, impoverished, albeit talented, country.

On the other hand, Soviet sport did provide a sporting focus for Georgian patriotism. The most successful of Georgian football clubs, Dinamo Tbilisi, although associated in the usual way with the security forces, was an undoubtedly Georgian institution which was always represented by an overwhelming majority of Georgian players. Just as Catalan, Basque and Galician teams in the Spanish Football League can to a very considerable degree rely on a regional-national identity to provide them with consistent and passionate support, so could teams in the Soviet League from outside the Russian

Federation: Dinamo Tbilisi and Dinamo Kiev were the most notable and successful examples. Indeed they were the only Soviet winners of European club competitions.

In a sense, Dinamo played 'in Europe' every week, because they were always playing 'foreign' teams and could be assumed to be the standard bearers for Georgian pride and national identity. The parallel with Barcelona as a symbol of Catalan identity is limited, however. Under Franco's regime, between 1939 and 1975, the Spanish state did attempt overtly to suppress regional identity; in these conditions "Barça" became a sanctuary in which you could talk, sing and chant in Catalan and support for the team was a kind of subversion. But Soviet nationalities policy did not seek to repress identity in this way nor to deny that Georgia was a nation; it left language and folk culture (though, paradoxically, not sport) as legitimate symbols of the smaller national identity. Dinamo's greatest achievement was to win the European Cup-Winners' Cup in 1981 beating the East German side Karl Zeiss Jena 2-1 in Dusseldorf. Given that this was two clubs from Communist countries playing in West Germany, the crowd was actually the lowest ever recorded for a European final: the official figure is 9,000. This was something of a disappointment as Dinamo were used to playing home games in front of as many as 81,000 people. Perhaps what felt like the greatest achievement for Dinamo was when they knocked the otherwise all-conquering Liverpool out of the European Cup 4-2 on aggregate in 1979-80. Georgian reaction to this victory is amusingly described by Colin Thubron, not a football fan, in *Where Nights are Longest* (quoted in Rosen, 1991).

Before the beginning of the 1990 season the Georgian F.A. withdrew its teams from Soviet competition, established a Georgian Soccer Federation and instructed national players to play football for Georgia. The Soviet authorities did not accept this situation and it was only in 1993 that FIFA and UEFA recognised the Georgian Federation. There are, thus, two candidates for "first Georgian international match": 27 May 1990, a 2-2 draw with Lithuania and 7 September 1994, a 1-0 defeat by Moldova in a European Championship qualifying game.

In many respects, the break-up of the Soviet Union has been a disaster for Georgian sport. The whole system was a Soviet creation; it was within that system that institutions worked and individuals formulated and pursued their ambitions. Dinamo Tbilisi playing in a Georgian league is like Barcelona playing in a Catalan league or Newcastle United playing in a Northumbrian league. In November 1995 I watched the club's league game, against Durugi, a small-town club. I counted approximately two hundred people in the stadium, many of whom were more interested in asking me about the progress of Georgi Kinkladze at Manchester City than they were in the game and I left when the score was 8-0 to Dinamo.

Sadly, that was a fairly representative experience. Because Georgian sport was always a state activity and not based in a civil society, it has proved to have little durability. School and amateur teams have died and the sight of broken basketball hoops and overgrown football pitches is depressingly common in the Georgian countryside. In attempting to research a possible revival of Georgian sport, conducting interviews in late 1996 I often found myself talking at cross-purposes with my interviewees. I wanted to know what were the signs of Georgian sports moving on to a voluntary, spontaneous basis, of people organising teams and clubs despite hardship. The replies often failed to understand the idea of voluntary activity: sport could not be prioritised in circumstances of poverty and disorder such as Georgia had experienced. Georgian sport would revive when real capitalism came to the country and large firms were prepared to subsidise sports facilities and activities.

Thus the de-Sovietisation of Georgian sport and, for example, the creation of the Georgian Football Federation were anything but a shift to a system of sport founded in civil society. Indeed, at one extreme it was a shift from state communism to state gangsterism. For the first half of the 1990s the committee of Dinamo Tbilisi consisted, with one exception, of members of the Mkhedrioni, and in 1995 when it seemed as if a genuinely privately owned club, Samtredia, might win the Georgian championship there were rumours of dire threats if they actually were successful. I cannot vouch for the truth of the rumours, but Dinamo Tbilisi were again victorious. The Soviet period may have ended, but its *étatiste* assumptions live on; for example, after Georgia's perceived failure in the Atlanta Olympics of 1996 the Minister of Sport, Kakhi Asatiani, called for the restoration of greater state control over sport[6].

Because the Georgian economy and Georgian sport are both in such a parlous state sportsmen of professional standard are either in exile or aspire to be in exile. The Georgian sporting press is full of tales of the unimaginably high wages paid by Manchester City, of the equally unimaginable inhospitable attitudes of Germans (and of their constant cheating!), of the iniquities of the British regulations on work-permits, which insist on a player having played in three quarters of internationals in a two-year period, when applied to a war-torn country and so on[7].

The question of ethnic tension in post-Soviet Georgian football is complex. It would be quite easy to mount a case that it had been considerable. Spartak Tskhinvali (South Ossetia) and Dinamo Sukhumi (Abkhazia) withdrew from the Georgian championship in 1990, the latter to take part in 'CIS' competition as, for example, Neftchi of Baku did (though they have not yet played against the Armenian team Ararat Yerevan who also play in the larger competition). Georgian football is undoubtedly more ethnically homogenous than it was in Soviet times, though there are Azeri and Armenian players. On the other hand, Georgian football has always been dominated by Kartli-Khaketians and relations with Ossetes still seem cordial in many respects. A number of Georgians now play for Alania Vladikhavkaz in North Ossetia in the Russian Federation. Their trainer is Ahrik Tsveiba, formerly of Dinamo Tbilisi who is an Abkhazian from Gudauta, the centre of Abkhazian separatism. He has spoken in moving terms of his nostalgia for the old multi-ethnicism of Georgian football, just as people have told me of life in Soviet Sukhumi, when Georgians, Abkhazians, Russians and Greeks mixed as friends and neighbours. (For that matter, it is all reminiscent of descriptions of Sarajevo under Tito). Given the emotions surrounding the Abkhazian situation it would be difficult to imagine Tsveiba working in Georgia at the moment, but an Ossetian, Sergei Gutsaev, is currently coaching the Georgian youth team. Georgian journalists habitually ask the Georgian players who play in Vladikhavkaz how surprised they are to find themselves playing in the Russian Federation, given that Russia and Georgia were perceived (by Georgians, at least) to be fighting a proxy war over Abkhazia in 1990-93 and the issues are still not resolved. In April 1997, to celebrate the centenary of Russian football, an inter-parliamentary tournament was held in Sochi in Southern Russia, near Abkhazia. The Georgian parliament was invited to send a team (which included the MP Menucher Machaidze who had been a Dinamo player in the 1970s). But the Georgian team were faced with the presence of an Abkhazian team which was clearly unacceptable to them. In the end, the Russians declared that the Abkhazians could remain but not compete, which was satisfactory to the Georgians.

The mixture is complex, but also familiar. The natural spirit of sportsmanship demands that everybody should be able to compete fairly with everybody else. There is nostalgia not only in general for Soviet ethnic mixing, but in specifically football terms for the days in which a Tbilisi fan only cared about whether a player was giving his all for Dinamo and not about the ethnic implications of his surname. Many people (including Tsveiba) regret deeply as a footballing issue the absence of Georgian clubs from a wider CIS-Russian framework of competition. At the same time although some footballers have led peace missions (Gutsaev to South Ossetia, for example) others, as Tsveiba points out, have taken up arms and fought against the nationalities of former team mates. We are left with the old banality that sport aspires to be above ethnic and other social conflicts, but more often than not it is dragged down by them.

It is likely to be decades rather than years before Dinamo Tbilisi bestrides Europe again and their decline is in many respects typical of what has happened in Georgian sport. However, it would be wrong to conclude that there is no basis for the revival of any sport. Wrestling has shown a capacity for spontaneous grass roots organisation; it is one of the few sports with genuine roots in Georgian society going back to pre-Soviet times; it is also, of course, a sport which requires relatively limited resources. In 1994 student unions began to organise their own sporting competitions, starting with a national student basketball league. The generation born since about 1975, which has had much of its education in the post-Soviet period, is, in my experience, markedly different from its elders in that its members have a more intuitive grasp of the nature of market economics and of spontaneous activity.

Finally, I think the power of international civil society should not be underestimated. In a very important way international football matches against major countries open Georgia up to the values and practices of the west. This was the emphasis of the press treatment of the Georgia–England World Cup qualifying game in November 1996. Attending the game, I found that the predominant reaction of Georgians was not a great will to win, but a desire that it should be a high quality sporting contest, though many people were surprised by the fanaticism of the England fans, believing people from prosperous and important countries like England to be neither particularly passionate nor particularly patriotic. My abiding memory of the game, in which Glen Hoddle's England shut the Georgians out completely in a 2-0 win, is of England fans demanding (in a sort of song) "Can you hear the Georgians sing? I can't hear a fucking thing" as the Georgian crowd politely clapped England's passing.

Perhaps the best example of the connection to an international civil society is the Georgian Rugby Union which organised itself on an independent basis with a full range of officials, including junior and veterans sections, in 1995. Paradoxically, the Georgian R.U. portrays itself as the inheritors of an ancient, partly Georgian game called Lelo, though is happy to be aided considerably by the International Rugby Board and is aiming to compete at the World Cup in 1999 and the Olympics in 2000 (see Georgian RFU, 1996). In sport, as in other fields, I am convinced that the best hope for the development of a healthy civil society in Georgia and in other post-Soviet states lies in close contact with international and western organisations which alone can "normalise" the situation.

Notes

[1] For a story about the Georgian-Abkhazian situation and its background, see Allison and Kukhianidze (1995). A highly polemical reply by George Hewitt, not used by the *New Statesman*, has been circulated on email from the address <GH2@soas.ac.uk>.

[2] For an account of his intensely dramatic world-view see Gamsakhurdia 1991.

[3] This is true of Professor Hewitt.

[4] For a full account of these events see Aves 1991.

[5] See Drone and Robinson 1995, p. 12.

[6] I would like to thank the following Georgian journalists for talking to me and introducing me to further contacts: Alexander Breyadze, Slava Sologhashvili, Akami Grimadze and Sandro Bregadze, all of the *Georgian Times* and Zviad Kozidze (editor) and Bidzina Makashvili of *7 Days* magazine.

[7] I am grateful to my friend Alexander Kukhianidze for finding and translating interviews from a variety of Georgian press sources.

References

Allison, L. (1997) 'The concept of civil society in Georgia, Thailand and South Africa', *South African Journal of International Affairs*: Vol. 4, No. 2: pp.18-39.

———— (forthcoming, 1998) 'Sport and civil society', *Political Studies*.

Allison, L. and Kukhianidze, N. (1995) 'Letter from Georgia: An everyday story of ethnic cleansing', *New Statesman* 27 January: pp. 12-13.

Aves, J. (1991) *Paths to national independence in Georgia 1987-90*. London: School of Slavonic and East European Studies, University of London.

Coppieters, B. (1997) 'Georgia in Europe: The idea of a periphery in international relations', in B. Coppieters, D. Trenin and A. Zverer (eds) *Commonwealth and independence in Eurasia*. London: Frank Cass.

Drone, K. and Robinson, A. (1995) 'Strong growth forecast for Eastern Europe', *Financial Times*, Thursday November 2nd: p. 12.

European Bank for Reconstruction and Development Transition (1995) *Annual Report*.

Gamsakhurdia, Z. (1991) *The spiritual mission of Georgia*. Tbilisi: Ganatleba.

Gellner, E. (1983) *Nations and nationalism*. Oxford: Blackwell.

Georgian RFU (1996) *Georgia's Rugby Union* pamphlet.

Nodia, G. (1995) 'Georgia's identity crisis', *Journal of Democracy* Vol. 6, No. 1: p. 104.

Riordan, J. (1991) *Sport, politics and communism*. Manchester: Manchester University Press.

Rosen, R. (1991) *Introduction to the Georgian Republic*, Odyssey, Hong Kong, quote p. 106.

Smith, A. D. (1983) *Theories of nationalism*. New York: Holmes and Muer.

———. (1986) *The ethnic origins of nations*. Oxford: Blackwell.

Stalin, J. (1947) *Marxism and the national and colonial question* English Edition. Moscow: Moscow Publishing House.

FOOTBALL IN THE YEMENS:
INTEGRATION, IDENTITY AND NATIONALISM
IN A DIVIDED COUNTRY

Thomas B. Stevenson
Anthropology, Ohio University-Zanesville

Abdul-Karim Alaug
Department of Sociology, Sana'a University

In global terms, 1990 is probably most notable for the official collapse of Soviet style communism, Iraq's invasion of Kuwait, and the reunification of the two Germanys. Often overlooked amid these events was another national reconciliation, the May 22 unification of the Yemen Arab Republic (YAR — North Yemen) and the People's Democratic Republic of Yemen (PDRY — South Yemen) as the Republic of Yemen. Outsiders frequently portray the Yemens as an Arab version of the Germanys and superficially the joining of these long-divided nations seems similar. Like Germany, Yemen was divided between capitalist and socialist elements. But the differences were significant. The German separation lasted 45 years and was concluded by the Federal Republic of Germany wholly absorbing the bankrupt German Democratic Republic. The Yemens were last united in 1658. South Yemen was a British colony and protectorate for more than a century. The Ottomans occupied North Yemen and, after that Empire's defeat, the nation was an isolated, Muslim theocracy. Their union was a power sharing merger of financially troubled nations.

How could two states with such divergent historical and contemporary backgrounds merge successfully? Despite the "laissez-faire" and "state control" labels and rhetoric, each state's economy had comparable mixes of public and private enterprise. Carapico (1993) suggests that as third world nations and clients of industrial states, the Yemens followed very similar development courses. It was not their differences but what both Yemens shared — poverty and dependence — that dictated economic planning. Despite substantial progress, on the verge of union, the Yemens remained among the world's least developed countries[1], had comparably low per capita incomes, counted migrants' remittances as a major portion of gross domestic product, and relied on foreign aid.

Economic similarities may explain the mechanics of unification but of much greater significance was the popular appeal of a single Yemen. Historically, Yemeni identity was based on claimed common heritage associated with the glories of the Sabean, Qataban, and Himyarite kingdoms. Although local and regional relationships took precedence over other, broader associations, the influential 'one Yemeni people' category was a designation drawn upon situationally. Each government encouraged affiliation with its polity, but they recognized the symbolic power and resonance of this more inclusive, albeit elusive, identity.

In the twenty years preceding unification, the Yemens pursued nation-building. State policies sought to integrate all areas into national systems, create connections that transcended traditional identities, and demonstrate national status on the international stage. At the same time, each Yemen competed with the other to extend its hegemony. Football matches were venues in which the states tried to score their goals. Despite strained finances, each government invested a portion of its limited resources in athletic programmes.

The Yemens were hardly unique in using sports for political purposes, especially to incorporate autonomous regions, mold national identity, and encourage nationalism. During the past quarter century, all the Arabian Peninsula states have funded sports development. The best financed and most successful programmes are in the Gulf Cooperation Council (GCC) states (Oman, Saudi Arabia, Kuwait, United Arab Emirates, Qatar, and Bahrain), each of which used oil revenues to underwrite clubs and to construct first-class facilities (Younger, 1977; *Physician and Sportsmedicine*, 1978; Reed, 1980; Wagner, 1980; Jenkins, 1984; Hunnicutt, 1985; Chakra, 1988; Shamleh, 1989; Rosandich, 1991; Wagg, 1995).

Like other emerging states, the GCC countries recognized the domestic and international importance of sports. Internally, sports contests divert attention from social, economic, and political problems[2] in part because their structure suggests equality and so presents the illusion of democracy, a consideration perhaps more salient in these monarchies[3]. Competitions encourage the formation of civil associations that are a basis for regional integration into the state. Externally, a team legitimizes statehood just as do a flag, a national airline, or United Nations membership. Whatever its prospects for success, participation in the Olympics or other international tournament approbates the state's status. This may be particularly significant for Middle Eastern countries whose citizens are more often imagined by Westerners as terrorists or camel-riding shaykhs. Beyond their foreign policy implications, international competitions promote nationalism.

Sport as agency of integration, identity and nationalism

Our understanding of these sociopolitical roles of sports is informed by Janet Lever's (1983) analysis of football in Brazil. In a nation rent by regional, cultural, and racial differences, Brazilians defined their loyalty and identity through local rather than national allegiances. This insular focus inhibited the development of the broader-based, civil connections necessary to the creation of a modern, integrated state. Lever argued that football contributed to societal integration, national identity, and nationalism. Sports were a bridge, drawing on elemental, regional connections while encouraging the formation of more inclusive associations. "Sport's paradoxical ability to reinforce societal cleavages while transcending them makes soccer, Brazil's most popular sport, the perfect means of achieving a more perfect union between multiple groups. Local soccer teams publicly sanction and express society's deepest primordial sentiments, while the phenomenal success of the national team has enormously heightened all Brazilians' pride in their citizenship" (Lever, 1983: pp. 6-7).

Competition is a key to understanding sport's powerful, if ambiguous, integrative roles. We were led to this realization while reading Korr's (1986) history of the British football club West Ham United. Members' financial and emotional investments are overt expressions of their attachment to and pride in their team, but, we deduced, their identification with their club could be validated only in relation to other teams. The paradox is that while clubs represent regional loyalty or identity, endorsement of this position requires admission to the state's sports system. Even if a club opposes the state, making this statement depends on participating in the state structure, an act implying acceptance of the government's dominance and validating its legitimacy. As agents of integration, sports teams and contests convey multiple symbolic messages whose meaning is heightened in the ritual settings of matches.

Gramsci (1988) labels this acceptance of the views of those in power as hegemony. It is a balance between the force of political society, the formal institutions of power, and the consent of civil society, the semi-autonomous organizations of popular culture. Dominant social groups try to manufacture consent in civil society. As Hargreaves (1986: pp. 205-223) notes, because of the importance attached to sports, they are a significant factor in achieving hegemony and so encouraging identification with those in power. However, since civil organizations are outside formal control, these associations may express opposition or resistance to the power structure.

Baker's (1987) examination of sports and nation-building in recently independent African states suggests how sport extends a government's hegemony and establishes a basis for a new identity. He argues that because European sports are free of ethnic associations, they serve as a common denominator that crosscuts traditional loyalties. Support for clubs cultivates consent, extends hegemony, and so fosters integration and identity. Moreover, when governments certify sports stars as national rather than local heroes they promote citizens' identification with them and encourage a national consensus. Stuart's (1996) analysis of football's pan-ethnic attraction in colonial Rhodesia (now Zimbabwe) illustrates many of Baker's generalizations, especially integration and identity through sport, but in a society seeking to achieve independence. In revolutionary Cuba, the government sponsored sports programmes are ways to achieve two sociopolitical goals, promoting egalitarianism and national identity (Pettavino and Pye, 1994). The Nicaraguan government sought to develop a collective mentality through baseball (Wagner, 1988). In each instance, participation in civil associations extended governmental hegemony.

Participation in civil society contributes to national identity formation, the "subjective feelings and valuations of any population which possesses common experiences and many shared cultural characteristics" (Jarvie, 1993: p. 61). For example, Archetti (1996) shows how the largely illusory idea of a unique Argentinean style of football is emblematic of national identity. Sörlin's (1996) analysis of skiing in Sweden illustrates how an introduced sport was reconstructed as a national pastime tying important cultural elements to notions of identity. Jarvie (1991) and Sugden and Bairner (1993) discuss how unique sporting activities, respectively the Scottish Highland Games and the Gaelic games of hurling and football, shaped modern cultural identities.

Yet as MacClancy (1996) cautions, sport-based identities exist on many levels and with only a few exceptions, none are exclusive. This suggests both the fluidity of identity and constant reinterpretation of hegemonic relations. As civil associations, sports clubs provide a focus of communal identity. This may take many forms. "Sports, in sum, may be used to fulfil a plethora of functions: to define more sharply the already established boundaries of moral and political communities; to assist in the creation of new social identities; to give physical expression to certain social values and to act as a means of reflecting those values; to serve as potentially contested space by opposed groups" (MacClancy 1996: p. 7).

Nationalism is a strong emotional attachment to the idea of the nation; it is a bond welded through symbols. Benedict Anderson (1991: pp. 1-7) argues that modern nation-states are "imagined communities", bound together not by actual ties but shared national cultural elements. Llobera (1994: pp. ix-xi) notes that the nation is conceptualized as a culturally-defined, quasi-sacred community, qualities that may explain the seemingly visceral response to national symbols. Recently Klein (1997: p. 9) has added clarity by introducing autonationalism, a self-referential term, describing "political and social relations that foster an identity with the nation-state". A state's social and cultural institutions provide this identity by arousing feelings of loyalty and pride by focusing on national accomplishments or by engendering cohesion through hostility to outsiders.

Speaking of Europe, Hobsbawm (1983: p. 1; 1990: pp. 140-142), contends that identification with the nation and nationalism are expressed through the media and sports. According to Kellas (1991: p. 21), "The most popular form of nationalist behaviour in many countries is sport, where masses of people become highly emotional in support of their national team". Nowhere is this more apparent than in international competitions such as the Olympics where citizens, seeing their nation accorded status on the world stage, experience autonationalist feelings.

Even the success of individual athletes can stimulate national pride. Klein's (1991) analysis of Dominican baseball shows how the game and its players are an important national focus in a country whose culture and economy are dominated by the United States. Unable to compete on equal terms, Dominicans resist American hegemony and find expression for their nationalist sentiments through the success that individual baseball players achieve in the American major leagues.

Baker (1987) argues international sports competitions are a source of visibility and prestige for newly independent African states[4] even when their athletes are not victorious. Nevertheless, often, winning is an important source of legitimation. For Cuba's leadership, their athletes' phenomenal performances in regional and worldwide tournaments confirm the success of their revolution, counter the hegemony of the dominant powers, and stimulate national pride.

As many scholars note, national identity and nationalism can exist even without a formally recognized polity[5]. In colonies the indigenous population may use sport as a vehicle for expressing opposition to the colonizer[6]. Stuart's (1996) Rhodesian case illustrates how the sports field became the ground upon which colonizer and colonized contended for control of a nation whose status was in transition. James (1984), Patterson (1969), and St. Pierre (1995) explain that for West Indians defeating their former British colonizers sparks nationalist passions that transcend the boundaries of the individual states from which their team's players are selected. Here the 'nation' refers to a geographic region. Outside the sports context, Trinidadians or Jamaicans identity with their states, not a West Indian entity.

The reverse situation, where national sentiments exist within a segment of a state, also obtains, as is shown in another chapter in this book. Afrikaner nationalism was closely tied to rugby. Victories over South Africans of British ancestry gave substance to Afrikaners' feelings of identity and nationalism. Jarvie and Walker (1994), Duke and Crolley (1996), and Moorhouse (1996) each address nationalism within the countries comprising the United Kingdom. Boyle (1994), Finn, (1991), and Murray (1984) illustrate how supporters of Celtic, a Glasgow football club, exhibit strong Irish nationalist sentiments. In none of these cases does the nation correspond with the state.

This literature review suggests that sports competitions promote political integration, shape multiple identities, and encourage nationalist sentiments. In this article, we use data from the People's Democratic Republic of Yemen and the Yemen Arab Republic to illustrate these points. After establishing the historical and social settings, we address sport in the two states. The primary focus is the twenty-year period before unification during which each country used sport organizations to counter regionalism, foster national identity, promote nationalism, and compete with each other. Finally, we speculate on why their sports systems were similarly structured and how these contributed to the sense of nationalism manifested at unification.

Background and social setting

Yemen occupies the southwest corner of the Arabian Peninsula (see Map 1). The quadrant is not all desert, but much of the topography is harsh. Climate and natural resources favour the area bordering the Red Sea (the former North Yemen) over the region lying along the Arabian Sea coast (the former South Yemen).

North Yemen's Red Sea coastal littoral and eastern desert abutting Saudi Arabia are arid zones, but these regions are bisected by a rugged, monsoon-watered mountain range. These highland areas enjoy a temperate climate and most parts receive sufficient annual rains to support a cereals-based economy. The majority of Yemeni live in this region known by the Romans as Arabia Felix. Historically these highlanders lived in dispersed, often isolated agricultural villages. While this pattern continues, since the late 1970s improvements in transportation and infrastructure have spurred population shifts into the principal cities of Sana'a, Ta'izz, and al-Hodeidah.

Map 1:   Administrative Map of the Republic of Yemen

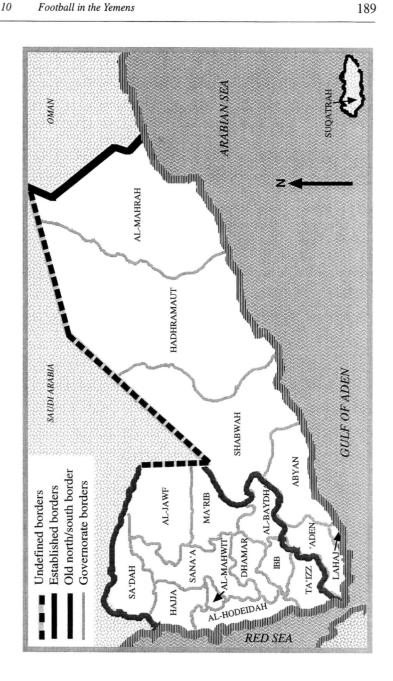

South Yemen's mountains lie outside the monsoon rain shadow. Apart from the vast, verdant, and densely populated Wadi Hadhramaut, most of the region is arid. Population size and distribution reflect the country's limited natural resources. Geographically larger than the north, the south has only one-quarter as many people. Most inhabitants live in Arabian Sea coast cities, such as 'Aden and al-Mukalla, or in the Hadhramaut towns of Tarim or Shibam; the remainder of the population is dispersed.

Yemeni society is crosscut by cultural, religious, and political divisions. All Yemeni speak Arabic, are Muslims, and share a sense of common identity, but the appearance of homogeneity is superficial. There are many local dialects of Arabic, and although the theological and ritual differences are slight, Yemeni are divided along sectarian lines. Inhabitants of the northern half of North Yemen follow the Zaydi school, a moderate form of Shi'a Islam from whose ranks that nation's religious and political leader used to be selected. Residents of South Yemen and the southern portion of North Yemen adhere to the Shafi'c legal school of Sunni Islam.

Despite recent infrastructural improvements, rugged terrain has sustained many variants of Yemeni culture. These differences are apparent in subsistence, attire, residence, and affiliations. These are not muted distinctions. Just as the coastal dweller is identified by his dialect, dress, and food so the highland tribesman is distinguished by his speech, diet, costume, and dagger. Parochialism is institutionalized. The most widespread feature of Yemeni culture and a core identity component (Varisco, 1986) is the daily chewing of qat leaves (Kennedy, 1987: pp. 100-1). Political leaders often used regional and social differences as grounds for pitting one group against another. While modern communication has lessened regionalism, Yemeni continue to define themselves through kinship and local affiliations.

External forces also shaped identity. The Ottomans twice occupied portions of the country (1538-1636 and 1849-1918) but owing to an often rebellious populace, Yemen's integration into that empire remained marginal. In 1839, the British established a coaling station in the southern port of 'Aden. A brief war in 1873 curbed Turkish designs on South Arabia, legitimized British organization of 'Aden's hinterlands into protectorates, and established the limits of each side's control. In 1904, these spheres of influence were formally demarcated by the Anglo-Ottoman line[7] that created North Yemen and South Yemen. This border was recognized by tribes living along it and by the international community. When the Turkish defeat in World War I forced their withdrawal, the traditional religious and political leader, the imam, regained power. The imam challenged British control in the south but the division of the Yemens was reconfirmed by the 1934 Treaty of Sana'a.

The British forged agreements with tribal leaders, creating two buffers around the seaport, and gradually expanded their suzerainty from the Bab al-Mandab to Oman. In 1963 the Federation of South Arabia was formed when the Eastern and Western protectorates were joined with 'Aden Colony. At the same time, liberation groups began an armed struggle that, in 1967, resulted in independence for the People's Republic of South Yemen (PRSY). In 1970, the socialist-leaning state was renamed the People's Democratic Republic of Yemen (PDRY).

In the north, the imam's xenophobia kept the Kingdom of Yemen ideologically and technically isolated until the 1962 coup d'état installed a modernist, republican government. The Yemen Arab Republic (YAR) that emerged in 1970 from an eight-year long civil war followed the capitalist economic model.

The border between the states was an important political symbol but the flow of Yemeni in either direction was generally unhindered. As a result, during the imamate, heavily taxed Shafi'c farmers and businessmen from the southern part of North Yemen sought less repressive conditions and better opportunities in 'Aden (Halliday, 1975). After South Yemen adopted socialism, many 'Adeni businessmen moved to the YAR.

Relations between the Yemens were strained and grew more so in 1970 when each adopted new constitutions placing them on different ideological paths. The states fought a brief border war in 1972 that concluded with their signing the Cairo Agreement, a treaty that included a plan for union. However, over the next 18 years political differences and stormy relations precluded its implementation. Ideologic differences, verbal skirmishes, attempted subversions, a 1979 border war, and coups d'etat and assassinations thwarted unionists' dreams. It was not until 1990 that the two presidents officially reconciled their differences and formed a power sharing government. The union was fragile and the balanced power arrangement short-lived. A two-month civil war in 1994 resulted in the defeat of the forces of the former south.

On the popular level Yemeni embraced union enthusiastically (Sobh, 1991) and saw it as the fulfillment of a long held dream. Yemeni seemed to hunger for unification, but this sensation resulted more from a created than a real sense of deprivation. "Since the end of World War II, modern political discourse has increasingly focused on the notion of one Yemeni nation and the sacred goal of its unification — i.e., *wahida*" (Burrowes, 1995: p. 398). Although at times unity seemed an indeterminate objective grounded in ancient history, the connections were stronger and contemporary. For most of this century, strong trade and labour relations linked North Yemen and 'Aden Colony. Indeed, the family origins of many PDRY political figures were across the border.

Football in Yemen

Before union the Yemens used football competitions as instruments of integration, identity, and nationalism. In the 1950s, some South Yemeni football clubs[8] were linked with Arab nationalism. In the 1960s, anti-colonialism was evident in clubs' connections with liberation movements. After independence, sports promoted integration, identity, and socialist ideology. In North Yemen, football was a minor force before 1962 when the game became an expression of the revolution. After 1970, football's role was similar to that in the south, integrating autonomous areas and identity formation. In both countries, football's penetration of rural areas corresponded with the expansion of government hegemony. While national teams represented statehood and nationalism, matches between the two states promoted national identity and pan-Yemeni nationalism.

Football in South Yemen: The pre-independence era

European sports, particularly football, were introduced to South Yemen in the 1880s. Although sports were segregated, with only the native elite playing alongside the colonists (Ma'tuq, 1981: p. 23), other Yemeni competed for clubs sponsored by expatriates, often Indian nationals. Initially limited to 'Aden, football soon diffused into the surrounding areas. The sport's growth was less dramatic in the separately-administered, largely rural protectorates.

From the 1920s, when ordinary Yemeni were permitted to form sanctioned clubs[9], until World War II the number of clubs grew steadily. Typically teams were loosely organized neighbourhood associations. In response to the increase in clubs, in 1934 the colonial authorities appointed the 'Aden Sport Committee (ASC) to oversee sports. One of the committee's responsibilities was to guard against clubs turning into political platforms. The government's concern stemmed from its experience with nationalist clubs in Cairo (Marks, 1985: p. 36). These incidents suggest that, like cricket in the West Indies, football in the region was associated with resistance to colonialism.

The Committee organized a popular annual championship in which six Yemeni clubs participated (Ma'tuq, 1965: p. 41-42)[10]. After World War II, these tournaments were opened to expatriate teams. The ASC pursued an integrative policy and arranged matches between teams from 'Aden and Hadhramaut.

In the 1950s Yemeni were increasingly persuaded by Arab nationalist and anti-colonial ideas that drew inspiration from the 1952 Egyptian Revolution. Arab unity and national independence were discussed in clubs and members are credited with helping to orchestrate the struggle against colonialism[11]. In 1955 club leaders challenged British control and established an independent sports council, the Sport Federation. Shortly this group was reconstituted as the 'Adeni Football Federation (AFF). Apparently because these new associations were symbolic of the era's nationalist and anti-colonial posture, most clubs in 'Aden aligned with the new association.

No tournaments were held until 1958 when the ASC regained ascendency over the AFF. However, the lack of sanctioned competitions did not dampen, and may have increased, interest in football clubs, although probably not for athletic reasons. The number of clubs in the 'Aden area rose to 30 clubs by 1958 (Ma'tuq, 1965: pp. 118-119)[12]. It is likely that the suspension of official competition added weight to the notion that clubs were forces of unity, identity, and nationalism.

Sports clubs began to take overtly political actions in 1959 when they boycotted the South Yemen football championship as a protest against French colonial policies in Algeria. This was followed by clubs supporting an 'Aden labourers' strike in 1960, boycotting a match to protest the 1963 formation of the Federation of South Arabia[13], and organizing and participating in riots and strikes in solidarity with the 1962 coup d'état in North Yemen. Nationalist sentiments were furthered by visits of teams from Sudan and Egypt and an 'Aden team tour to Egypt.

During the 1960s, sports figures were active in the armed struggle against the British (ar-Riyadhah, 1991: p. 4) and clubs were allied to independence groups, principally the National Liberation Front (NLF) and the Front for the Liberation of Occupied South Yemen (FLOSY). As Table 1(following page) shows, the number of clubs increased dramatically — from 49 in 1962 (Ma'tuq, 1965: p. 137) to 62 in 1965 and to 100 when independence was achieved in 1967 (Ma'tuq, 1981: p. 130). Growth alone may not indicate widespread nationalism, but the 22 clubs in Hadhramaut suggest its penetration.

Football in the People's Republic of South Yemen: Consolidation and integration

On November 30, 1967, the British granted independence to the People's Republic of South Yemen. In the same year, the new state's sport organization affiliated with FIFA. Article 28 of the 1970 constitution established the state's responsibility

Table 1:   South Yemen and PDRY sports clubs, 1958-1990

Governorate[1]*	1958	1962	1965	1968 Consolidation		1973 Consolidation		1975 Consolidation		1985
				Before	After	Before	After[6]	Before	After[9]	
'Aden	30	48	61	64	15[4]	23	8	7	5	7
Lahaj	1	1	1	8	8	8	4	4	2	6
Abyan	-		6	6	4	4	4	4	6
Shabwah	-		-	-	-	-	-	-	7
Hadhramaut	-		22/17	13[5]	13	11[7]	11[8]	11	12
al-Mahrah	-		-	-	-	-	-	-	4
Totals	31[2]	49	62	100[3]	42	48	27	26	22	42

*Prior to 1967 there were three administrative areas: 'Aden, the Western Protectorate, and the Eastern Protectorate. After 1967, six governorates were established. Abyan, Lahaj, and the western portion of Shabwah were created from the Western Protectorate. The remainder of Shabwah, Hadhramaut, and al-Mahrah were created from the Eastern Protectorate.

Notes:
1. See Map 1 for governorate locations.
2. All clubs were in the vicinity of 'Aden city; the Lahaj club was counted as an 'Aden club in some records
3. There is an unreconcilable variation in club numbers; but the total is reported as 100.
4. Six clubs were closed and three of the 15 were specialized in sports other than football.
5. Eight clubs were in coastal towns and five clubs in rural areas.
6. This consolidation only occurred in 'Aden and Lahaj governorates.
7. Two clubs appear to have disbanded.
8. Six clubs were in coastal towns and five clubs were in rural areas.
9. Only one club was permitted per district. This does not apply to major cities.

Source: Compiled from Ma'tuq (1965; 1981) and Ministry of Youth and Sports records

for the all-around development of the younger generation (Bäskau, 1981)[14]. Sports governance was reorganized to conform with state ideology. The 'Aden Sport Federation (the former AFF) was dissolved and replaced by the Yemeni Football Federation (YFF). To promote integration into and identification with the state, clubs that had supported the opposition parties were disbanded. This pared the number of clubs from 100 to 42 including a 76 per cent attrition in the number of 'Aden clubs. These reductions showed that the rules applied uniformly, that the capital city was not a special case, and that all regions were treated equally.

The YFF was superseded in 1973 by the Supreme Council for Sports. To hasten integration, the SCS reduced the number of clubs through mergers. Again, the most dramatic decrease, from 23 clubs to eight, was in 'Aden. In 1975, SCS carried out a second, smaller round of consolidations and decreed a limit of one club to each regional centre.

Merging clubs forced disparate groups together. Whether in provincial capitals or district centres, coalescence as a single team weakens parochialism, establishes a new basis for loyalty, and requires participation in civil society. Although each team has a regional identity, validation of its uniqueness requires joining the club system, a process that encourages the transition from traditional ties to national affiliation. As in Brazil, Yemeni football matches dramatize symbolic conflict between regions even as they instil a sense of common identity among previously separated people.

With these policies in place, the number of clubs grew steadily from the mid1970s until 1990 (see Table 1). The 22 clubs in 1975 increased to 42 by 1985. At unification there were 47 clubs, 17 in urban areas and governorate capitals, the remainder in district centres. Both growth and distribution suggest widespread rural penetration, participation in civil society, and political integration.

Like other socialist states, the PDRY advocated physical culture — a combination of physical and mental development. However, this ideology was not integral to club structure. The state sponsored its youth ideological and cultural activities through the Union of Democratic Yemeni Youth. This government-controlled, well-financed organization oversaw cultural programmes.

Club structure was governed by the Supreme Council for Sports. The often symbolic office of club president was held by locally prominent men[15]. Clubs were sanctioned by SCS but received little financial support. Clubs sponsored non-sport activities such as underwriting public lectures, organizing trips to other areas of the country, or subsidizing theatre, dance, or musical groups' performances during national holidays.

Football in North Yemen: The imamate era

Comparatively little is known about football in North Yemen (Kingdom of Yemen) before the revolution. Returning migrant workers repatriated the game to the Ta'izz area by 1900 and expatriates introduced it in Sana'a by 1930 (Stevenson, 1989a). Probably because of its modern connotations, the game achieved some popularity. By the mid-1940s, Sana'a, Ta'izz, and al-Hodeidah each had one well-known team[16]. While the number of clubs in these principal cities increased during the late 1950s — Sana'a had at least seven clubs — the rate of growth was well below that in 'Aden where nationalism found voice in sports.

North Yemen's imams were isolationists yet they took only passing notice of the growing interest in football. Like the ASC, the imams' preeminent concern was that clubs might participate in or serve as covers for political activity. A 1950s incident justifies his concern. The team associated with the School of Islamic Sciences named itself "Republic" (al-Jumhuriyah). The imam correctly interpreted this as a political statement, was angered by it, and forced the club to change its name. Al-Marwani (1987) intimates that clubs were relatively safe havens for reformers, but the imam was no fool, had a history of suppressing opposition, and was attentive to the implications of foreign influences. While clubs may have opposed the theocracy, their statements were muted and not heard by most people.

Football in the Yemen Arab Republic: Revolution, integration, and identification

The 1962 coup d'état overthrew the imam and established the Yemen Arab Republic. The republican government inaugurated organized sports and, through the extension of education, introduced them to newly built schools in rural areas. For the new state's youthful supporters, football emphasized a new, modern, Yemeni identity.

In the 1960s, Egyptian advisors established "Sports and Cultural Centres" in Sana'a, Ta'izz, al-Hodeidah and Ibb. In 1965, the Egyptian Army football team toured war-free areas of Yemen, easily defeating teams composed of the best players in the three major cities. Yemeni sports officials contend these exhibitions awakened the populace to the importance of football. Although indebted to Egypt for military and economic aid, Yemeni disliked the Egyptians' superior attitude and assumption of authority. Egypt's victories generated nationalistic sentiments and enthusiasm for international sports competitions. Perhaps as with cricket in the West Indies (Stoddart 1988a; Stoddart 1988b; Soomer 1995) or baseball in the Dominican

Republic (Klein 1991), the contests expressed hostility to Egyptian cultural hegemony.

The government created the Council for Youth and Sports in the early 1970s. Mandated to build a national sports infrastructure, the council installed central sports committees in the most populous governorates, those with Sports and Cultural Centres[17]. Like the policy in the PDRY, these committees were charged with expanding and consolidating the club system.

Increasing participation in sport was a key to overcoming the effects of the civil war and achieving the goals of integration and identification. The first national championship in 1972 included teams from those southern and central governorates, Sana'a, Ta'izz, Ibb, and al-Hodeidah, in which identification with the republican regime was strong. By the end of the decade the participation of most governorates in divisional tournaments suggests the extension of government control.

In the late 1970s the government intensified its sports emphasis. The number of clubs increased and, in 1980, the YAR was admitted to FIFA. Using sport to encourage identity was an important, implicit goal of the renamed Supreme Council for Youth and Sports (SCYS)[18] that in 1981 was elevated to ministerial status. The council argued that sport expanded contacts between people from all areas of the YAR, promoted understanding and pride in the state's cultural diversity, and replaced the potentially destructive aspects of regionalism with a new basis of identity.

SCYS expansion plans encouraged the formation of football clubs in all areas, but especially in parts of the northern and eastern governorates that remained outside government control. Since unregulated expansion would license teams to represent narrow regional or social constituencies, SCYS policy, like that adopted by its counterpart in the PDRY, was to sanction only one team in each regional centre. This practice forced interaction between players and fans from neighboring areas, weakened micro-regional attachments, and incorporated these groups in the state system. As in the PDRY, football's penetration of rural areas accompanied the incorporation of these regions into the national system (see Table 2 following page). During the 1980s, the nearly 100 per cent growth of clubs, from 61 to 118, paralleled the expansion of government control (Stevenson, 1989b). At union, there were 26 clubs in urban areas and 92 in district centres. The explicit message was that a district had a team to represent it but the implicit meaning was tacit acceptance of state authority.

Table 2:   Yemen Arab Republic sports clubs, 1981-1990

Governorate[1]	1981[a]	1981[b]	1983[c]	1984[d]	1985[e]	1987[f]	1988[g]	1989[h]	1990[h]
Sana'a	10	14	9	12	15	16	15	18	20
Ta'izz	9	25	10	12	12	12	12	12	12
al-Hodeidah	14	20	5	17	16	17	17	18	17
Ibb	11	16	10	15	16	16	16	18	20
Dhamar	3	4	2	7	7	8	8	8	7
al-Baydha	5	7	8	9	9	11	11	11	10
Sa'dah	3	6	3	4	6	7	7	7	7
Hajja	4	5	4	6	6	9	10	9	9
al-Mahwit	2	2	2	2	2	6	7	6	8
Ma'rib	-	-	-	3	3	3	3	3	4
al-Jawf [2]	-	-	-	-	-	-	-	-	4
TOTALS	61	99	53	87	92	105	106	110	118

1   See Map 1 for governorate locations.
2   Al-Jawf was designated a province about 1980.

a   Central Planning Organization (1982: p. 291)
b   Central Planning Organization (1983: p. 302)
c   Supreme Council for Youth and Sports (1983: p. 49)
d   Central Planning Organization (1985: p. 346)
e   Central Planning Organization (1986: p. 366)
f   Central Planning Organization (1988: p. 318)
g   Central Planning Organization (1989: p. 253)
h   Ministry of Youth and Sports Records

While SCYS policy promoted sports, clubs were formed by local initiatives, were headed by highly regarded local men, and were independent. However, to be eligible for modest government subsidies and to participate in sanctioned competitions, they had to comply with Supreme Council rules and receive official recognition.

The government's sports philosophy was close to the socialist ideal of physical culture. As articulated by SCYS officials, sports develop a person physically, but a well-rounded individual and good citizen must be developed mentally as well.

This doctrine was evidenced both in club names, such as "Unity Club for Sport and Culture," and in club organization. Clubs conducted non-sports activities including art, geography, and history programmes, and participated in celebrations of national and religious holidays. Beginning in the 1980s, the SCYS conducted social and cultural tournaments with teams competing in Islamic education, Arabic literature, geography and history, and sports and physical education.

The government hoped that sports would reduce the daily chewing of qat, thereby improving citizens' physical and mental well-being, and economic productivity (Stevenson, 1992). While the YAR was often under pressure from donor states to control qat use, these initiatives may have been influenced by the PDRY's restriction of qat chewing to one day per week.

PDRY and YAR participation in international competitions

In the 1970s and 1980s neither Yemen could field successful national football teams. The YAR sent teams to some regional competitions with the intent of bolstering nationalism and making some foreign policy gains (Stevenson, 1989a) but their performances were not memorable. A similar pattern seems to hold for the PDRY. FIFA records (see Table 3) from 1985 reveal limited international competition and few victories in the years preceding union.

Moreover, those matches played did not attract much interest. In part this may owe to lack of media coverage but also suggests public chagrin. Rather than engendering nationalism, the poor performance dramatized national weakness especially in relation to neighboring states[19]. The primary path to achieving national goals was competition between the Yemens.

Table 3: YAR and PDRY international match results, 1985-1989

Country	1985 w–l–d	1986 w–l–d	1987 w–l–d	1988 w–l–d	1989 w–l–d
Yemen Arab Republic	1–6–0	No matches	No matches	1–1–3	0–2–1
People's Democratic Republic of Yemen	0–1–1	No matches	No matches	0–4–0	1–2–0

Note: Only includes "A" level matches
Source: FIFA Secretariat (personal communication)

Football matches between the two Yemens

Despite the constant tension that marked their relationship, sports were one of the few communication channels between the Yemens. These links, forged when South Yemen was a colony, began with individual players from the north and south making cross border visits. The first officially organized team tour was in 1969 when an 'Adeni football team played three matches in al-Hodeidah. Though the visitors won all the games, the exhibitions were popular.

More football exchanges were conducted in 1970. The YAR military football team traveled to 'Aden losing matches against the PRSY[20] military team and an 'Aden All Star team. The PRSY military team reciprocated by playing two matches in Sana'a. While these contests drew large audiences, it was the reception of the visiting team by YAR President al-Iriyani and his call for further sports exchanges that added significance to the event.

These inter-Yemen team exchanges continued in 1971 with the Revolution Cup tournament held in celebration of the ninth anniversary of the YAR's September Revolution. A Libyan team, the YAR national team, and the victorious PDRY national team competed in Sana'a for the title. A southern club from Lahaj won matches in Ta'izz, Ibb, al-Hodeidah and Sana'a. In these contests, the PDRY was clearly superior and this may be a partial explanation for the YAR's decision in the late 1970s (see above) to devote more resources to sports.

In 1979 the Yemens fought a border war which ended with the Kuwait Agreement, according to which the states reaffirmed the 1972 Cairo Agreement's (see above) call for unity. Following this resolution, in June 1980, the two sports councils held discussions on enhancing interaction and understanding of youth in the two Yemens. These talks produced an agreement to hold an annual football tournament called the Yemen Cup, a competition with a clear political objective[21]. The tournament began in Sana'a during the celebration of the YAR's September Revolution and ended in 'Aden during the anniversary of the PDRY's October Revolution. The trophy was inscribed with "The Unified Yemen Cup" and the players' medals had "The Unified Yemen Tournament" engraved on one side and "1980 Celebration of the September and the October Revolutions" on the other.

As part of its elabourate staging, the competing teams represented the major governorates in the YAR (Sana'a, Ta'izz, Ibb, and al-Hodeidah) and in the PDRY ('Aden, Lahaj, Abyan, and Hadhramaut) One match between teams from 'Aden and Sana'a was the first YAR televised football contest. The first Yemen Cup was won by an 'Adeni team.

The second Yemen Cup tournament, held in 1981, was organized differently with only the regular season football champion and the runner-up team from each country competing. The reasons for these changes are unknown although it is likely they were to increase the chances for a YAR victory and to reduce costs. Surprisingly, the two YAR teams won their matches and played each other for the Cup. The PDRY President, Ali Nassir Mohamed, was scheduled to attend the title match in 'Aden. When he did not appear, there was speculation that he was trying to avoid conceding political advantage to the north.

To avoid a similar crisis, in 1982 the rules for the third Yemen Cup were revised dramatically. Four teams competed for the Cup but each team included a mix of YAR and PDRY players.

Building on this structure, in 1988 a unified Yemeni national football team was formed as an advanced step in the process of merging the two Yemens[22]. The players were selected equally from both countries. This team conducted a training camp but did not compete internationally. Matches were played against club teams in Sana'a and 'Aden in celebration of the two Yemeni Revolutions.

These successive rules modifications point to the political maneuvering behind the tournaments. Political leaders appear to have supported these events because they were popular, gave the impression of willingness to unite, and with victory would suggest the validity of their political ideology. Despite their pan-Yemeni emphasis, politicians were using these matches to address their constituents. Through the device of competitions, each state wanted first, to generate identity with and national sentiments for their own side, and second, to extend its hegemony to gain support for their ideology in a united Yemen.

If our understanding of the politicians' intentions is accurate, they did not have the desired effect. Influenced by the rhetoric of unity, and perhaps guided by Arab media declarations of these matches as steps toward unification, Yemeni citizens cheered both teams and used slogans confirming their desire for unity. Rather than promoting national identity, the matches seem to have fostered pan-Yemeni nationalism.

Discussion

Despite their different political systems, both the YAR and PDRY promoted sports competitions to involve youth in the national systems, to reduce a legacy of regionalism, to gain international recognition, and to declare the success of their ideology to their fellows across the border. Achieving these goals required two interrelated strategies. One approach focused on integration, and the acknowledgment of regional ties within a state regulated system. The other course simultaneously called for identification with the state as well as the idea of a Yemeni nation. In fulfilling these objectives, both Yemens created similarly structured agencies and adopted comparable policies[23], such as each state writing new constitutions in the early 1970s or attempting to regulate qat use. The equivalences between the PDRY's Supreme Council for Sports and the YAR's Supreme Council for Youth and Sports are deeper than their names. These agencies had the same mandate.

The Yemens followed parallel courses because they shared common problems. For example, although each nation's borders were defined before their republican eras, the governments did not control all areas within these limits. Sport was important in integrating semi-autonomous areas into the nations. By calling attention to existing teams and their locally prominent officers, staging national championships, and sending teams to compete internationally, each state legitimized the importance of sport and encouraged football club formation.

Sports teams enable regional identification but make its expression dependent on competing against others in a national system. Allegiance to a team is how affiliation with a community is imagined. To use Gramscian categories, football clubs are part of civil society through which governments manufacture consent and extend their hegemony. The steady increase of Yemeni clubs, particularly in remote or semi-autonomous areas, suggests penetration of state control.

Encouraging clubs partially achieved the objective of integration, but permitting many clubs in an area perpetuated and strengthened multiple identities and undercut national consensus formation. By limiting clubs to regional centres, participants were encouraged to abandon their narrow local ties and to form new broader connections. The merit of these strategies is clear in the YAR's decision in the early in 1980s to structure its consolidation and limitation on the policies established by the PDRY a decade earlier. Beyond fulfilling similar goals, copying each other's programmes may have had political implications as well. These included creating similar structures following official policy favouring union or preventing one state gaining an advantage over the other.

While each state achieved regional integration, to what degree did this promote national identity and nationalism? Although the governments supported both, here the answer is ambiguous. Citizen connection to either the YAR or PDRY was essential to that state's ability to govern. As a result, each state used secular education, the media, and popular culture to stress important events such as the YAR's overthrow of the imam or the PDRY's defeat of the British as elements in creating a national consensus. Archetti (1994: p. 37) suggests identity is positional and strategic. This accords with the largely situational nature of Yemeni notions of the nation. Beyond their histories and ideologies, the Yemens lacked a clear basis for unique national identities. Moreover, Yemeni were drawn to the claims of common heritage to which, at least rhetorically, each government appeared sympathetic. This is evident in sports clubs' cultural and historical activities that highlighted state specific and shared Yemeni elements.

Sugden and Bairner's (1993) examination of the two Irelands attributes the permanence of the division to three different notions of identity and nationalism — Irish, British, and Ulster — within the two populations. Abetted by government policy, sports encourage and reproduce these ethnic and religious distinctions. Although very real differences existed between the Yemens, these were phrased in ideological terms rather than as a core or fundamental disparity.

Kellas (1991) identifies three facets of nationalism in sport: nationalist behavior, national consciousness, and national ideology. The Yemen case is best described by the second type derived from Anderson's (1991) notion of nations as "imagined communities". Anderson argues that symbols such as markets, printed language, the arts, and common heritage are the ties which bind people. But as Sugden and Tomlinson (1994: p. 3) suggest, "Sport in many cases informs and refuels the popular memory of communities, and offers a source of collective identification and community expression for those who follow teams and individuals". This aptly conveys the core of the nationalism Anderson describes and that is found in Yemen.

Klein (1997: p. 9) notes that "autonationalism fosters collective identification both through the inclusion of those living within fixed borders and the exclusion of neighboring entities or others". In Yemen, the border was pliable, at times expanding to include both states, at other times contracting to the internationally recognized lines. Sports contests incorporate both versions. Intra-Yemen competitions served the goal of promoting national identity without alienating those attached to a pan-Yemeni identity. Moreover, at regional and international sports conferences, officials representing the two states overcame their ideological differences and took a unified position on many issues. Despite the focus on doctrinal distinctions, Yemeni autonationalism was a more powerful ideology. Duke and Crolley (1996: p. 4) observe, "football captures the notion of an imagined community perfectly. It is much easier to imagine the nation and confirm national identity, when eleven players are representing the nation in a match against another nation". In the Yemens, while each government may have been represented by eleven players, all twenty-two competitors represented the imagined nation.

Conclusion

At the outset we posed the question of why the Yemens, seemingly very different states, were able to merge so easily. We have argued that contrary to appearances, because of common problems and solutions, the states were quite similar. Moreover, while both governments were intent on building a national consensus, they were also laying the foundations for union. National identity was a component in the creation of Yemeni nationalism. Sports were one of the few visible expressions of the peoples' desires for one nation. In this sense the community Yemeni imagined was based on a limited set of common elements and required them to set aside a host of differences that had in the past been the basis of division.

Nevertheless, there are clear limits to the national or nationalist feelings engendered by sports competitions. Kellas (1991) observes the sentiments promoted by sports contests rarely convert to political action. Indeed, in Yemen the euphoria of union waned as the political leaders were unable to relinquish their personal ambitions as easily as they had merged governmental institutions. Ultimately power sharing failed, civil war erupted, and parties once drawn together easily changed the bases of their identity and fought each other. But not long afterwards, a new national championship season was again underway.

Notes

Thomas Stevenson conducted research on sports in the Yemen Arab Republic in 1987-1988 as a secondary project supported by a Fulbright Islamic Civilization Award. Abdul-Karim Alaug collected and made a preliminary analysis of data on football in the People's Democratic Republic of Yemen and the Republic of Yemen in 1995. His research was supported by funds obtained by the senior author from Ohio University Regional Higher Education, the Ohio University Research Enhancement Fund, and the Ohio University Foundation. The article was written by Thomas Stevenson who is fully responsible for the interpretations presented.

[1]   While there were equivalences, as Dunbar (1992) observes, the YAR had made dramatic economic gains since 1962 while the post-1967 PDRY had stagnated.

2   This diversionary effect is well illustrated in the Cameroonian film *Mr. Foot* (Teno, 1991).

3   A possible indication of sports' effectiveness in conveying national sentiments is that at important matches in the Gulf states supporters wave pictures of their national rulers (John Peterson, 1997, personal communication).

4   This point was made clear as I watched the opening ceremonies of the 1988 Seoul Olympics with students from the Yemen Arab Republic. Knowing no members of their team would advance to the televised finals, my friends were intent on seeing their countrymen march in the parade of nations.

5   Howell (1995) presents the unusual case of baseball along the northeast coast of North America. Sports-based identity is tied to this maritime region and so transcends the border between the United States and Canada.

6   Hobsbawm (1990: pp. 137-138) suggests former colonies have a 'made-up' nationalism.

7   Despite the agreement, this line was not ratified until 1913 (Burrowes 1995: p. 76).

8   Although organized to promote all types of sports, in both Yemens most clubs had football as their primary focus.

9   The "Mohamedan's Union Club," founded in 1902 (ar-Riyidhah 1990b: p. 10; Ma'taq 1965: p. 28), was apparently the only exception.

10 The ASC did not provide financial or organization support to clubs. It organized tournaments by finding sponsors among local business leaders. The cups awarded were named according to the wishes of the benefactors.

10 This is a common interpretation of events (see ar-Riyadhah, 1990a: p. 9).

12 Almost certainly there were clubs in Hadhramaut but corroborative data are not available.

13 The match was chosen for boycott because one of the teams was named "The Federation".

14 Through cooperative agreements East German experts conducted sports clinics (Sports in the GDR, 1982).

15 The practice of locally prominent men serving as sports club officers is common in the Middle East and may result from Egyptian influence. In the GCC states, members of ruling families are frequently presidents of football clubs (Rosandich, 1991; John Peterson, 1997, personal communication).

[16] There were certainly many other clubs in these cities but informants do not recall them.

[17] No committees were established in the northern and eastern regions (Sa'dah, Hajja and al- Mahwit) and the yet to be designated, Ma'rib and al-Jawf governorates) where antipathy to the government and modernization was strong. The absence of football indicates that government control had not penetrated these areas.

[18] Sport oversight in the YAR has changed frequently. After the revolution, sports were overseen by the Prime Minister's office. In the late-1960s supervision shifted to the Department of Social Affairs, Labor, and Youth. Through the mid-1970s an independent agency, the Council for Youth and Sports, made sports policy. In the late 1970s, sport was part of the Ministry for Social Affairs, Labor, and Youth. Since the early 1980s the Supreme Council for Youth and Sports has overseen all sports.

[19] All the GCC states have made dramatic gains in sports, especially football. The Saudi national team won the Asian Nations' Cup in 1984 and 1988 (Murray 1994) and reached the finals of the 1994 World Cup. The Kuwait national team won the Asian Nations' Cup in 1980 and qualified for the 1982 World Cup (Chakra 1988; Murray 1996). Qatar finished second in the 1981 World Youth Championship and the national team won a berth in the 1984 Los Angeles Olympics (Salahi 1982: p. 32; Qatari Ministry of Information 1987).

[20] The People's Republic of South Yemen changed its name to the People's Democratic Republic of Yemen on November 30,1970.

[21] Memos from the meeting of the two delegates in 'Aden, December 7, 1980, pp. 2-3.

[22] A number of agencies, including the postal office, central bank, and news services, merged prior to the official date of union (Braun 1992).

[23] In terms of sport, some of these parallels result less from mimicry than from international standards.

References

Anderson, B. (1991) *Imagined communities: Reflections on the origin and spread of nationalism.* Revised edition. New York: Verso.

Archetti, E. (1994) 'Argentina and the World Cup: In search of national identity', in J. Sugden and A. Tomlinson (eds) *Hosts and champions: Soccer cultures, national identities and the USA World Cup.* Aldershot: Arena, pp. 37-63.

———— (1996) 'In search of national identity: Argentinian football and Europe', in J. A. Mangan (ed) *Tribal identities: Nationalism, Europe, sport.* London: Frank Cass, pp. 201-219.

Baker, W. J. (1987) 'Political games: The meaning of international sport for independent Africa', in W. J. Baker and J. A. Mangan (eds) *Sport in Africa: Essays in social history.* New York: Africana Publishing Company, pp. 271-294.

Bäskau, H. (1981) 'Körperkultur und Sport in der VDR Jemen', *Köpererziehung* Vol. 31, No. 10: pp. 449-455.

Boyle, R. (1994) 'We are Celtic supporters. Questions of football and identity in modern Scotland', in R. Giulianotti and J. Williams (eds) *Game without frontiers: Football, identity and modernity.* Aldershot: Arena, pp. 73-102.

Braun, U. (1992) 'Yemen: Another case of unification', *Aussenpolitik* Vol. 43, No. 2: pp. 174-184.

Burrowes, R. D. (1995) *Historical dictionary of Yemen.* Lanham, MD: The Scarecrow Press.

Carapico, S. (1993) The economic dimension of Yemeni Unity', *Middle East Report* No. 184 (Sep-Oct): pp. 9-14.

Central Planning Organization (Prime Minister's Office) (1982) *Statistical Yearbook, 1981.* Sana'a, Yemen Arab Republic.

———— (1983) *Statistical Yearbook, 1982.* Sana'a, Yemen Arab Republic.

———— (1985) *Statistical Yearbook, 1984.* Sana'a, Yemen Arab Republic.

———— (1986) *Statistical Yearbook, 1985.* Sana'a, Yemen Arab Republic.

———— (1988) *Statistical Yearbook, 1987.* Sana'a, Yemen Arab Republic.

———— (1989) *Statistical Yearbook, 1988.* Sana'a, Yemen Arab Republic.

Chakra, A. A. (1988) 'Sport', in T. Mostyn (exec. ed) *The Cambridge Encyclopedia of the Middle East and North Africa.* Cambridge: Cambridge University Press, pp. 156-157.

Dunbar, C. (1992) 'The unification of Yemen: Process, politics, and prospects', *The Middle East Journal* Vol. 46, No. 3: pp. 456-476.

Duke, V. and Colley, L. (1996) *Football, nationality and the state*. Essex: Addison Wesley Longman, Ltd.

Finn, G. P. T. (1991) 'Racism, religion and social prejudice: Irish Catholic clubs, soccer and Scottish identity — II. Social identity and conspiracy', *International Journal of the History of Sport* Vol. 8, No. 3: pp. 370-97.

Gramsci, A. (1988) *A Gramsci reader: Selected writings, 1916-1935*. David Forgacs (ed). New York: Shocken Books.

Grundlingh, A. (1995) 'Playing for power: Rugby, Afrikaner nationalism and masculinity in South Africa', in A. Grundlingh, A. Odendaal and B. Spies (eds) *Beyond the tryline: Rugby and South African society*. Johannesburg: Ravan Press, pp. 106-135.

Halliday, F. (1975) *Arabia without sultans: A political survey of instability in the Third World*. New York: Vintage Press.

Hargreaves, J. (1986) *Sport, power and culture: A social and historical analysis of popular sports in Britain*. New York: St. Martin's Press.

Hobsbawn, E. J. (1983) 'Introduction: Inventing traditions', in E. Hobsbawm and T. Ranger (eds) *The invention of tradition*. Cambridge: Cambridge University Press, pp. 1-14.

—————— (1990) *Nations and nationalism since 1780: Programme, myth, reality*. Cambridge: Cambridge University Press.

Howell, C. D. (1995) *Northern sandlots: A social history of maritime baseball*. Toronto: University of Toronto Press.

Hunnicutt, B. (1985) 'Recreation among the oil wells: Saudi Arabia develops its leisure services', *Parks and Recreation* Vol. 20, No. 7: pp. 50-55.

James, C. L. R. (1984) *Beyond a boundary*. New York: Pantheon.

Jarvie, G. (1991) *Highland Games: The making of a myth*. Edinburgh: Edinburgh University Press.

—————— (1993) 'Sport, nationalism and cultural identity', in L. Allison (ed) *The changing politics of sport*. Manchester: Manchester University Press, pp. 58-83.

Jarvie, G. and G. Walker (1994) 'Ninety-minute patriots. Scottish sport in the making of the nation', in G. Jarvie and G. Walker (eds) *Scottish sport in the making of the nation: Ninety minute patriots*. Leicester: Leicester University Press, pp. 1-8.

Jenkins, I. (1984) 'Los Angeles '84: Can Arab teams reach the gold standard?', *Middle East Economic Digest* (20 July): pp. 24-25.

Kellas, J. G. (1991) *The politics of nationalism and ethnicity.* New York: St. Martin's Press.

Kennedy, J. (1987) *The flower of paradise: The institutionalized use of the drug qat in North Yemen.* Dordrecht, Holland: D. Reidel Publishing Company.

Klein, A. M. (1991) *Sugarball: The American game, the Dominican dream.* New Haven: Yale University Press.

Klein, A. M. (1997) *Baseball on the border: A tale of two Laredos.* Princeton: Princeton University Press.

Korr, C. (1986) *West Ham United: The making of a football club.* Urbana: University of Illinois Press.

Lever, J. (1983) *Soccer madness.* Chicago: University of Chicago Press.

Llobera, J. R. (1994) *The god of modernity: The development of nationalism in Western Europe.* Oxford: Berg.

MacClancy, J. (1996) 'Sport, identity and ethnicity', in J. MacClancy (ed) *Sport, identity and ethnicity.* Oxford: Berg, pp. 1-20.

Marks, J. (1985) 'Dashed hopes of Egypt's football fans', *The Middle East* No. 131 (September): pp. 36-37.

al-Marwani, A. H. (1987) Speech to al-Ahli Club for Sport and Culture. Sana'a: Yemen Arab Republic. February 25.

Ma'tuq, 'A. al-R. (1965) *The history of sport in 'Aden* [in Arabic]. 'Aden: Dar al-Hanna.

────── (1981) *Football in Democratic Yemen* [in Arabic]. 'Aden: Ministry of Culture.

Moorhouse, H. F. (1996) 'One state, several countries: Soccer and nationality in a United Kingdom', in J. A. Mangan (ed) *Tribal identities: Nationalism, Europe, sport.* London: Frank Cass, pp. 55-74.

Murray, W. J. (1984) *The Old Firm: Sectarianism, sport and society in Scotland.* Edinburgh: John Donald Publishers Ltd.

────── (1994) *Football: A history of the world game.* Hants, England: Scolar Press.

────── (1996) *The world's game: A history of soccer.* Urbana: University of Illinois Press.

Patterson, O. (1969) 'The cricket ritual in the West Indies', *New Society* No. 352: pp. 988-989.

Pettavino, P.J. and Pye, G. (1994) *Sport in Cuba: The diamond in the rough.* Pittsburgh: University of Pittsburgh Press.

Physician and Sportsmedicine. (1978) '"Sports City" under way in Saudi Arabia', *The Physician and Sportsmedicine* Vol. 6, No. 3 (March): p. 27.

Qatari Ministry of Information, Press and Publications Department (1987) 'Sports and leisure: The blend of past and present: A new force on the scene', in *Glimpses of Qatar. 2nd Edition*. Doha: Ministry of Information.

Reed, J. D. (1980) 'The name of the game is petrosports', *Sports Illustrated* Vol. 53, No. 21: pp. 90-94; 96-98; 100; 102; 104.

ar-Riyadhah (Sports Newspaper) (1990a) 'Idris Hanbalah and the sports movement' [in Arabic]. No. 11: pp. 9. [August 5].

———— (1990b) 'The story of an 85 year old sport club' [in Arabic]. No. 23: pp. 10. [October 28].

———— (1991) 'The first martyr in 'Aden' [in Arabic]. No. 73: pp. 4. [October 27].

Rosandich, T. J. (1991) 'Sports in society: The Persian Gulf countries', *Journal of the International Council for Health, Physical Education and Recreation* Vol. 27, No. 3: pp. 26-30.

St. Pierre, M. (1995) West Indian cricket as cultural resistance', in M. Malec' (ed) *The social roles of sport in Caribbean societies*. Amsterdam: Gordon and Breach Publishers, pp. 53-84.

Salahi, K. (1982) 'Young footballers put Qatar on the map', *The Middle East* No. 87 (January): pp. 32.

Shamleh, O. (1989) 'Leibesbungen und Sport in der arabischen Golfregion', in H. Uberhorst (ed) *Geschichte der Leibesbungen Band 6*. Berlin: Verlag Bartels and Wernitz GmbH, pp. 610-624.

Sobh, S. (1991) 'Yemen an 1: Où est passée l'euphoie de l'unification?', *Arabies: Le Mensuel Du Monde Arabe et de la Francophonie* (June) pp. 46-53.

Soomer, J. (1995) 'Cricket and the politics of West Indies integration', in H. McD. Beckles and B. Stoddart (eds) *Liberation cricket: West Indies cricket culture*. Kingston: Ian Randle Publishers, pp. 256-268.

Sörlin, S. (1996.) 'Nature, skiing and Swedish nationalism', in J. A. Mangan (ed) *Tribal identities: Nationalism, Europe, sport*. London: Frank Cass, pp. 147-163.

Sports in the GDR (1982) 'Great prospects for sport in PDR Yemen', *Sports in the GDR* Vol. 1: pp. 22-23.

Stevenson, T. B. (1989a) 'Sport in the Yemen Arab Republic', in E. A. Wagner (ed) *Sport in Asia and Africa: A comparative handbook*. Westport: Greenwood Press, pp. 27-49.

———— (1989b) 'Sports clubs and political integration in the Yemen Arab Republic', *International Review for the Sociology of Sport* Vol. 24, No. 4: pp. 299-313.

————— (1992) Sport and qat in North Yemen: A cultural context analysis of a plan to change attitudes and reduce consumption. Unpublished manuscript.

Stevenson, T. B. and Alaug, A.- K. (1997) 'Football in Yemen: Rituals of resistance, integration, and identity', *International Review for the Sociology of Sports,* Vol. 32, No. 3: pp. 251-265.

Stoddart, B. (1988a) Caribbean cricket: The role of sport in emerging small-nation politics. *International Journal* Vol. 43, No. 4: pp. 618-642.

————— (1988b) 'Cricket and colonialism in the English-speaking Caribbean to 1914: Towards a cultural analysis', in J. A. Mangan (ed) *Pleasure, profit, proselytism: British culture and sport at home and abroad, 1700-1914.* London: Frank Cass, pp. 231-257.

Stuart, O. (1996) 'Players, workers, protestors: Social change and soccer in colonial Zimbabwe', in J. MacClancy (ed) *Sport, identity and ethnicity.* Oxford: Berg, pp. 176-180.

Sugden, J. and A. Bairner (1993) *Sport, sectarianism, and society in a divided Ireland.* Leicester: Leicester University Press.

Sugden, J. and Tomlinson, A. (1994) 'Soccer culture, national identity and the World Cup', in J. Sugden and A. Tomlinson(eds) *Hosts and champions: Soccer cultures, national identities and the USA World Cup.* Aldershhot: Arena, pp. 3-12.

Supreme Council for Youth and Sports. (1983) *Accomplishments of the Supreme Council for Youth and Sports, 1982-1983* [in Arabic]. Sana'a, Yemen Arab Republic.

Teno, J.-M. (dir) (1991) *Mr. Foot.* London: South Productions and Channel Four Television.

Varisco, Da. M. (1986) 'On the meaning of chewing: The significance of qat (Catha edulis) in the Yemen Arab Republic', *International Journal of Middle East Studies* Vol. 18, No. 1: pp. 1-13.

Wagg, S. (1995) 'Mr. Drains, go home: Football in the societies of the Middle East', in S. Wagg (ed) *Giving the game away: Football, politics and culture on five continents.* Leicester: Leicester University Press, pp. 163-178.

Wagner, C. B. (1980) 'Sport in Saudi Arabia', in W. Johnson (ed) *Sport and physical education around the world.* Champaign: Stipes Publishing Co, pp. 523-527.

Wagner, E. A. (1988) 'Sport in revolutionary states: Cuba and Nicaragua', in J. L. Arbena (ed) *Sport and society in Latin America: Diffusion, dependency, and the rise of mass culture.* Westport, CT: Greenwood Press, pp. 113-136.

Younger, S. (1977) 'The Saudis go for goal', *Middle East International* No. 74: pp. 28-29.

BETWEEN SALEEM AND SHIVA: THE POLITICS OF CRICKET NATIONALISM IN 'GLOBALISING' INDIA

Ian Mcdonald

Centre for Sport Development Research, Roehampton Institute London

Introduction

On the stroke of midnight, 15th August 1997, millions of Indians throughout the world celebrated India's 50th year of independence. However, for many people, celebrations were tempered by the fact that independence was won from the British at a massive human cost – Partition. Partition meant the division of colonial India into two nations, 'secular' India and 'Muslim' Pakistan. It exacerbated tensions between Hindus and Muslims, leading to riots, mutual recriminations, and the death of nearly a million people. It led to one of the largest forced migrations in history, with Indian Muslims fleeing to Pakistan, passing long shuffling columns of homeless Hindus and Sikhs streaming the other way into India. It was to prevent such slaughter and misery happening again on the subcontinent that a new non–denominationalist, non–religiously affiliated state in India was created, with a constitution calling on Indians to "transcend religious differences" while preserving the nation's "composite culture".

Under the leadership of the Indian National Congress, the new state set about creating an inclusive national identity based on the Nehruvian Consensus – a political project contoured by the values of socialism, democracy, secularism, and non–alignment in foreign policy matters. It was a project which sought to embrace all of India's ethno–religious and language groups, whilst privileging none. If the low level of Hindu–Muslim violence in the ensuing twenty years is an indicator, then the pluralist conception of Indianess implied by the Nehruvian Consensus, enjoyed a wide degree of legitimacy. However, following the failure of the Congress *Raj* to solve the country's socio–economic crisis and the

213

consequent collapse of the Nehruvian Consensus, and in the midst of global forces penetrating deep into Indian society, the spectre of Hindu–Muslim communalism is again on the political agenda. The recent successes of right–wing, chauvinistic anti–Pakistan/Muslim, Hindu organisations in shedding their pariah status, and in entering the mainstream of political life, resurrects the spectre of the country being torn by the forces of communalism. This chapter will trace the impact of the emergence of communalist forces on the relationship between sport and national identity.

In the relationship between sport and national identity, cricket is invested with more significance than any other sport in India, and is therefore the key site for the investigation of divisions over national identity. Hockey is often seen as India's premier sport, based on the fact that India dominated international hockey for decades, (not losing a match in the Olympics from 1928 to 1960). However, a combination of the introduction of artificial pitches in the 1970s, which quite literally created a level playing field to undermine India's superiority, and the low international prestige associated with success in hockey, has divested hockey in India of significant political importance. Football is another popular sport in India. However, its popularity is as a local sport where it attracts mass support. Also, unlike in cricket, the national football team is far from one of the world's best. Traditional game forms such as wrestling and kabbadi are also keenly played and followed, but without an international profile, they provide little scope for success in a global arena. In the relationship between sport and national identity in India, cricket has no parallel.

As India's national sport, cricket's role in contributing to national unity within civil society during the early post–independence years was significant. Although there were divisions and conflicts in cricket from the 1950s to the 1970s, these tended to be based on regional rivalries expressed, for example, in perceptions of selector bias for the national team. (Cashman 1980) However, in line with wider social changes, and the more volatile political situation in the last two decades, the inclusive, pluralistic cricket nationalism is being increasingly strained. The relationship between national identity and cricket in India is now much more contested, with the rise of extreme forms of Indian national identity based on the politics of right–wing Hindu chauvinism exerting an increasing influence. Sitting at the centre of this right–wing cricket nationalist ideology is a conjoining of Hinduness with Indianness, and a questioning of the status of indigenous Muslims as 'true' Indians.

This chapter analyses the context for the emergence of this 'new cricket nationalism' – the assertion of a narrower national identity through cricket – and the ways in which it sows divisions between Hindus and Muslims. Incidents from the 1996 Cricket World Cup, held on the Indian subcontinent, will be drawn on to illustrate how one day international and test cricket tend to promote Hindu chauvinist forms of national identity in India. It is not simply a question of cricket being hijacked by outside extreme nationalist political forces, but, it is also related to a project that is championed by India's top cricket administrators – the globalisation of cricket. Essentially then, the chapter is concerned with some of the main ways in which social divisions and hostility between Hindus and Muslims have been expressed in cricket in recent times. The analysis focuses on how cricket nationalism is being re–shaped by the politics of Hindu communalism and by the globalisation of cricket. At a more theoretical level, it is argued that the 'internal' political dynamic of communalism, and the 'external' process of globalisation are not autonomous processes, but are, in the main, symbiotically related.

Saleem and Shiva: the janus–faced politics of Indian national identity.

The two competing forces of, on the one hand, a secular, pluralist national identity, and on the other, an exclusively Hindu–defined national identity, are embodied in Salman Rushdie's novel *Midnight's Children* (1995) in the fictional characters of Shiva and Saleem. In this political parable, Rushdie argues that neither Saleem nor Shiva, on their own, capture the essence of Indianess. This essence is found in the workings of their perpetual but ultimately doomed conflict with each other; "Shiva and Saleem, victor and victim; understand our rivalry, and you will gain an understanding of the age in which you live". (Rushdie; 1995: p. 432). The battle between Shiva and Saleem raises the issue of cultural authenticity. As he was born just as Nehru was ushering in political independence on the stroke of midnight, 15th August 1947, the ambivalent secularist Saleem is presented as the true child of India. Shiva, who was born just after midnight in the same hospital ward, develops into a Hindu militant with a menacing presence over the life of Saleem. However, the dark secret truth is that just after being born, a disturbed Christian nurse deliberately and unnoticed, swapped their name tags – thus making Shiva not Saleem the true 'Midnight Child'. India's national identity has no essence and is not static. It emerges out of a process of struggle between secular and religious forces. As the Indian social scientist Achin Vanaik states, "Indian cultural nationalism is neither 'naturally' a Hindu nationalism, nor 'naturally' a secular nationalism or composite nationalism. What it is and will be is what we fight to make it be" (1997: p. 151).

An indicator of the balance of forces in this 'fight' over India's national identity can be discerned from a brief analysis of the results of the 1996 General Election. The right–wing Hindu chauvinist Bharatiya Janata Party (BJP) gained the largest number of seats, with 161 out of the 543 contested. Despite the fact that it got only 20.8% of the votes cast in the election, the BJP, having improved on its showing at the 1991 elections when it secured 119 seats, now claims to be the rising nationalist force in Indian politics. The electoral gains of the BJP stand in sharp contrast to the sorry plight of the Indian National Congress party. It emerged discredited and humiliated from the elections to see its percentage share of the vote fall from 36.5% in 1991 to 28.1% in 1996, which is larger than the percentage share of the vote for the BJP, but translated into only 139 seats. (Vanaik, 1997: pp. 342–53). The emergence of the BJP in the 1990s as a serious political force, and the corresponding disintegration of the Congress hegemony, not only reflects a period of parliamentary instability, but also a significant ideological shift in the battle for the soul of Indian nationalism. This is a shift away from a conception of Indian national identity based on the ethno–religious pluralist vision of Mahatma Gandhi and the secularist aspirations of Jawarlahal Nehru, which prevailed as part of the Nehruvian Consensus within independent India until the 1970s. Since the 1980s, the discourse over Indian national identity has been increasingly influenced by the ideology of Hindutva. The central tenet of Hindutva is that the essence of Indianess is Hinduness, and therefore to be a true Indian is to be a Hindu. This is an ideology that unites a number of political organisations into what is known as the Sangh Combine. At the heart of the Sangh Combine sits the Rashtriya Swayamsevak Sangh (RSS), a uniformed militaristic cadre of volunteers with fascistic traits, which influences other organisations in the Combine such as the BJP, the Vishwa Hindu Parishad (VHP) and the Bajrang Dal. In defining the essence of India in religious terms, the ideology of Hindutva is not only nationalist, but communalist also. Vanaik has defined communalism as, "a process involving competitive desecularization (a competitive striving to extend the reach and power of religions), which – along with non–religious factors – helps to harden the divisions and create tensions between different religious communities" (1997: p. 36). Using this definition, the politics of the BJP and the rest of the Sangh Combine can be labelled as communalist. In contemporary Indian society, neither the secularist nor the Sangh conception of national identity enjoys hegemony – rather, both are locked in a critical ideological struggle for predominance.

One of the most significant factors in stimulating debate over national identity stems from the adoption in 1991 of the New Economic Policy (NEP) by the then Congress government of P.V. Narasimha Rao. Post–independent India has until recently been dominated by high levels of state control and investment, complete with Soviet style five–year plans. This has now been supplanted by an unequivocally neo–liberalist approach designed to open up the Indian economy to the global market. Thus, among other measures, the state has relinquished its strategic control over the domestic operations of the market, taxes have been reduced, the government has pruned social welfare programmes and a rapid privatisation of the public sector has been implemented. (Kurien, 1994: pp. 94–104). In turn, the global market, in the form of multinational companies, has been quick to recognise the development potential in India, where an estimated market of over 200 million people with money to spend, puts it on par with the USA or Europe. For example, Coca–Cola have recently set up installations in India at cost of 700 million dollars; this is one of more than 1, 270 foreign investment projects approved since July 1996 by the Indian government. (India Weekly, 1997: p. 13).

Such foreign investment in India inevitably brings with it the values of commerce and consumerism. The appetite for Western goods and lifestyle is particularly strong among the educated, urban middle classes, whose massive numbers and affluence offer a vast outlet for such goods. As Jeremy Seabrook notes in his account of the brutalising effect of economic liberalisation on the wealthy Indian middle class, "the lives of this group of people are increasingly articulated not to India, but to the global market" (1995: p. 52). Not surprisingly, the high levels of change that have swept India in the 1990s have prompted resistance from organisations opposed to the impact of this 'new imperialism' on 'traditional' Indian culture. Two of the highest profile incidents in this context have occurred in Bangalore, known as the 'Silicon Valley of India'. Early in 1996, a branch of Kentucky Fried Chicken was burned down by Hindu extremists, supported by angry farmers concerned about the adverse impact of factory–farmed chickens on agricultural development and the Indian diet. Later in the year, in November, protests against the staging of the Miss World competition, led by women's groups opposed to the commodification of womens' bodies, and religious organisations concerned with the betrayal of traditional notions of Indian womanhood, led to clashes with the authorities. (Frontline, 1996). However in a telling statement on the contradictions and conflicts caused by globalisation, the head of the multinational giant Microsoft, Bill Gates, was feted and honoured by politicians, business leaders and millions of ordinary people during a visit to India during March 1997. (India Today, March 31st 1997: p. 48). "It is said", writes Ian Jack about the recent and rapid modernisation of India, "that villagers in the remotest part of India know who Bill Gates is, would recognise him if he stopped by the well one day to beg a glass of water" (1997: p. 3).

However, of significance for the present discussion is the fact that for the beneficiaries of globalisation – the urban middle classes, and in particular upper–caste and educated Hindus – issues of national identity have not decreased in importance. On the contrary, it is these groups, the most modernised section of India's vast and segmented population, which have been most inclined to the xenophobic Hindu–centred campaigns of the Sangh Combine. A breakdown of the social profile of voters for the BJP and its allies in the 1996 elections illustrates that the Sangh Combine received 52% of the upper castes and highly educated Hindu votes (Vanaik, 1997: p. 342). Furthermore, it is this same group that supplies the social base of support for extreme forms of Hindu nationalism in cricket, as will be illustrated later. In order to understand why it is that the most modernised sections of the population are also the most nationalistic, and why international level cricket provides such a suitable vehicle for their (Hindutva) world view, it is necessary to look more closely at the political ideology of contemporary Hindu nationalism.

The emergence of Hindu nationalist forces since the late 1980s has been supported by a number of contingent factors. The most important has been the integration of India in the global market, which has exposed the failure of the bureaucratic Nehruvian–state to sufficiently modernise the country. The same period has seen India's so–called third path of development between capitalism and communism rendered obsolete with the ending of the cold–war. In the wake of these global transformations, India has found itself as a marginal player in world politics, with its status as *de facto* leader of the developing world no longer recognised. These developments have left India's Hindu aspirant and 'globalised' middle classes feeling marginalised and disorientated, as the promise of inclusion as respected equals in the global modernity remains unfulfilled. Moreover, they feel increasingly threatened by state abetted domestic developments. The emergence of political confidence amongst Muslims, (compounded by the rise of Islam on the global stage), backward castes and the Dalits (previously known as Untouchables). in India, has added fuel to a sense of social fragmentation and fear amongst India's Hindu middle class. This desire to emulate the West, coupled with a perception of the state pandering to minority non–Hindu groups and backward castes, has left the Hindu middle class succeptable to the rhetoric of Hindutva. In his examination of the growth of Hindutva since the late 1980s, Thomas Blom–Hansen (1996). identifies how this discourse has been able to enter into the popular Hindu imagination:

> To the Hindu nationalists, as well as to millions of people around the world, the imagining of modernity is inextricably connected to notions of power and consummation: economic prosperity, a strong state and 'full' and unequivocal cultural and national identities. In this phantasmic construction, the strong, homogenous nation is a sign of modernity; it bestows protection, sovereignty, self–confidence and political integrity on its citizens. (Hansen: p. 603)

A strong homogenous Hindu–state, residing over an economically prosperous nation with a clear cultural identity, is advocated by the Hindu nationalists as both the means and reward gained from assimilating into, and scaling the 'new world order', an 'order' which is perceived as a metaphor for subordination to the west. It is a strategy that is predicated on the putative Hindu essence of India. According to Hindutva, to be a true Indian is to be a Hindu. Vanaik refers to a *chain of reasoning*, behind such an assertion:

> Ethos/spirit is the heart of Hinduism, which is at the heart of, or coterminous with, Hindu culture (which defines Indian culture), which is at the heart of the Hindu nation (which defines the Indian nation). Four concepts – ethos, religion, culture, nation – are the key elements of the discourse. (1997: p. 151)

Hindutva arouses a sense of deprivation among Hindus, by using a similar rationale to white racist groups throughout Europe. The usual argument of white racists is not that blacks and immigrants oppress whites, but rather that white people are unfairly treated, and that the country is suffering because of a supposed favouring by the state towards these minority groups. In India, Hindu nationalist argue that the 'pandering' by the state to Muslims has betrayed and stifled the Hindu essence of the nation, thus preventing the country from taking its place as an equal partner inn the global modernity. For India to take its place in the global modernity as an equal partner, it needs to adopt the imagined forms of western modernisation, (a strong state, economic growth etc), but emphasise its philosophical and cultural (Hindu) distinctiveness. Such a position leads to a quest for cultural strength and purity. The logical conclusion of this quest was seen in the campaign by the Sangh Combine throughout the 1980s for the destruction of a sacred mosque in Ayodhya in north India and its replacement by a new temple dedicated to Lord Rama. The mosque was demolished by Hindutva fanatics in December 1992, and was the catalyst for the most serious communal riots, or more accurately anti–Muslim progroms, in January 1993 since partition.

Clearly then, in a multi–ethnic, but crisis–ridden society such as India, the emergence of the Sangh Combine under the banner of Hindutva signals the threat of communal divisions and conflicts. This is especially threatening to the status of Muslims as Indians, as they have been defined in Hindutva ideology as the 'enemy within'. Sociologically speaking, if the West is defined as the 'significant other' of Hindutva, then Indian Muslims are the 'operational other'. Although the blame for India's backwardness is levelled at the state, the substance of Hindutva politics are based on an inventory of myths concerning the anti–national mentality of Indian Muslims, their latent loyalties to Pakistan, and the promiscous and primitive sexuality male Muslims. In their discussion of the communalism and the media in India, Gupta and Sharma note that:

> The Hindu right in India has made an ambitious attempt to popularise the idea of the Indian nation as a 'Hindu' nation, in a meticulously organised manner. Ostensibly cultural, the project is, in fact, deeply political – building a typology of prejudices regarding the Muslims and remoulding every sphere of society. It has constantly brought out leaflets highlighting the 'inferiority' of minorities, especially Muslims, and emphasising the glory of Hinduism. (1996: p. 1)

Thus, contained within the Hindu nationalist project of Hindutva is an anti–Muslim hostility, which lays the basis for communal tensions and divisions. Economic liberalisation and the rise of Hindu nationalism provide the context for the rise of strident and aggressive forms of cricket nationalism that can easily stoke the embers of communalism. As both a global game, and the premier national sport in India, cricket is a 'sphere of society' which has provided opportunities for anti–Muslim hostility based on the myths outlined above. Fundamentally, this is possible because international level cricket offers a means of gaining respect within the global modernity through the assertion of a strong, militant form of Hindu nationalism.

Hindu nationalist influence is increasingly evident in various ways in international cricket, for example, in the partisan nature of crowds, in the press reportage of cricket and cricket related incidents, and in some cases, the occupation of key administrative positions in cricket by supporters of Hindutva ideology. Although this Hindu nationalist influence is often more contradictory than coherent, the consequence of this process of politicisation is that communal tensions in international cricket in India are likely to increase. What then is the impact of these tensions on cricket in India?

Cricket and divided national identity

Ramachandra Guha, an Indian social historian and cricket fan, has neatly captured the popularity of, and passion for cricket in India:

> In the years since India became independent in August 1947, cricket has grown spectacularly in mass appeal. During big matches normal life comes to a standstill: Offices and roads are empty, with hundreds of millions of Indians glued to their television or radio sets. This game is now patronised as much by the Maharaja as by the milkman, by the snob as well as by the socialist. The spread of satellite television has greatly expanded the game's reach. In this respect, television has effectively bridged the divide between city and country and between man and woman, with both peasant men and upper–class women numbered among the fanatical followers of India's Test side. India's most successful cricketers have been elevated to iconic status, worshipped as only film stars and Hindu deities have been. Cricket is not so much India's national game as its national obsession. The only opponents of cricket still around are the economists, who call it the opium of the people and do calculations of its negative impact on GNP. (Guha, 1994/5: p. 257)

The widespread popularity and, therefore, the commercial nature of international test and one day cricket in India can be discerned from a comparison with the game in England. Whereas the sponsors of English cricket have traditionally been banks and insurance companies, Pepsi and Coca–Cola vie for predominance amongst the benefactors of Indian cricket. Whereas traditionally some public figures in England have expressed a modest enthusiasm for cricket, for India's public figures a passion for the game is considered mandatory. In contrast to the 'official' tradition of rural and suburban cricket in England, urban India provides cricket's geographical base. And while the English cricket authorities content themselves with maintaining its base of support among the established middle classes, cricket in India is aggressively sold to, and embraced, by urban India's aspirant and affluent consuming classes. It is the binding forces of nationalism and commerce over the cricket–mad middle classes in India that account for the popularity and the deeply symbolic importance of cricket in contemporary India. Moreover, it is in the context of India's policy of globalisation that 'capitalist modernisation' of cricket becomes particularly prone to exploitation by communalist forces. Although this is a development that has intensified in the 1990s, the communalising of cricket nationalism was foreshadowed in the 1960s, as the story of Abbas Ali Baig illustrates.

The kiss of Abbas Ali Baig (revisited)

In 1960, a small yet symbolic incident occurred during the India – Australia Test match at Bombay's Brabourne Stadium. With the series level at 1–1, the match appeared to be going in favour of the visitors. However, a spell of batting by Abbas Ali Baig retrieved a dire situation for India and, ultimately, forced a draw. When the Oxford–educated Muslim batsman reached his half–century, he was rewarded with a kiss from a young Hindu woman who ran onto the field. However, in the subsequent Test series between India and Pakistan, Baig failed to reproduce this heroic performance, with scores of 1, 13, 19 and 1. Although all 5 Test matches in this series were drawn, Baig suddenly found himself on the receiving end of a stream of poison–pen letters accusing him of deliberately throwing his wicket to help his fellow Muslims from Pakistan. From being acclaimed as an Indian hero, Baig had become a Pakistani fifth columnist in the space of three matches, and was dropped from the national team. This was despite the fact that Baig had emulated the great Ranjitsinhji in making a century on his Test debut, and was heralded as the man around whom the next generation of Indian batting would be built. (Bose, 1990: p. 221)

In the few books on the history of Indian cricket, (for example, Cashman, 1981; Docker, 1976; Ramaswami, 1975) hardly any attention beyond the mere narrative of events as retold here, is given to the Baig episode. In revisiting the kiss of Baig and his subsequent travails through the lens of the sociological imagination, we can see a microcosm of the fissures and tensions of globalisation, commerce and nationalism developing in Indian society from the 1960s. Although not reflected in the cricket history books, the shock waves caused by a wealthy young Hindu woman kissing the Muslim Baig has been evocatively portrayed by Salman Rushdie, in his novel *The Moor's Last Sigh*. It was, he writes:

> ... a gasp provoking, scandalous kiss, a kiss between beautiful strangers, perpetrated in broad daylight and in a packed stadium, and at a time when no movie house in the city was permitted to offer audiences so obscenely provocative an image. (1996: p. 228)

Official India may have been offended, but it was a kiss that reflected the arrival of Test cricketers like Baig in the 'filmi' culture of Bollywood. It was a kiss that signalled the emergence of cricket at the cutting edge of a nascent consumerist Indian youth culture; a kiss which confirmed cricket as *tamasha*. In short, although apparently spontaneous and certainly fleeting, it was an immensely symbolic kiss, which highlighted a key characteristic of cricket in India; cricket as modernity. More ominously however, the kiss of Baig and his subsequent failures against Pakistan also provided fertile terrain for communalist politics to grow through the reinvocation of Hindu nationalist myths about Indian Muslims.

The kiss offended the prejudiced ideology of Hindutva, not only because it was a public display of sexual impropriety, but also because it represented a pollution of Hindu spiritual purity by Islamic lust. The mythical sexual/masculine excess of the virile and primitive Muslim community is a prominent theme of Hindu nationalism — it is an excess which will weaken the Hindu nation, and an excess which threatens to overpower Hindus and to dominate the Indian polity. For Hindu nationalists, the imagery of a Muslim saving the Indian nation from defeat, celebrated in a casual 'sexual' encounter with a Hindu woman, followed by the poor performances against Pakistan, merely rekindled older fears of Indian Muslims as the enemy within. International test cricket is an institution ideally placed for the articulation of the communalist politics of Hindu nationalism in the era of globalisation. Thus the scapegoating of Abbas Ali Baig can be seen, not as the expression of a backward and residual force, but as an expression of an incipient and modern form of Hindu communalism. Furthermore, as cricket has emerged as a global game, with the one day format leading the way, nationalist and communalist pressures have correspondingly been magnified in the game. Thus, the globalisation of cricket, and the role of India's cricket administrators in this project, are important factors.

Going global; Jagmohan Dalmiya and the 'disneyfication' of cricket

Until 1981 when Sri Lanka were admitted, the ICC still had six full members only. In 1991, the end of apartheid allowed the re–entry of South Africa, and, in spite of England's objections, Zimbabwe was also voted in. After almost 90 years, a supine ICC, under the stewardship of the MCC, had, and still has today, only nine full members. Outside this 'elite' club, there are 22 associate members, thus making the ICC one of the smallest international sporting organisations. However, outside the official structures of the ICC, the globalisation of cricket is firmly underway. However, it is not the traditional five day Test that is being diffused globally, but the televisual gladiatorial spectaculars of the one day match and the abbreviated six and eight–a–side contests. In these matches, players are kitted out in colourful 'pyjama' outfits, which, (some people say) is as close to the soul of baseball as of traditional cricket. The one day format also redefines the role of nationalism in cricket. The Indian sociologist, Ashis Nandy (1989), has argued that Test cricket is an ideal vehicle for nationalist expression because the role of fate in cricket provides convenient excuses to explain away defeat (e.g., vagaries of the weather, umpiring decisions, etc). In addition, although victory tastes sweeter where both the opponent and fate have been vanquished, Nandy asserts that the priority is not to lose. In one day cricket, however, a draw is not an option. There are only winners and losers, so that without the face–saving option of a draw, nationalist expression is forced to the extremes of triumphalism or despair.

Major influences on the development of the one day game have been the global commercial considerations of satellite television networks, such as the Hong Kong based Star TV owned by Rupert Murdoch, and its close rival, ESPN, which is owned by Disney Corporation. These networks have taken international cricket to new venues such as Toronto, Hong Kong, Nairobi, and Kuala Lumpur in Malaysia, where countries as diverse as Japan, the United Arab Emirates, Thailand and Papua New Guinea met in a Pepsi–sponsored tournament in 1996 (Cozier, 1996). The biggest market for these televised cricket extravaganzas is without doubt the Indian subcontinent, and in particular, the massive Indian middle classes. Televised international cricket provides the ideal vehicle for multi–national corporations (MNCs) like Coca–Cola, Pepsi, Sony, Shell, and ICI, to reach this vast and lucrative market, taking advantage of India's recent liberalising measures.

Alongside the satellite television networks and the sponsorship of MNCs, other important cog in the globalisation of cricket are the promoters. These are the 'middle men' who purchase the television rights of cricket tournaments, and market their coverage to the television networks. World Tel, sole purchasers of the rights to the 1996 World Cup, lead the field, with Mark McCormack's International Management Group also closely involved. It was the IMG that brought an India–Pakistan series in Toronto, live to prime time television in South Asia (Tiruchelvam, 1997). The initiative for promoting the globalisation of cricket, however, has come from astute and ambitious South Asian cricket administrators and entrepreneurs. Foremost among them is I.S. Bindra, senior civil servant and a former President of the Board of Control for Cricket in India (BCCI), and Jagmohan Dalmiya, Calcuttan business tycoon and a former secretary of the BCCI. Recently, Dalmiya was quoted as saying, "The game of cricket must be globalised. I have already demonstrated that it is possible" (*The Guardian*, 10 July, 1996). He was referring here to the staging of the 1996 Cricket World Cup on the subcontinent, which was organised by Pilcom (made up of the cricket boards of the three host countries, India, Pakistan and Sri Lanka).

Dalmiya and Bindra understand that by developing the commercial potential of sub–continental cricket through the strategy of globalisation, they also develop India's political influence in the cricket world. This is a not a strategy to create an alternative centre of power to the ICC, however, but, as Dalmiya's accession to the Presidency of the ICC in April 1997 illustrates, is one based on assimilation and innovation; it is the quest for 'equality through difference'. The significance of Dalmiya's appointment (making him the first Indian ever to head a world sports body) for many people in India was spelled out in *Sportstar*, the biggest selling sports magazine in India:

> Jagmohan Dalmiya's accession to the top ICC *gaddi* is reason to celebrate and rejoice. Only a few years ago this election seemed unlikely because Indians had no chance of reaching there, they were not considered good enough even to be in the line of succession. In a way this is Indian cricket's greatest success for a long time, though only off field. His appointment is an honour for India, for Indian cricket. It shows

conclusively that in world cricket the pendulum has swung irreversibly away from the traditional leaders. Lord's ceases to be the nerve centre of modern cricket, the dark days of control and veto are gone forever. With vigorous crowd support and large corporate funding, fresh cricket impulses emanate from India the thrust area could be globalisation, with more nations sucked into the cricket orbit. As the game spreads, interest grows and TV audiences become large. More money will flow in. For this to be done in a coordinated manner, the ICC needs strength and vision. JMD has both. (Mathur, 1997)

From the denial of access by the 'significant other' — the anglo–saxon cricket bloc — through the triumphalistic reporting of Dalmiya's success on the global stage, and finishing with a tribute to the 'strength and vision' of 'JMD', it is an account that is redolent of Hindutva ideology. In this sense, Dalmiya can be considered a Hindutva role model for aspiring Indian entrepreneurs and civil servants in and outside of sport. However, as the 1996 Cricket World Cup highlighted, there is a dark side to this strategy. As with the aforementioned global cricket tournaments, the World Cup was first and foremost a global television spectacle, but by Indian standards it was also a tournament of unprecedented glamour and hype. For big business, the tournament was a marketing strategy to reach the hearts and pockets of the affluent and materialistic cricket–mad South Asian middle classes. For India's cricket administrators, the tournament was part of a political strategy to facilitate sub–continental supremacy over England as the new epi–centre of cricket as a global game. For India's political elite, the tournament was an opportunity to entice multi–national interest and investment. In tune with the Indian government's policy of economic liberalisation, the World Cup was a carnival of globalisation generating a financial profit of £21 million (*Asian Age*, 1996). According to *Business World*, the 1996 World Cup was "the biggest marketing extravaganza in India this decade" (cited in Marqusee, 1996: p. 88). With the high levels of hype to match the levels of financial investment made by the MNCs, combined with the global exposure of the tournament, the World Cup was also a veritable cauldron of nationalist, and at times, communalist fervour.

World Cup controversies: The cases of Bombay, Bangalore and Calcutta

Attending one of India's matches during the 1996 World Cup, the respected Indian economist and cricket lover, P. Patnaik, was moved to ask whether cricket is still a force for bringing together the diverse communities of India (1996). He was provoked by the sound of anti–Pakistan chants coming from sections of the Indian crowd during a match not even involving Pakistan. The dominant assumption, which Patnaik is questioning, is that cricket contributes to national unity. However, the idea that cricket does mould the "societies of India" into an "Indian society" (Stern, 1996), has always been more a cliché than a reality pedalled by the vested interests of India's cricket officials and politicians. There is, nevertheless, a widespread acceptance that cricket at least *ought* to represent the nation as a whole – to promote what Patnaik calls a "progressive, inclusive nationalism" (1996). Sport in general, and cricket in particular, have traditionally been seen as exceptions to the segmentation of popular culture and recreation along religious and caste lines. Indeed, Patnaik believes that cricket still does promote a form of inclusive nationalism, but warns that the experience of the World Cup illustrates it is under increasing strain from the twin pressures of communalism and commerce:

> On the one side are the Hindutva forces, which in the name of nation-alism are out to promote communal–fascism. On the other side are the forces of commerce of which the satta operators [*illegal gamblers*] disrupting the match represent the crudest manifestation. (Patnaik: p. 14)

There were other occasions when communalism affected the experience of the World Cup. These include the sidestepping of Bombay as a key venue, the nationalist celebrations following India's victory over Pakistan in Bangalore, and the nationalist despair following India's defeat by Sri Lanka at the Eden Gardens stadium in Calcutta.

Bombay

Bombay is known as the cradle of Indian cricket. The city is India's foremost cricketing centre both on and off the field. It was in Bombay that Indians first took to cricket in the 1840s and where the top cricket tournament of colonial India – the Pentangular – was staged in the 1930s. 1933 saw the first test played on Indian soil take place in Bombay. Many of the greats of Indian test cricket including the current star, Sachin Tendulkar, have been born and nurtured on the maidans of Bombay. India's first modern cricket stadium, the Brabourne, and one of her current Test grounds, the Wankhede, are sited less than a mile apart in Bombay. Yet, during the 1996 Cricket World Cup staged on the sub–continent, Bombay was bypassed as a venue for any of the prestigious and important matches, and played host to just one first–round league tie between India and Australia. Bombay was snubbed because the organisers of the tournament, PILCOM feared, with justification, that should Pakistan need to play there, anti–Muslim prejudices, systematically encouraged in cricket and elsewhere by the Maharashtra state's ruling Shiv Sena–BJP alliance, could explode into ethnic and communalist violence. For example, Bal Thackeray, leader of the Maharastrian regional party Shiv Sena had declared in 1991 that there would be no match between India and Pakistan in Bombay. True to his word, a scheduled visit from the Pakistanis in October 1991 was cancelled after Shiv Sena activists poured oil on the Wankhede pitch. Thackeray has declared that "it is the duty of Muslims to prove they are not Pakistani" (cited in Marqusee, 1996: p. 107). He has even invented his own Indian version of the notorious 'Tebbit Test', stating that he wanted to see tears in the eyes of Muslims whenever India lose against Pakistan.

Following the 1995 state election victory by the Shiv Sena–BJP alliance, the city, which has the greatest religious diversity of all India's large cities, changed its name from Bombay to Mumbai, summoning up a resident Hindu deity, Mumbadevi. The organic link between Hindu communalist politicians and cricket is highlighted by the position of Maharastrian chief minister, Manohar Joshi, who is also the vice–President of the BCCI and President of the Mumbai Cricket Association. Although, in the interest of securing a quarter or semi–final, Joshi was willing to embrace a foreign presence and foreign investment in the city, he was unable to convince PILCOM that the communalist invective of Thackeray would be controlled. The tournament organisers were simply not prepared to risk images of communalist fervour beamed around the world. Pilcom officials probably still remember the tensions from the World Cup held in India and Pakistan in 1987, when communalist celebrations erupted amongst Hindus in Bombay and Delhi following Pakistan's semi–final defeat in Lahore. The next day in these same cities and Ahmedabad also, riots broke out when Indian Muslims celebrated England's victory over India in the other semi–final. On other occasions, Pakistani umpires incurred the wrath of sections of Indian supporters when they felt decisions went against Indian national interest (Nandy, 1989: pp. 111–13).

Bangalore and Calcutta

In spite of PILCOM's best attempts, the World Cup did fuel outbreaks of ethnic and communalist intolerance amongst India's large, partisan and demanding crowds. Not unexpectedly, the first real display of extreme Hindu nationalism came with the victory by India over Pakistan in the quarter–final match at Bangalore's Chinnaswamy Stadium. Political tensions between the two countries, not least over the disputed territory of Kashmir, meant that this was the first meeting in either India or Pakistan between the two arch–rivals for seven years. Pakistan came to the match as the reigning World Champions and, coupled with a superior record over India in recent contests, were consequently clear favourites to win. Victory for India was therefore greeted with national surprise and delight, but also with nationalist hysteria and celebrations. It was the vengeful nature of the celebrations that was striking, as Guha witnessed when he stood to applaud the exit from international cricket of one of Pakistan's great batsmen Javed Mianded after his dismissal, which effectively secured the match for India:

> "What are you clapping him for" yelled a man behind me. Through a long evening I had stood the crowd's shameful partisanship, now, I responded. "You should clap him too. He is truly a great player and we shall never see him again". The short, definitive reply – "Thank God I'll never see the bastard again". (Outlook, March 24, 1997: p. 64)

Victory precipitated an orgy of national celebration, which seemed to be less about progressing to the semi–final, and more about victory over a nation considered a political, military, social and economic inferior. In his insightful account of the 1996 Cricket World Cup, Mike Marqusee reported on the atmoshphere following India's victory:

> Imran Khan's windscreen had been smashed as he returned to his hotel ... Muslim areas were placed under curfew ... a small group of Hindutva fanatics raised the tricolour in an attempt to provoke an incident. "The tension was palpable, " said police, but no violence ensued. Sometime overnight, there was another exchange of fire along the Kashmir border. Casualties went unreported. (1996: p. 103)

Appropriately enough, the match at Bangalore was advertised as "War minus the Shooting". One article declared that "Winning the Bangalore battle, in style, almost equalled the thrill of winning the war for India" (Prasad, 1996: p. 71).

After reaching this 'high point', the ferris wheel of Indian cricket descended rapidly with the equally hysterical response to the semi–final defeat by Sri Lanka in Calcutta at Eden Gardens. With India heading for certain defeat, trouble erupted when a small section of the crowd began throwing bottles on to the field and lighting small bonfires in the stands. The referee was forced to abandon the match and award Sri Lanka their deserved victory and a place in the final. After the 'riot of Eden Gardens', as the media labelled it, the national mood swung from elation to despair in a matter of days. Headlines such as "Calcutta Crowd Shames the nation" (The Times of India), "Shame in Calcutta" (Indian Express) (cited in Marqusee, 1996: p. 264) were accompanied by articles full of self–flagellation and despair for Indian cricket. The reason for this over–reaction had little to do with the actual events that occurred, which involved at most 200 spectators amidst a capacity crowd of 110, 000, and was, according to the BBC commentator Christopher Martin Jenkins only "...a mild form of what goes on with say, British football hooligans". (Bahal, 1996). Under the telling headline of "The Disgracing of India" Vinod Mehta provides the real reason for the feeling of national shame:

> Like millions, I sat glued to my TV set last Wednesday; and as happy evening progressed into ugly night, one watched with stunned disbelief the concluding scenes. Tony Greig's periodic reminder, 'this telecast is being watched by 600 million people all over the world, ' took on an urgent menace: we were making a spectacle of ourselves on a global scale. (1996)

Marqusee concurs that the sense of national shame seemed to stem from the fact that the 'riot' at Eden Gardens was globally televised, commenting that:

> The World Cup, which was to project India as a modern competent nation doing big trade in the world marketplace, had ended up displaying the country at its most 'barbaric'. (1996: p. 267)

It also demonstrated that the principal protagonists of disorder and the least tolerant of defeat, came from the affluent sections of the ground. "This was not", Marqusee observed, "a riot of the dispossessed but a perverse protest by a small and relatively privileged minority". (*ibid.*: p. 117). Similarly, in India's first defeat by Sri Lanka earlier in the tournament at the Feroz Shah Kotla stadium in Delhi, anti–Pakistan taunts poured from the expensive seats occupied by members of the capital's middle classes.

The emergence of a 'lumpen middle class' cricket support confirms the political trajectory of India's cricket crowds outlined by Richard Cashman (1980) in his scholarly history of Indian cricket. Cashman has contrasted the mood and behaviour of the Indian cricket crowd between the "cheerful, sporting and tolerant assemblies of the 1930s to the more vociferous and demanding audiences of the 1970s" (1980: p. 132). The increasing partisanship and violent turn in crowd behaviour cannot be blamed on a larger lower class presence, a common explanation for deteriorating crowd behaviour in other sports and in other countries. The culprits of the 'offensively rude' response by a section of the crowd to a poor Indian performance at a test held in Bombay in 1977 "...were not the occupants of the cheaper stands, but the elite in the members' enclosure" (*ibid.*: p. 131). The World Cup confirmed and illustrated that it is the section of the population that is most integrated into the global market place, the affluent, highly educated, middle classes, who are also the most *influenced* by the politics of Hindutva. It is among the obstreperous nationalist supporters in Bangalore, among the 'rioters' at Eden Gardens in Calcutta and the anti–Pakistan chauvinist chanters at the Feroz Shah Kotla in Delhi, that the Sangh combine can rely on most for its support.

Conclusion

This chapter has sought to analyse the recent increase of communalism in contemporary Indian cricket. Although, many pertinent questions and issues surrounding communalism and nationalism in Indian cricket have not been covered, it is possible to draw some tentative conclusions. Far from being an anti–modernist swipe at the invading forces of globalisation, Hindu nationalism is an example of a post–colonial nationalism, which is a *product* of the intensification of globalisation, and thus a project of modernity. In the context of a polarising society and the disintegration of a hegemonic Indian National Congress, the ideologists of Hindutva have been able to find significant support for both their diagnosis and cure to the problem posed by modernisation through globalisation. By promoting a strong homogenous Hindu nation, the desire for respect and equality within the global hierarchy (ie from the West) can be achieved.

Recent developments confirm that the forces best positioned to capitalise in this new era of 'global' India are those on the political right based around the Hindu chauvinist Sangh Combine. Due to its place in civil society, and as a significant element of popular culture, international one day and test cricket offers fertile terrain for the articulation of Hindu chauvinist and communalist ideologies. The globalisation of cricket fuels the communal tensions and divisions between Hindus and Muslims. To fully understand how cricket is likely to develop and to assess the prospects for divisions between Hindus and Muslims increasing will require a more comprehensive study than has been possible in this chapter. Such a study will necessitate a consideration of the ways in which social divisions are contoured by the specific socio–historical trajectory of cricket in India since the colonial period. It will also involve an understanding of the relationship between sport and the politics of nationalism, national identity and communalism, especially in the last thirty years. Then it will be possible to properly weigh up the strengths but also the weaknesses, the coherence but also the contradictions, facing the forces of Hindu communalism in cricket.

The question that is constantly posed in Marqusee's book (1996) and which was to give its title is: is cricket in the subcontinent "War Minus the Shooting" or is it a vehicle for peace and unity? Marqusee concludes that events during the World Cup support both positions. If the theoretical analysis of Hindu nationalism as the expression of Indian modernity in the era of globalisation has substance, it can be argued that, the forces of communalism and division in cricket are more likely to prevail over the calls for peace and unity. Vanaik argues that; "In the last twenty years, the communal phoenix has risen from the ashes and spread its wings to cast a growing shadow over India's body politic" (1997: p. 3). In the context of a policy of economic liberalisation, and India's quest to become the centre of cricket as a global game, a case for investigating more fully how the shadow of communalism extends over cricket, and sport generally in India, should be made.

References

Asian Age newspaper, July 1, 1996: 1.

Bahal, A. (1996) 'And it rained mineral water', *Outlook* magazine, New Delhi. March 27th: 72.

Bose, M. (1986) *A maidan view: The magic of Indian cricket*. London: George Allen and Unwin.

———— (1990) *A history of Indian cricket*. Suffolk: Andre Deutsch.

Cashman, R. (1980) *Patrons, players, and the crowd: The phenomenon of Indian cricket.* New Delhi: Orient Longman Ltd.

Cozier, T. (1996) 'A cricket revolution', *The Sportstar* magazine, Bombay, 9th November: 38.

Docker, E.(1976) *History of Indian cricket.* Meerut: Macmillan Company of India Ltd.

Frontline (1996) magazine cover story, November 30–December 13: 4–17.

Frontline (1997) magazine editorial Bombay, 21st March.

The Guardian (1996) 'Asian tiger tweaks Lord's by the tail', July 10th: 23.

Guha, R. (1994/5) 'The Empire plays back' *Wissenschaftskolleg – Institute for Advanced Study Berlin – Jahrbuch 1994/5*: 253–263.

Guha, R. (1997) 'Those little gladiators', *Outlook*, New Delhi, May 26th.

Gupta, C., and Sharma, M. (1996) 'Communal constructions: media reality vs real reality' *Race & Class*, Vol. 38, No. 1: pp. 1–20.

Hansen, T.B. (1996) 'Globalisation and nationalist imaginations: Hindutva's promise of equality through difference', in *Economic and Political Weekly*, Vol XXXI, March 9: 603–616.

India Today, 'Hardsell highway', 31st March: 5–51.

India Weekly, 'Coca–Cola's plan gets government nod', 11–17 July, 1997: 13.

Jack, I (1997) 'A passage to the new India', *The Guardian* newspaper supplement. April 1st: 2–4.

Kurien, C.T. (1994) *Global capitalism and the Indian economy.* New Delhi: Orient Longmann Ltd.

Marqusee, M. (1994) *Anyone but England: Cricket and the national malaise.* London: Verso.

———— (1996) *War minus the shooting: A journey through South Asia during cricket's World Cup.* London: Heinnemann.

Mathur, A. (1997) *The Sportstar* magazine. April 12th.

Mehta, V. (1996) 'The disgracing of India', *Outlook* magazine, New Delhi. March 27th: 73.

Nandy, A. (1989) *The tao of cricket: On games of destiny and the destiny of Games.* Calcutta: Viking.

Patnaik, P. 'Of cricket, communalism and commerce', in *Frontline* magazine, Bombay, April 5th, 1996: 14–15.

Prasad, K. (1996) 'Pride and passion', *Outlook* magazine, New Delhi. March 20th.

Ramaswami, N.S. (1975) *From Porbander to Wadekar.* Delhi: Shakti Malik Abhinav Publications.

Robertson, R. (1992) *Globalization: Social theory and global culture.* London: Sage.

Rushdie, S. (1996) *The Moor's last sigh.* London: Vintage.

————— (1995) *Midnight's children.* London: Vintage.

Seabrook, J. (1995) *Notes from another India.* London: Pluto Press.

Stern, R. (1993) *Changing India.* Cambridge: Cambridge University Press.

Tiruchelvan, N. (1997) 'On the box', *Inside Edge: The new voice of cricket* magazine, Issue 8, April.

Vanaik , A. (1990) *The painful transition: Bourgeois democracy in India.* London: Verso.

Vanaik, A. (1997) *The furies of Indian communalism: Religion, modernity, and secularization.* London: Verso.